AN
AMERICAN
COVENANT

AN AMERICAN COVENANT

A Story of Women, Mysticism, and the Making of Modern America

LUCILE SCOTT

TOPPLE
BOOKS

Published by TOPPLE Books & Little A, New York

www.apub.com

Amazon, the Amazon logo, and TOPPLE Books & Little A are trademarks of
Amazon.com, Inc., or its affiliates.

ISBN-13: 9781542091275 (hardcover)
ISBN-10: 1542091276 (hardcover)

ISBN-13: 9781542091299 (paperback)
ISBN-10: 1542091292 (paperback)

Cover design by Zoe Norvell

Printed in the United States of America

First edition

For the girl on the stairs.

We are told in 1 Samuel 15:23, "Rebellion is as the sin of Witchcraft."

—*Cotton Mather, Massachusetts, 1693*

CONTENTS

A NOTE FROM TOPPLE BOOKS

When the patriarchy's suffocating grip has tightened around us, women have found a way to persist. In *An American Covenant*, journalist Lucile Scott conjures a journey into the past, exploring the way witches, healers, and diviners have created powerful paths forward, despite the insistence that their work and lives were dangerous, frivolous, or heretical.

As our collective rage rose up amid the Women's March and #MeToo, Scott found herself drawn to mystic traditions as a path toward understanding the history of feminist resistance. As she investigated, a clear trend emerged: women have been harnessing their own control since the dawn of time, altering the course of their lives, and helping shape this country's future.

In this perfect addition to our TOPPLE Books imprint, Lucile battles the oppressive heritage of patriarchal society, gathering her own historical coven of radical women who have persevered throughout the ages. By tapping into the powerful, complicated stories of Marie Laveau, Cora L. V. Scott, Helena Petrovna Blavatsky, Zsuzsanna Budapest, and Marianne Williamson, Scott shatters the masculine lenses of history that have gazed upon these women and so many others. In *An American Covenant*, heroines pass on their long legacy of courage, queerness, and defiance, inspiring us to bring our own transformational magic to the revolution.

—Jill Soloway, TOPPLE Books editor-at-large

THE COVEN

"We proclaim Jesus Christ Lord over Brooklyn," boomed a plastic megaphone in the night. "We're not here for Brett Kavanaugh; we're here for your soul."

"Lavetur in nobis sanguis tyrranus" (We bathe in the blood of tyrants), we thirty ensconced inside a candlelit converted Brooklyn garage chanted back in unison.

Despite the multiple phoned-in death threats and the mob of protestors just outside vastly outnumbering us, we then followed the lead of Dakota, our red-mohawked high-priestx, and calmly prepared to hex Supreme Court Justice Brett Kavanaugh. We arranged our Kavanaugh poppets for cursing in effigy, placing them on the altar beneath the thickening incense and sage smoke licking at a goat skull, a few white penis candles run through with coffin nails, and a jar of piss and grave-yard dirt that had charged under a full moon. Dakota told us that tonight, we would channel our collective rage toward the justice denied us elsewhere. Tonight, we would feel power despite a government that had dedicated itself to stripping us—the female, the queer, the brown—of it. We would touch the spark deep within that we needed to keep up the fight for however long it took to win it, or so Dakota said.

Meanwhile, thanks to online news reports, I knew that a different group of Christian soldiers based in California was diligently performing a "counter-exorcism" to protect the eternal soul of the afore-mentioned justice, sworn into office two weeks prior despite allegations of sexual assault and perjury. I imagined an outpost somewhere in the dust-swept rural interior of the state, where a smattering of desert Holy Rollers clustered in front of a TV mounted at the edge of their exorcism circle to watch the live scene outside this occult shop—brought to them by the ample right-wing media presence that had joined the sidewalk swarm. Perhaps they'd even broadcast a shot of my face, grimacing at the camera that had been shoved into it as I'd entered the shop. I pictured I came with a caption, "Brooklyn Witch" or maybe "Satan's Minion, New York City." Then I smiled.

One highly disconcerting aspect about living in America during fall 2018 was that every day on the street everything seemed so normal. People walking through busy intersections contentedly texting, people petting rescue dogs, people drinking CBD-infused slow-drip coffee as they talked about Tinder dates. Life went on. In the end, a slow slide toward authoritarian rule didn't feel Orwellian at all.

Still, despite the external banality, I felt some constantly raging cosmic battle of good v. evil, light v. dark, freedom v. control—like in Lord of the Rings or Harry Potter or World War II—swirling just beyond sight. That night, at that ritual, the clash somehow manifested before me, poof. Given, each side disagreed on who'd been cast in which role, but we all concurred on the celestial stakes. And living, actually walking into that unseeable space in the in-between, well, that felt magic.

This is a story about the liminal, where real v. fake, belief v. disbelief, and other earthbound binaries do not apply. This is a story about America and five mystic women who transformed it—though by and large we've forgotten their names. This is also a story about a slight, blonde lesbian in her midthirties trying to parse a way through both her personal and cosmic chaos—me.

The Salem witch trials of 1692 inextricably linked theology, gender, and control in the cultural fabric of our burgeoning nation. Yet despite the best efforts of those seminal Puritan purges, the mystic has persisted in America, an ever-present flow just beneath the surface of the national psyche. And from time to time, like the bubbles of a cauldron, that constant undercurrent has erupted into the cultural mainstream.

Those surges usually occur at, and underscore, pivotal moments in the fight for liberty that define our better angels in America—especially during each feminist wave. In fact, women have often been the de facto heads of these more or less headless movements. But though this clear historical pattern exists, most Americans don't know about the feminist mystic's role in our cultural and political battles. Like reflex, the mainstream order has consistently and quickly dubbed these movements the province of the *weak* and *muddleheaded*—of women—then ground them down to a spectral footnote or punch line.

In the 20-teens, one day no one was talking about witches. The next, we feminists casting to #HexThePatriarchy had bubbled up everywhere—at least in candlelit converted Brooklyn garages and on Instagram. Statistically speaking, approximately 1.5 million Americans identified as Wiccan or Pagan,[1] meaning there were more self-identified witches than Presbyterians (1.4 million) in America. Legions more had adopted the title "witch" more ephemerally, including many among the 27 percent of Americans, and rising, who were proclaiming themselves "spiritual but not religious." In 2018, the Ariana Grande single "God Is a Woman" hit the summer top-ten list, while the Netflix headliner *Chilling Adventures of Sabrina* (of teenage witch fame) conjured enough streams to warrant a separate Christmas special. Sundry other witch-themed movies and TV series materialized. There were some definite misfires,

---

1   Most Americans who identify as witches consider their spirituality descended from Pagan nature- and peace-loving religions far older than the Christian God or his devil; however, the nation also contains a contingent of satanic witches (who are not counted in the 1.5 million or discussed in this book).

especially when corporate entities attempted to cash in. Sephora, for one, announced the planned launch of a "Starter Witch Kit" that it quickly canceled after throngs of DIY, small business–oriented #witches focused their online evil eye its way.

Prior to that witchy moment, the mystic and I had developed a touch-and-go relationship. I first felt her lunar pull as a Kentucky teenager, removing an old leather-bound Wiccan tome from beneath my friend Beth's flower-duvet-covered bed. I further submerged myself in my early twenties while basking in the glitter of urban queer culture for the very first time. Back then, my enthusiastic chatter about visiting my Intuitive Reader or the power of candle magic often elicited a slight shunning, a repulsion, but also a titillated sort of curiosity, from my usually female conversation mates—much as if I'd just shown the person porn. But over the years, I'd slowly, then completely, moved away from all things mystic. Then the winds of the zeitgeist shifted circa 2016, and I was not immune. I found myself drawn back into the liminal's embrace.

However, I still shied away from explicitly proclaiming myself a true devotee, a loud and proud witch. And I wondered why. Was it some kind of internalized misogyny, a desire not to be seen as *that kind of a woman*? Perhaps some bone-deep terror of accessing the depths of myself, both light and shadow, as mystic journeys generally necessitate?

Part of the power and pull of religion is the bridge it builds to a tradition and history bigger than you. But this can prove tricky with the American feminist mystic, due to all the blotting out of its legacy. So I began digging about the past, to see if by unearthing and connecting the lineage of the divine feminine and the feminist mystic in America for myself I might alter my own POV.

What followed is the story of roughly one year. From November 2017 to January 2019, I frequented the New York Public Library and the multitudinous mystic offerings then available throughout the five boroughs and beyond. I chatted with wise witches in NYC, LA, West

Virginia, Texas, Salem. I listened to a feminist astrologer portend that in 2020 humanity would begin transitioning into a two-thousand-year era of either matriarchy or chaos, communal peace and love or tribal fear and loathing—the choice was ours. I frequented that converted Brooklyn garage, learning a panoply of ancient Pagan ways to touch that ancient mystic flame of personal freedom Dakota uncloaked for me during our hex.

Out of the centuries of female mystic leaders shrouded, instead of held up, by history, five soon called to me: Marie Laveau, the "Voodoo Queen" of New Orleans; Cora L. V. Scott, superstar nineteenth-century Spiritualist medium; Madame Blavatsky, enigmatic Russian immigrant and cofounder of the Theosophical Society; Zsuzsanna Budapest, author, activist, lesbian witch, and founder of explicitly feminist Goddess worship; and Marianne Williamson, New Age spiritual sage and 2020 Democratic primary presidential candidate. I wanted to immerse myself in their stories and traditions, form a sort of ancestral spirit coven, and see what effect it might have on me—see how, or if, it would transform me and my relationship to the mystic; how, or if, my ancestral spirit coven could help me transcend, rise up, and break free from my fears and more-questionable life choices that, at the time, I felt calcifying around me into something rather like a cage. What follows is that story, mostly theirs but also mine.[2] It's a story about resistance, just like Dakota said it would be. It's a story about power, control, and freedom. What follows is my American coven(ant).

---

2   Some names and identifying details of people in my portion of the story have been changed to protect their identities. Others haven't been changed at all.

KEY TERMS

Patriarchy (n.): 1. A war-based, dominator model of society based on the rigid binaries and hierarchies necessary to divide, conquer, and control—e.g., men over women, men over nature, straight over gay, rich over poor, and, often, white over black and brown.

> Sentence examples: 1. The first rule of *patriarchy* is don't talk about *patriarchy*; instead, act like it is the natural order and call all that threatens it the devil's work. 2. Since Stonehenge first greeted the dawn of *patriarchy*, women who have dared to demand autonomy, to challenge the way of things, have been branded witches in some form or fashion.

Matriarchy (n.): 1. A partnership model of society, where descent passes through the female line, based on cooperation, self-responsibility, personal freedom, and the idea of the inherent equality, dignity, and sacredness of all life.
2. The devil's work.

> Sentence examples: 1. *Matriarchy* is not a reverse patriarchal hierarchy with women on top instead of men, but an entirely different societal model. 2. In *matriarchy*, there are no

Madonnas and whores, slaves and masters, or even good and evil, just the maelstrom of life and death, creation and destruction, all holy, all intertwined.

Mystic (n.): 1. Spirituality rooted in an ecstatic search for unity with the divine.

Sentence example: 1. In the *mystic*, the divine can only be glimpsed, not fully comprehended or codified and then bound in leather.

Magic (n.): 1. Energy moved with the intention of transforming reality, often via a spell, also known as a prayer.

Sentence example: 1. Only *magic* can save us now.

PART I

MARIE LAVEAU, THE VOODOO QUEEN OF

NEW ORLEANS

1

Becoming American

The small girl with big eyes and brown skin watched the flag bearing fifteen stripes and fifteen stars as it lurched like the head of an inebriated chicken up the pole anchoring the Place d'Armes. Or maybe she didn't watch at all. The historical record doesn't actually say. What the record does relay is that many of New Orleans's eight thousand residents did watch on December 20, 1803, eve of the darkest day of the year, when they were suddenly proclaimed American—after having in a span of just forty years been French, then Spanish, then French once again. The city surrounding them, less than one square mile in size, stood fortified by a brick rampart and a rough pentagram of five forts. It served as a remote island of cold military might in the midst of a breathing, teeming swamp that often remained hot as a cauldron well into the Louisiana fall.

The crowd that December day contained European faces, African faces, Native American faces, and blends of all the above, packed into that central square so tightly they must have looked, from where the flag flew, like a multihued carton of eggs. Some people's eyes, upturned toward Old Glory, softly spilled over with tears. Others turned imploringly toward the old St. Louis Cathedral, its high turrets then sloped like two conquistadors' helmets, looming over the northwest edge of the plaza. Though of such varied roots, the congregants had long considered themselves one people, Creole people, struggling to survive together on the military outpost that seemed both on the shores of the Mississippi and the edge of the world—until they were informed they'd suddenly become American people.

To New Orleanians, *creole* did not refer to the color of a person's skin but to a person who'd been born in Louisiana—and usually born free. In the early 1800s, approximately 40 percent of New Orleans's population was considered white, 20 percent *gens de couleur libre* (free people of color), and 40 percent enslaved and of color. And though white men ran the city, the *gens de couleur libre* owned property, ran businesses, and dressed in the finest Parisian fashions. They had the liberty to build their own culture, replete with music, cuisine, and religion. It was also a culture in which women, who constituted two-thirds of the free people of color residing in the city, could hold property and maintain a level of social and economic independence unprecedented for women in their new nation.

So while there is, in fact, no historical record of whether Marie Laveau was in the Place d'Armes that day, I picture the two-year-old free Creole girl of color in the arms of her mother, Marguerite—a woman born enslaved to the man who was, most likely, her father, then sold to a new master who later freed her. The handsome mother-daughter duo would have exited the Place d'Armes, the black sulfurous smoke from the US Army rifle salute still lurking over it, and proceeded down St. Ann Street to a chorus of Creole gentlemen of color politely tipping their tall beaver hats. They'd have continued past Burgundy Street, to the edge of New Orleans and the foot of the rampart wall that delineated city from swampland, where a four-room Creole cottage, with a red tile roof and a smattering of banana trees, stood. The cottage belonged to Marie's grandmother Catherine Henry, who built it in

1798, shortly after she'd purchased her own freedom, at age forty-two, for six hundred pesos.

Marie would have made that same journey many a Sunday after attending Mass at the cathedral. As she approached her grandmother's cottage, she would have heard music carrying over the ramparts from Congo Square—vibrant, driving, distinctly African music played on instruments fashioned from wood, sun-stretched leather, and animal bone. When the ramparts were then demolished by the new American authorities and replaced by Rampart Street, young Marie, then approximately four years old, could have finally glimpsed the brown bodies dancing, laughing, free—for that one afternoon a week at least.

This square, where African culture could persist publicly, had sprouted out of a six-acre lot that tumbled into the Delta swamp during French, then Spanish, then French colonial rule. Its existence and culture were near anomalies in America. Under French and Spanish colonial laws, slavery was a system of labor based on brutal corporal punishment and dehumanizing mental, physical, and sexual control, but it was not considered a permanent state. A person had the legal right to buy themselves out of it. They also got Sundays off from any duties. And many people enslaved in or near New Orleans spent their Sundays in Congo Square. In addition to performing music and dance that lent itself to the soulful variety of *liberté*, they sold goods and services to save money toward buying their legal freedom. When they did, they became *gens de couleur libre*. *Gens de couleur libre*, however, still could not vote or hold public office or marry white people, leaving their status somewhere in between enslaved subject and full citizen.

I envision Marie, still in her best Sunday dress with puffy sleeves, standing just outside Congo Square, transfixed as the music surrounds and fills her, offering the same exaltation she'd discovered among the incense and smoke and the more staid, ethereal choral music of the cathedral. And with that ecstasy came a certainty obtained as instinctively as that of her liminal position in the Creole caste system, that no one institution had a monopoly on rapture or the divine.

Each Sunday, small groups, made mostly of women, broke away from the main marketplace to gather behind Congo Square in the thick of the cypress swamp, with its boggish, brackish water and veil of Spanish moss. There, far out of sight of white eyes, or any who might pry, they'd perform the holy ceremonies those Congo Square songs and dances were derived from. When people first began convening on Congo Square, no later than 1740, the rituals likely remained pure West African Vodun, but slowly the traditions of that long-standing religion fused with those of other old worlds and into something brand new—something that would come to be known as New Orleans Voodoo.

Marie's great-grandmother—the family's first Marguerite—likely knew this power of Vodun firsthand. As best as scholars can tell, she was born neither enslaved nor a Marguerite. She was, most likely, born in or near the Senegal River basin, before being abducted circa age seven and shipped through the Middle Passage, with all its horrors designed to make a person forget their body was ever their own, to New Orleans on a French slave ship called *St. Ursin*.

The Middle Passage, however, failed in its mission to fully sever enslaved people from their humanity, due in no small part to the power of West African Vodun and then New Orleans Voodoo—a force able to fuel that soul-deep sense of *liberté*, even in chains. And little Marie Laveau would eventually grow up to become the nation's most famous Voodoo Queen. To some, this would make her a near saint; to others, she was synonymous with the devil; but to all, she was a cosmic force to be reckoned with. Though she had the power of the God-Force at her fingertips, no one ever gave Marie, a girl of color, the power of the written word. And without journals or detailed letters, there are a lot of *likely*s and *probably*s in the story of Marie Laveau.

Some concrete details are a matter of public record: the date of Marie's baptism when she was six days old and by extension her birth date, September 10, 1801; her marriage at age seventeen to a free Haitian of color, Jacques Paris; the date of her death; and the first published reference to her as "head of the Voodoos" in an 1850 article. Many of the documents are branded with the only remaining remnant directly from Marie, the steady *X* she used to sign her name.

Official documents also convey that after gaining her freedom, Marie's mother lived in plaçage with a much older Frenchman named Henri D'Arcantel. In plaçage, a white man could maintain both a white family, who constituted his legal wife and heirs, and a family of color—from whom he could withdraw his financial support whenever he pleased, as such support was offered as a point of chivalry and honor, not as a condition of legal marital bond. This tenuous arrangement Marguerite had with D'Arcantel also meant Marie's own father, Charles Trudeau Laveaux, a prosperous free man of color, could never marry Marguerite. However, he could provide his daughter with a last name and her husband, Jacques Paris, with a dowry of a small house on Love Street.

Marie knew the house, and her father's ability to bequeath it, made her lucky. It provided a stability, its own kind of freedom, elusive to many free women of color, especially those living in or born out of plaçage—including her mother and her half siblings fathered by D'Arcantel. Long before she was the powerful Queen of Voodoo, Marie Laveau was all too aware of how little stood between her, a woman of color, and drowning.

Then, gradually, the always slight structure keeping her afloat grew smaller. After 1803, rigid American laws based in binary ideas of race and notions of justice that didn't include people with dark complexions at all slowly replaced the more flexible French and Spanish ones. In the mid-1820s, Marie's mother died of unknown causes, her husband vanished, and the two children Marie and Jacques are believed to have had together also passed to the other side of the veil. To Marie, it likely seemed that the only way to survive, if one even wanted to, was by

15

learning to walk on water. It was then that Marie Laveau met Sanité Dédé—and made a choice.

2018
Boston

I descended wooden stairs into a crypt-like concrete basement a little after 9:30 p.m. on a Saturday in November, just in time for the annual Festival of the Dead, or Fête Gede. I'd been invited to Boston to attend this Vodou (as it's spelled in Haiti) ceremony, generally the grandest of the year, by a man I'd met in New Orleans two months prior. I'd traveled there to the Big Easy on a mission to better understand Marie Laveau and her Voodoo tradition.

My research showed that like its parent, West African Vodun, and its sibling, Haitian Vodou, the New Orleans Voodoo of Marie's time was a shamanic religion, a cosmology based on direct communication with spirits via possession or divination—the latter often done with tarot cards originally brought over by Europeans or with the bones used in many African traditions. In West African Vodun, there is one all-powerful creator too remote and vast to commune with directly, so humans call upon an array of lesser spirits who serve as intermediaries to the ultimate deity. This cosmology directly reflects Roman Catholicism, with its almighty Creator God and his host of saints whom the faithful commune with. When West African people were enslaved in primarily Roman Catholic cultures, like New Orleans and Haiti, the religions easily fused into a new entity, along with their saints and spirits. Limba, the guardian of the Crossroads and escort for the recently deceased (better known by his Haitian Vodou name Papa Legba), joined with Saint Peter, who holds the keys to heaven's gate; Daniel Blanc, the spirit of luck and love, with Saint Michael; the divine feminine with the Virgin Mary; and the list goes on. In addition, in New Orleans, elements of Native American spirituality—another shamanic religion with a reverence for nature—melted into this medley, along with some flecks from then-popular European occult movements like Masonry and mesmerism.

Despite their similarities, however, Vodun and Catholicism remained strikingly different. The Christian Creator God is an emphatic *He*, existing above and before natural cycles, including being born of a woman. The West African Creator is generally androgynous, bigger than gender, though if one must choose, for many, past and present, the preferred pronoun is *she*—as mystics say the cosmic macrocosm reflects the natural microcosm, and in the microcosm women birth life. In West Africa, both priests and priestesses could traditionally serve the spirits, while in mainstream Christianity, only men could function as a surrogate for the male God—and by extension, only men could truly be holy. In eighteenth- and nineteenth-century New Orleans, where women constituted the majority of people of color and had a degree of autonomy unusual for the time, the system grew more matriarchal even still.

At the center of that subterranean room in Boston sat a middle-aged black woman, our Mambo, or high priestess, softly chanting while shaking a brown gourd rattle. She was small in stature but huge in spirit and dressed all in white. Her folding chair rested on the hard, gray floor, dotted with flames that floated in hemispheric orange peels filled with oil. Amid those flames glimmered intricate patterns—*veves*—constructed with cornmeal, along with other cornmeal-sketched symbology—skulls, crosses, pyramids.

Carefully, platter by platter, like proud waiters dressed in matching light-purple shirts, the pious members of her Vodou House began setting out a feast—whole crabs, tropical fruits, cake, fritters, a skull made of icing—on an altar that spanned the entirety of the fifty-foot back wall. Behind the grand platters rested a dense conglomeration of Catholic saint statues, fresh flowers, votive candles, liquor bottles, sequins, and natural skulls of bone. All of it was an offering for the spirits alone. No human touched the food that night.

Surprised by the calm, I took a seat in a folding chair among a handful of meditative onlookers, some in traditional ceremonial attire of white or purple lace and bandana fabric, some in street clothes like me. Sitting at the periphery, I thought of the Episcopalian services I'd attended from time to time in my youth. Though Protestant, they'd still employed a fair amount of Catholic ritualistic flair—incense, candles, bright silk robes, ornate golden talismans—to conjure the divine.

But the calm was just the warm-up, the opening invocation of the spirits that lifted the veil to move this basement to a space between worlds and, I've been told, outside time. Soon the drumming started, as people, most all Haitian immigrants, trickled in and milled about, sharing rum and Coronas. By midnight, about one hundred women and men stood packed together, chests to backs, forearms against elbows, our sweat mingling. Then we began swaying while stomping to the drumbeat, as the dozen members of the house, led by their Mambo, processed down the stairs in choreographed motion and into the pulsing throng of us. Soon our dancing gave way to something even more ecstatic and unencumbered—as the hour pushed on to 3:00 a.m. and then 4:00, then later still.

As we crossed further into the wrong side of midnight, as my southern mother used to call it, lines blurred into what started to feel like some waking dream in my sleep-hungry mind. In that subterranean concrete space between worlds, I watched a ceremonial melee of purple and white, lace and linen, small coffins and full-size swords, machetes and crosses. Flames erupted on the floor from rum poured in circles. People danced around the fire as it licked at their clothes. A woman writhed beneath a white sheet while eating a hard-boiled egg coated in flour. A man lay prostrate and frozen, wrapped in a shroud, cotton up his nose, rendering him deceased, ceremonially speaking, for a number of minutes.

In New Orleans Voodoo, and also Haitian Vodou and West African Vodun, spirit and matter are not binary: one sacred, one profane; one living, one accessed only through death or a cleric. Instead, divinity resides in all things living and inanimate, including all of us, regardless of race and gender. Voodoo is about channeling the spirits to balance and heal both an individual and their community. In Voodoo, each dance, each word, each intention, be it a blessing or a curse, reverberates through the divine ether connecting all. Each action also sparks a commensurate reaction upon the doer—basically the same idea as karma. So, if someone messes with the more aggressive side of the spiritual forces—curses, hexes, and the like—they must be willing to pay the price, in terms of negativity in their own life. Therefore, such work is generally done sparingly. In fact, what would become known as "Voodoo dolls" were actually poppets brought over by Europeans who used them in folk magic from time to time to ward off malevolent forces. The dolls aren't an actual fixture of Voodoo; however, priestesses and priests have employed them to focus healing energy on a certain part of a person's body, almost always at that person's request, by using those infamous pins.

In that basement, I watched bodies around me fill with something otherworldly. I watched them shake, push, fling, and occasionally free-fall, hitting the concrete with a bruising crack. Sometimes someone would catch me off guard, send me tumbling into the drums, onto a chair. Other times, when I was on guard, I tried to break someone's fall, hold the weight of their flailing, struggling body, then lay them onto my lap as they relaxed, their voice deepened, changed, their eyes unfocused, taken over by some force that seemed elemental and vast, savoring of and hungry for life but less specific than the human conscious it had replaced. A woman standing next to me said the possession feels like rapture, like returning from the moon.

There was a woman making penance, groveling wormlike across the concrete floor, as our Mambo, then possessed by the male spirit Ogun and dressed in a royal red, smacked her with an antique machete. A man told me it really stings. There was someone eating money and rubbing hot peppers on her bare chest, her skin growing red and inflamed. These were not polite spirits, ethereal and cerebral; they were life and death, creation and destruction, exaltation and debasement, the sum total.

And always the drumming, songs, movements, calling forth the spirits. The Mambo, when not possessed by Ogun, guided it all, conducting, offering parameters, barriers, a sense that there was control, that there was power in that room, and that we, our bodies pressed tightly together yet unencumbered and with spirit, possessed it—not just vice versa.

Marie Laveau, now a woman in her twenties, walked through the hot, dark streets of a French Quarter lit only by tar-filled barrels capped in flames made wild by a river wind. She walked past the wrought-iron balconies and loping Renaissance-colonial roofs, past the cemetery gates, where corpses, swollen and jaundiced by yellow fever, were piled high—their smell thinly masked by the blooming jasmine. She exited the Quarter onto Congo Square and the newly established Tremé neighborhood, home primarily to free people of color, then walked farther still.

New Orleans was fast transforming from a remote military outpost into America's wealthiest port city, its formerly near-nonexistent economy supercharged by steamships, the cotton gin, and the largest slave market in the nation. But even in the 1820s, late at night in the farthest reaches of town, it could still feel like the edge of a fragile world sinking into an eternal swamp. Marie lifted her full white skirt away from the mud, then stooped to enter an abandoned brickyard out there on the fringe, ensuring her white tignon, folded in seven cloth points atop her head, avoided the deteriorating archway.

Though describing her alternately as brown, black, golden, cream, and red, all historical accounts agree that Marie Laveau was beautiful, arrestingly so—that she had the power to pull all focus without batting a large, obscurely deep eye. And there the striking Marie stood, inside a brickyard hut, after three days and three nights of fasting, purified and burning with life. Surrounded by walls tangled with trumpet creeper vines slowly reclaiming the crumbling brick, some sixty people, also dressed in white—roughly ten white Creole women, the rest people of color—watched as Marie Laveau prepared for her initiation. Before her stood a makeshift altar alight with fire and adorned by two stuffed black cats and a black statue, its upper half a woman, its lower half a snake. The presiding priestess, Sanité Dédé, signaled an older black man to begin beating a homemade drum. Slowly the crowd began to move and sway and pass a large serpent from person to person as it wriggled and coiled around their upstretched arms.

"Come Voudou, come Voudou," the crowd beckoned as their swaying gave way to dancing and that dancing became a frenzy. People were taken over, in almost painful ecstasy, as they stripped down to their underclothes and the drumming grew faster. Sanité Dédé threw more fuel onto the flame and prepared her cauldron.

At least that's how I imagine the day Marie Laveau joined the Voodoos, reconstructing the account from a description of an 1822 initiation ceremony conducted by Sanité Dédé, who historians theorize initiated Marie around that time—though some argue it was in fact the priestess Marie Saloppé who presided over Marie's rites. No actual record of Marie's initiation remains, but it was likely very similar to these proceedings. In fact, almost all written firsthand accounts of nineteenth-century New Orleans Voodoo rituals that do remain come from white men, taught to see Satan's work at play, who were not Voodooienne themselves. The account of that initiation was given to a reporter some fifty years after the fact by a white man who'd been just a boy when a woman enslaved by his family brought him to the ritual to ease her passage through the night policed for "runaways" and "trouble-makers" of color. So when he talks of "orgies" and "the devil," modern-day interpreters are left to wonder what that might have meant to a buttoned-up nineteenth-century American boy. Likely "orgies" actually meant ritual dancing, akin to modern-day twerking, not group sex. And Voodoo has nothing to do with the devil, who is a Christian invention, as are ideas of the inherent evils of the flesh, be it sex or just dancing unencumbered in one's underclothes.

Before she stood amid the flames during that "satanic orgy," Marie Laveau would have spent months studying all things Voodoo. She would have learned how to honor and respect nature and all its spirits. She would have learned the drumbeats and colors and offerings—tobacco, whiskey, or a hard-boiled egg doused in flour—that conjure each spirit and how to hold that spirit once it arrived, channel it as it entered her body, instead of letting it knock her sideways, a tin soldier flicked by a Goddess.

Critically, Marie also learned natural remedies for various ailments from her Mambo, her mother, and likely other Creole women of color. Marie then took that knowledge and expanded upon it with the help of local Choctaw well versed in the flora and fauna of their native land. At a time when male doctors trained in European medical tradition relied on bloodletting and other purgatives more likely to kill than cure a patient, Voodooienne were adept in treating, or at least easing the suffering from, the various plagues that perpetually struck the swamp city. They stood in high demand as fever nurses citywide, regardless of a patient's race or economic status. And Marie Laveau developed into one of the finest.

In short, Marie did not emerge from the deep waters of personal tragedy with just a religion, able to transform her perception of power within her liminal world; she also emerged with a solid, respectable live-lihood and the house on Love Street, which belonged to her alone after Jacques Paris vanished without a historical trace. And her new title, the

Widow Paris, freed Marie, still quite young and forever beautiful, from societal pressures to find a new mate—be it a legal husband of color or a white man to keep her in plaçage. There was only one reason Marie would need another man.

Perhaps they met at the opera, as the city had recently acquired one of the country's best. Perhaps it was at a quadroon ball, where white men sought out lighter-skinned, and therefore more desirable, lovers of color to keep in plaçage. Perhaps they locked eyes on a New Orleanian market street awash in mud and fortune-tellers, habited nuns, Choctaws, Creoles, self-described pirates, the occasional errant alligator, and a mix of Yankee, Southern, and European gentlemen—though generally not their cloistered white wives. However the meeting happened, it is clear what it led to was love. But there was one problem. Christophe Glapion was the white grandson of a French aristocrat who moved in the most elite New Orleanian circles.

For any other such lovers looking to commit as partners in full, not plaçage, the union would have been denoted star-crossed—not to mention illegal. Marie Laveau was not any such lover, but even a Voodoo Queen's power and influence had its limits under the scrutiny of the bright lights of white society. So Christophe Glapion, a man of pure French blood, took a step away from his birthright and into the liminal. With the help of Marie and his biracial half brother—the son of his father—Christophe began living as a *gens de couleur libre*, even signing official documents with his race designated as "colored."

1832 marked one of the worst cholera and yellow fever epidemics on record in a city with some of the worst cholera and yellow fever epidemics on earth. That year alone, eight thousand of the city's then fifty-five thousand residents passed to the other side of the Crossroads. It also marked the year that Marie Laveau and Christophe Glapion took legal possession of the Creole cottage on St. Ann's, shortly after Catherine Henry's death. They also maintained possession of the house on Love Street, and it's not entirely clear which address constituted the family's primary residence at which times. It is clear, however, that it was 152 St. Ann Street that would go down in both glory and infamy.

In that house, a stone's throw from Congo Square, Marie Laveau did the work that made her the go-to master for both the herbal remedies that could stave off Limba's entrance and for all mystic calls asking the spirits to reach into the chaos on one's behalf. In a world of death, Marie Laveau was the chosen one, touched, the Voodoo Queen of Voodoo Queens. The "illegitimate" daughter of a former slave became "the real boss of New Orleans," as one resident would later put it.

People claimed she could bring back a strayed husband, get a person out of jail or a court date, remove a curse, and bring abundance, a new horse, or freedom. It was said that fine horse-drawn carriages pulled up to her cottage on St. Ann's in the dead of night carrying wealthy white Creole women, their faces veiled to preserve their anonymity as they walked to her door. Once inside, they'd immediately strip out of their bone corsets and steel hoop crinoline "cages," all the way down to their loose, light underclothes, and start dancing, ecstatically, along with everyone else of color. It was said, as the legend grew, that Queen Victoria, the Marquis de Lafayette, and Aaron Burr all sought Marie's services. Others said they'd seen her on the road out of town late at night, leaving plates of food atop cypress stumps. Rumors swirled that she was offering food for the devil or for runaway enslaved people hiding in the swamp.

Slowly, though, increasingly repressive American laws were taking hold in formerly Creole New Orleans—including a new one outlawing mixed-race cohabitation, not just marriage. Amid this gradually gathering torrent, Marie and Christophe remained a fortress, an institution, illegally and flagrantly living, and raising a family, in a mixed-race union. The two never legally married. Instead, she remained protected by the honorific "Widow Paris," which allowed officials who feared her mystic wiles and guiles to easily cast a blind eye the couple's way—while he remained protected by the actual, even if no longer claimed, color of his skin.

By day, they attended Catholic Mass. Marie even served as the right hand and primary confidant of the Spanish head of St. Louis Cathedral, Père Antoine. By night, Marie led Voodoo rituals in the house on St. Ann's. It was said Marie regularly sat in Parish Prison, amid the screams and human rot, just a good Catholic, praying with men of all races who'd been condemned to die. It was said that, from time to time, she'd free one of those men who was poised to hang by invoking the storms, her spiritual signature, and making his noose so wet he'd slip through to the dirt below. It was said she cared for the poor, the hungry, the needy, and the orphaned, in addition to the sick. It was said she bought enslaved people on the market, only to free them.

Whether due to Voodoo, an intimate knowledge of every secret in New Orleans—passed from woman of color to woman of color to Marie Laveau—or the fact that she was expert in when and how to grease a palm, Marie Laveau mastered her shifting world. She also had Christophe at her side, a man not just literate but fluent in all the weak and sweet spots of the system and the men who ran it. Whatever the mechanism, the result was clear: "All the people—white and colored—start sayin' that's the most powerful woman there is. They say, 'There goes Marie Laveau!'"

But not even Marie Laveau, the most powerful woman there was, could stop what was coming. The 1830s gave way to the increasingly iron-fisted 1840s, then eventually to the 1850s and a nation divided and devouring itself like a disease over who, exactly, had a right to freedom in the free world. Soon enough, it again seemed that the only way for Marie and her world to survive in America was by learning to walk on water.

2

A (SNAKE) GODDESS RISING

2018
New Orleans

Oshun delivered me. Her Buick Encore smelled like mint and Doritos, and she proclaimed the purple Creole cottage where I had rented an Airbnb room, "cute." In New Orleans, a city forged in the spirit if not the name of Marie Laveau, people named for Yoruba Goddesses give Lyft rides. I tipped well.

The purple cottage sat just outside the Tremé and a twenty-minute walk from the location of the Laveaus' own Creole abode on St. Ann's. Far from being declared a historical landmark, however, the structure Marie's family had lived in for ninety-nine years was demolished in 1903. In its stead rose a shotgun duplex with pale-gray siding. In 2018, one of its "historic," "high-ceilinged" two-bedroom units rented for $1,800 a month. Still, I visited the plot to pay homage.

The first time I'd visited New Orleans, on a family vacation at age fifteen, I locked myself in a hotel closet. People say it's all the water in this city—built in a swamp below sea level, surrounded and bifurcated by a river, a gulf, and a lake, the air humid and thick as velvet—that makes it so haunted. Water, in Voodoo, is the spirits' realm. People say the spirits who dwell there talk to you in dreams.

After awakening from a dream of my own, I'd made my way into that dark closet. There, where my sleeping parents couldn't see me, I lay—or kind of fetal-crunched—pondering a newfound dissatisfaction with the word "that." I'd discovered my frustration some hours prior while staring at a leaf in the moonlight, suddenly profoundly sure said object was not a "that" but a continuation of me. Not knowing much about these things as an adolescent girl from Kentucky, I sketched out an angst poem attempting to define the mystically divine there in the dark on my knees.

That feeling, that balking at binary notions of reality, wasn't exactly new. I'd felt something similar the prior summer, as a crisp Appalachian waterfall pounded onto my head. My eyes had squinted, rather painfully, peering through the cascading water at a yellow butterfly that somehow hovered in the violent mist unharmed. This, in turn, somehow compelled me to swing naked on a vine over a small rocky chasm shouting, "Fuck all y'aaaaaalllllllllllllllllll," though no one but a chipmunk bore witness.

I'd felt it again after a Friday night spent consuming shoplifted bottom-shelf whiskey and Marlboro Reds in a field, as my friend Beth and I sat on her horse farm watching the huge Kentucky moon slide out of view as the sun began to rise. It's the one time of day the dewy grass actually glimmers its titular blue. Too young to drive, too old to hold faith in ABC's TGIF lineup, we sat as the gathering light slowly revealed the hills, shrouded in hazy blue, and the huge, sleek Thoroughbreds silhouetted atop them, simultaneously wild and gentle, as they stomped and snorted in the half glow.

But it was in New Orleans that the feeling congealed from some awareness flicking ghostily on the periphery of my mind. And I'd loved the city for it that first time I met it. It's a place where different ages and nations layered atop each other, then compressed into a dilapidated glory and something new. I felt drawn to the freaks, crusty punk squatters, freegans, and artists who inhabited the city, like ghouls and goblins, outcasts and renegades. To teenage me, it all felt like some truth people were always trying to hide beneath a shiny surface, the etiquette, starched shirts, and pressed pants of the respectable world. I discovered an honesty and comfort there in the demimonde, where shadows are left to flow free as the light.

In Voodoo, they say it's only when that door between worlds is left shut that what's on the other side, unseen and unheard, morphs into something scary. Before my first visit to New Orleans, I used to think a lot about suicide. After, I didn't so much.

Ever since, I've been drawn to that city. During one visit in the late aughts, on the Day of the Dead, I'd watched a person of indeterminate gender and race, dressed in a full body bag of loose black cloth painted with Day-Glo skeleton bones, jitterbugging about a dimly lit jazz bar in the Lower Ninth Ward. Outside, I'd seen blocks of abandoned houses, the watermarks from Hurricane Katrina still visible on their busted-up facades, along with spray-painted FEMA X codes denoting the fate of those who'd once lived inside, if they'd stayed or evacuated, lived or died.

In 2018, I saw a young black man in army fatigues perform an aerial spin around his wooden porch banister carved into looping fleur-de-lis, as a percussion-laden second-line parade processed past. On a Ninth Ward street more puddle than road, I watched a rooster, its plumage like a melting Creamsicle, bright orange and flecked with white, peck about in front of a pale-pink house with a pale-pink 1960s Cadillac parked in the driveway beneath a giant old magnolia tree. Standing there, I thought of my inaugural visit to New Orleans and of my current trip, the first one I had made specifically in pursuit of Marie Laveau. I wondered how, or if, providing my amorphous teenage epiphanies with a history and patron saint had reconfigured them into something new.

That night, the trumpets and trombones wafted after me through the Bywater, then the Marigny, down Frenchmen Street, past wrought-iron balconies, a drunken tourist throng lurching in flip-flops, and the closed, gated praline and souvenir shops at the fringes of the French Quarter, all the way to the Mississippi. Still thinking of Marie, I stared at that deep, muddy water and the distant lights, the music still faintly pulsing, but ever present, like blood. They say the spirits talk to you in dreams.

I have a tattoo of the Mississippi River snaking down my left side. I got it not long after Katrina. I couldn't really tell you why.

Back in the purple Creole cottage, I dreamed of a body, a skeleton in a fedora but somehow still whole, dancing beautifully, like a manic Fred Astaire, beneath a blue spotlight in an old bar. Rose petals tumbled down through the light from nowhere, like drops of blood, and a bright-orange eagle flew by. Somehow, we all knew it was the end of the world. But then a face came down from the stars, all glittering blue light, too, and it was no longer the end. It was just me lying in a field, next to a pet cemetery, looking up at this face of a woman, a saint or maybe a Goddess, of indeterminate race and place and age and made of stars. She offered no words, no wisdom, just a feeling of peace, of someone holding me, telling me silently I was not alone.

By 1850, Marie Laveau had acquired a pet serpent named Le Grande Zombi—thick as a cypress sapling, long as a gallows rope. Due to a constant flood of immigration—from the rest of America and countries like Ireland, Italy, and Germany—New Orleans ballooned to a population of 150,000 by the decade's end, up from eight thousand when it joined America. Free people of color constituted approximately 7 percent of the population—down from nearly 20 percent when the city joined the nation. To the tens of thousands of new Caucasian residents, New

Orleans was just another American city, one part of the antebellum American South.

In the early part of the decade, the city passed several laws curtailing assemblages of people of color, both free and enslaved. Congo Square was gated and frequently locked all Sunday. Voodooienne, both of color and white Creole women, were arrested in homes for gathering to conduct rituals. They were arrested on the Bayou St. John. They were arrested in their underclothes after scaling fences, in flight from the cops. And the press, once almost entirely silent on the topic of the "Voodoos," provided salaciously detailed reports, complete with names and addresses of the arrested. However, none of this stopped "the Negroes from assembling."

When Le Grande Zombi coiled himself around his mistress, the undulating circles of his long, glistening body gave the impression he was spinning into forever. Renegade gatherings of Voodooienne never tired of watching Marie dance with her pet infinity, kiss that deadly power, then coil it inside a box and carry it with her. Especially in Congo Square, a place that conjured up better, freer times, each woman and man dancing along with Marie and her serpent felt a rare moment of communal release and power, like they'd touched a piece of that infinity too—even as they heard the rhythm of the police boots surrounding their enclosure.

Then, with notions fast spreading that the nation's founding principle "all men are created equal" actually applied to all men, the enslavers tightened their grip on the Big Easy. And things went from bad to maniacal.

In 1857, the city decreed all emancipations of enslaved persons illegal; in 1858, that all religious services be led by a white person; and in 1859, that all free persons of color choose their own masters and hand themselves over to slavery. No one complied with that last edict, but throughout the ever-more-frenzied repression bonanza, many free people of color were kidnapped and sold into slavery. Many were forced to forfeit property or businesses, removing them completely from the bourgeoisie. Some were beat nearly unconscious or thrown in jail for no reason and with no recourse—at least not from the law.

Slowly, then all at once, the *gens de couleur libre* became black Americans. And just as their city was not the same Creole New Orleans, their hero, and Le Grand Zombi's mistress, was most likely not the same Marie Laveau at all.

In June 1855, just as the annual summer plagues began to collect their body count and the litany of laws against people of color to bludgeon down, Christophe Glapion died at age sixty-six. Of the seven children he and Marie had together, only two, their first, Marie Euchariste Glapion, born in 1827, and another daughter, Marie Philomène Glapion, born in 1836, had survived into adulthood. In the 1850s, these two Maries headed off down forking roads, like some bifurcation of their famous Creole mother into a black and white America. Though first, each had learned what it meant to be a nineteenth-century woman.

Marie Euchariste bore her first child at approximately age sixteen and her last of the five recorded at twenty-six. Most of her children seem to have died before reaching adulthood. The man believed to be their father, Pierre Crocker, was a free man of color twenty-four years her senior. He had a wife and an official mistress and therefore could not claim or support Marie and their kids—as even in New Orleanian Creole culture, a man could only respectably retain two families. It is unknown if he was kind. It is unknown if Marie loved him, or if Pierre, a man in his late thirties, forced himself upon the beautiful teenage girl who men "used to go kind of crazy lookin' at," knowing full well she would then be "ruined" and effectively belong to him—if he deigned to claim her.

As Marie grew from Pierre's teenage companion to an adult woman, she watched as everyone she knew of color, including the men, increasingly fell victim to the whim of any white man. She watched as their bodies increasingly became white men's province, not their own—their souls, too, subject to the dictates of a white male God. The message coming down every formerly Creole avenue was clarion: society had been hung a hierarchy and, in America, a woman of color occupied the basement rung.

But Marie Euchariste had a leg up. She had been raised by a Voodoo Queen, and in a house filled with love. And Voodoo Queens, like love and the spirits, are not confined by earthly dictates or violent attempts at psychological control. Marie Euchariste chose to accept her birthright. She chose to walk the path of Voodoo. And when she did, she rose up from the deep waters as rage made righteous, and enwrapped in Le Grande Zombi.

Marie Euchariste had seen the hellfires of death, oppression, and quite possibly rape, and learned they could not defeat her. And there's nothing more dangerous to the powers that be than that realization. Most likely, it was her, not her mother, who stood as straight and defiant as a middle finger on Congo Square, while holding Le Grande Zombi, a snake named after Nzambi, the God of all Creation in the Kingdom of Kongo. In Kongo, Nzambi was often symbolized by a serpent whose body formed the circle of life itself—long before the serpent's body came to connote Satan. Marie Euchariste arose Marie Laveau II—a whole new brand of Voodoo Queen.

In the 1850s, Marie Laveau II lived on Love Street in the house that had once been her mother's dowry to Jacques Paris. The Widow Paris, who was then living on St. Ann's, passed on far more than the powers of a Voodoo Queen to her eldest daughter. She passed on a tradition of financial security, without a man. She did not, however, pass on one key aspect of her priesthood. Marie II had no proper flip side palatable to the "respectable" world. Marie II was all fire and bugger you and rebellion, and she earned her living under that inherited roof by practicing a different sort of healing service than her mother, the famed fever nurse.

What many of us think of as Voodoo—Love Potion Number 9 (which Marie II allegedly first concocted), hot foot and Lucky Devil powders, Essence of Three Thieves, gris-gris (better known as the mojo bags one should avoid losing), and other such practical magic—is in fact Hoodoo. Hoodoo practitioners basically serve as cosmic pharmacists to Voodoo's spiritual cosmology. Hoodoo persisted in many places throughout America without a Congo Square or Creole culture, where the more religious aspects of African Vodun by and large didn't.

Day in and day out, clients flocked to Love Street. First, Marie II would invoke the storms, just as her mother did before her. Then, she would invite the great Good Mother spirit to take hold of her body—not possess her so much as fuse with her. Together with the Good Mother, Marie II became a being half-woman, half-snake Goddess, just like the statue on Sanité Dédé's initiation ceremony altar all those years before. Marie and the Good Mother would then chat with visiting clients about their troubles, their cheating lovers, or their exploitative landlords, and the Marie and Good Mother combo would proffer advice, both mystic and therapeutic—akin to a nineteenth-century Oprah.

During the proceedings, Marie II would whisper axioms, presumed satanic by outsiders, like, "Love is at the bottom of all things. Love rules the world." She would advise her clients to perform rituals, like lighting nine purple candles to honor the number of the spirit world and the waning moon and the color of power, magic, and the dead. Somehow, those lovers and landlords did have a consistent way of suddenly reforming, regardless of the exact tactics employed—be they spiritual or more earthly (e.g., bribes, threats, expert utilization of gossip). And this success sparked much hubbub regarding the dark powers of the Marie Laveaus. Some accounts claim that Marie II augmented her income and her cache of valuable secrets by working as a hairdresser, though there is no real evidence either confirming or disproving this.

Marie II's younger sister, Philomène, took a different approach. Sometime in the mid-1850s, when she was approximately twenty years old, Philomène entered into plaçage with Emile Alexandre Legendre, a white man. Legendre provided Philomène and their octoroon progeny with a well-appointed town house on Dauphine Street, in the Marigny. Unlike her sister, Philomène was a devout Catholic. Though she didn't attend Mass at the central Spanish cathedral where her mother still worshipped—despite the fact Marie Laveau was now immediately shuffled to the colored section in the back. Instead, Philomène frequented the newly constructed Catholic church in the Tremé designated for Creoles of color. Philomène also spurned all things Voodoo. Because by the 1850s, being associated with the "Voodoos" could make even a white lady into a pariah.

However, amid the arrests of Voodooienne—the majority women—there was one name that never appeared on the police rosters: Marie Laveau. Some speculate this was due to the Widow Paris's connections, which, though waning, still held some sway. But the legend tells another tale, one that is entirely a story of Marie Laveau II.

"I seen her make police [who had come to arrest her] get down and bark like dogs."

"Marie Laveau brought the people into the [Congo] Square with her, unmolested by the policemen. She hypnotized them and they could not do anything."

In public, Marie II always wore a guinea-blue calico dress with full skirts, a blouse with puffed sleeves, a bright tignon folded into seven points atop her head, and large gold hoop earrings. Outfitted in this classic Creole raiment, like a ghost from a fading world, Marie II walked through the new American one, with its freshly granite-paved streets lit by the latest gas lamps, "just like a queen," "like another Solomon, sent from the Almighty God above to come down here and help his people."

Eventually, Marie II took over the private Friday night ceremonies at her mother's home on St. Ann's—or maybe she started them, the exact line between the two Maries remains eternally blurry. She presided over the renegade ceremonies in Congo Square, usually held on Mondays—as the Square was padlocked on any given Sunday—often beneath a hollow tree that was immediately dubbed as some devil's lair by outsiders.

Not everything about Marie II's brand of Voodoo centered on love spells and a positive universal divine. But when she wanted to brave the more destructive side of the cosmic forces, to curse an abusive man or the powers that be, she did not do it out in the open, in Congo Square. Instead, she put on a brown dress, stuck Saint Anthony facedown in her yard, and retreated to a private back altar adorned with lions and tigers, instead of the Saint Pauls and Virgin Marys that covered the altar on full display in the front of her house on Love Street.

But not even hexes and hypnotizing lawmen could stave off the floods of white supremacy forever. By 1860, as America plummeted toward a climactic cracking open, the escalating oppression forced Voodooienne to stop gathering on Congo Square, that century-old symbol of black resistance and pride, entirely. The powers that be covered its open expanses in sycamores or developed them with buildings and chopped down the hollow tree. Then, in 1861, the cracks finally rent the United States asunder. Louisiana and ten other states seceded from the Union. The war followed, with its death and mayhem, rape, and brothers shooting brothers. In the end some 750,000 were left dead, the same proportion of the total population as some eight million today.

New Orleans, previously the wealthiest city in America, emerged from the fires of war with an economy and infrastructure in rubble, never to rebound. In the newly industrialized nation now crisscrossed with rail lines, the Mississippi, New Orleans's former lifeblood, had become more the subject of song than vehicle of commerce. Suddenly, everyone in the Big Easy felt on the down and out and in need of a symbol of power and rebirth.

On the firelit beaches of Lake Pontchartrain, a throng of people—white and black (as there was no longer the concept of in-between), men and women, poor and prominent—had already been waiting for hours. Just as they started to wonder if she'd ever show, Marie II emerged from the dark, far out on the vast placid water, perhaps floating on a wooden skiff or perhaps, as some attest, just walking on the water like Jesus, with a candle on her head and one in each of her hands, fully a Goddess. So it went on the eve of Saint John the Baptist's Day every June after the war.

When she reached the shore, Marie II would immediately drop, her tignon nearly touching the hard dirt as she rapped the ground three times, shouting "Father, Son, and Holy Ghost," while the exuberant crowd joined her. She'd demand they strip to their underclothes. She'd talk of what Saint John meant, that "he was a great man and always did what was right." She'd make a stew, likely sacrificing a rooster and possibly even a black cat—though the latter was reported by a white source of dubious veracity. Regardless of exactly what kind they were, animal sacrifices did occur, the energy of the creatures' blood an offering to the spirits and their flesh a meal for the human congregants. At midnight, after the scantily clad assembly danced toward peak ecstatic transcendence in the summer night, Marie would lead them into the deep, algae-filled waters of Lake Pontchartrain, like Saint John the Baptist once did for Jesus, offering a pungent rebirth from the ancient bayou waters.

Hundreds, then eventually thousands, would ride New Orleans's steam-powered railcars six miles from the city out to the lake, pursuing the Voodoo Queen. As time went on, actual sightings of her grew rarer and rarer, and then stopped entirely after 1872. But soon enough, the night boasted a constellation of other attractions. All along those shores, enclaves of people would gather, making music by torchlight while eating feasts of gumbo, jambalaya, and baked chicken, with few saintly icons or ritual skulls on display. It became something rather resembling today's famous New Orleans Jazz Fest.

But the respite of federal Reconstruction of the formerly Confederate states that had enabled these free displays of Voodoo—and a modicum of rights for black Americans—turned out to just be the eye of the storm. By the early 1870s, posses of angry white men, many armed with guns left over from the war, began killing men of color, especially men of color who tried to vote.

Soon, the already hyperbolized, and oft made-up, press accounts of the Saint John's Eve festivities grew even more fantastic, serving as a convenient ally to the white militias by offering evidence that people of color, as satanic primitives, did not deserve full citizenship. Soon the libel went off the rails. If a baby went missing, it was the Voodoos. Yellow fever? The Voodoos did it. If a black man ran for office, he could be sure one of his relatives would suddenly, and often unbeknownst to the relative, become "a known Voodooienne." The most frequent and damnable charge: Voodoos drove once-pure white women—those poor, weak, muddleheaded white women—mad. Because clearly any woman lusting for direct connection to the divine, a connection that required only her own body and mind, instead of the conduit of a male cleric and an acceptance that her body is sin incarnate, had to be a lunatic.

The death of Reconstruction, along with its promises of forty acres, a mule, and a free, integrated South, also brought the end to *la famille Laveau*. First, in 1872, Emile Legendre died, forcing Philomène and her children to move into the Widow Paris's cottage on St. Ann's. The

Widow Paris was by then in declining health and was soon confined to the high walnut bed she once shared with Christophe—placing Philomène firmly at the helm of the family abode. After Philomène moved in, there are no accounts of any Voodoo rituals on St. Ann's, on Friday night or any other night. It is also the last year any Marie Laveau is confirmed to have reigned over the annual Saint John's Eve festivities.

According to official records, Marie Euchariste Glapion had died in 1862, causing many historians to attest that someone else entirely, someone not even kin to the Widow Paris, must have become her heir and namesake who performed rituals into the 1870s. However, Marie II's alleged date of demise was not declared until her son, Victor Pierre Crocker, and his aunt Philomène went to court to legally make it so in November 1881. Nineteen years may seem a long time to wait to report a death. But 1862 offered several distinct advantages to the remaining Laveaus. Being in the midst of the tumult of war, a death that year stood nearly impossible to either prove or disprove. And, as the date occurred in advance of the infamous Reconstruction-era Saint John's Eve ceremonies, it conveniently freed the family from the taint of association. Finally, the Widow Paris, who might have objected to the premature erasure of her firstborn and her family's Voodoo legacy, had died, at age seventy-nine, some five months prior to the report.

"Marie Glapion was an outcast from her family. You see, that Madame Legendre, her sister, was so stuck up that she done denied her," said a neighbor when asked about the events some decades later.

But Philomène was not the villain. Like most any mother, Philomène wanted what she thought best for her children. And from their earliest days, as she stared at their faces sleeping softly in a bassinette, swaddled in cream-colored sheets, Philomène knew something about her offspring's futures. One drop of black blood or not, they would be able to pass as white. They could even—as long as no troublesome associations with the Queen of the Damned clung to them—transition over to the white world entirely. And as far as anyone can tell, they did. Her conviction about taking this path likely deepened after Reconstruction failed and Legendre died, taking with him the family's access to money and protection. By masterminding the official erasure of one sister, she would ensure all her children avoided the fate of New Orleanians of color—particularly the fate of the women—she'd come to know all too well.

2018
New Orleans

I learned of Erzulie Freda on Marie Laveau's 217th birthday. Erzulie Freda is a spirit, or *lwa* (as the spirits are called in Haiti), of Haitian origin, who has grown quite popular among Voodooienne stateside. As one bushy-bearded devotee told me in a Voodoo shop in New Orleans's upscale Garden District, Erzulie Freda is a gorgeous Creole woman who has lived in plaçage with a series of male spirits. She holds intellectual and artistic salons, the object of everyone in her demimonde's desire and attention. But now, and also eternally—as that's how it goes with spirits—at age forty or forty-five, the makeup is starting to flake, the corset is getting tighter. Or at least that's how this gay male Voodooienne thought of this spirit of love and luxury, as he informed me and the triumvirate of witches sitting at a table in the shop. Each of the women was roughly forty; none of them wore wedding rings.

Looking around at the walls lined with sequenced tapestries that depicted various lwa and their outsize—but very human—attributes, I wondered what his story of Erzulie Freda meant to the listening witches. Then, almost as an afterthought, I wondered what it meant to me—someone who'd had much more liberty to choose my path than Erzulie Freda, or at least than the many earthbound women who'd lived in similar circumstances. I don't pretend to comprehend spirits' notions of freedom and constraint.

I was a twenty-first-century single woman in her thirties, a lifelong lover of demimondes suspect of the "respectable" world, someone whose social media feeds were, nevertheless, increasingly full of other people's promotions, new homes, babies, and marathons virtuously run while I was still in bed hungover. Since graduating from college, I'd made a living writing in various ways, journalistic, artistic, and for nonprofits, but I'd never really dug in, or committed, professionally speaking—and also personally speaking. None of my post-collegiate romantic relationships had lasted past the two-year mark.

I knew I didn't actually want someone else's Facebook profile page. However, I couldn't repress the creeping feeling that by failing to glean these traditional trappings of adulthood—and in particular, womanhood—I had somehow failed at the mission called life. As a somewhat androgynous homosexual, I felt far less pressure aimed my way in that conventional regard than many women who, when single and childless at my age, face a pity closely related to ire specially reserved for them, even now.

Erzulie Freda's story, as it was told to me, felt pointed. Because what I'd apparently chosen was to live my life based on some idea that roots just bind a person to mud, likely to suck her down, six feet under. And that idea had reached the far side of viable. Sure, I had no professional or personal demands tethering me in place. I could go anywhere, do anything at the drop of a dime, quit a full-time job to take my chances freelance, stay out as late as I liked at a Brooklyn-hipster equivalent of a nineteenth-century salon, walk my tiny dog for hours, then spend a few more reading on my couch, or engage in copious budget travel. But at some point along the way, these formerly thrilling open expanses had started to feel hollow. At some point, freedom had indeed just become another word for nothing left to lose—while "busted flat in Baton Rouge," which is also in Louisiana.

Sitting there with those witches, I found myself wondering, *What exactly do I want then?* Per usual, I came up short. So I decided to employ some key terminology, as less academic tools that might elucidate my wants and desires remained stubbornly hard to conjure. *One can bad-mouth the patriarchy all day,* I thought, *but that doesn't necessarily nullify even we bad mouthers' adherence to subtler aspects of the path it has paved—a path most of us grew up believing had no exits.* I wanted to chart my own course out of my disquietude, not follow one based on the internalized dictates—the ghosts—of old men. But who, or what, could help guide me?

Some say Marie II died during a hurricane, sitting alone in a house she'd bought out on Lake Pontchartrain, la Maison Blanche, her White House. They say that's how she wanted it. That on Saint John's Eve sometime between 1872 and 1881, with her followers as witness, she stood on the shores of its deep waters, singing "I want to die in that lake," over a chorus of cicadas so loud they sounded electric. Then, Marie II knelt before her altar for three days praying for the storms, and when they finally came, they swept la Maison Blanche from its foundation in the porous bayou sod. They say Marie's body then washed onto the rocks in perfect angelic repose, arms crossed, eyes closed.

Others agree with most of this account. She raised the storms all right, but she did not actually die that day. Though she tried to stop them, the people who loved her pulled her out of a window at the last minute. She died some years later. And when she did, Le Grande Zombi, her faithful serpent, slithered right down off her altar and out into the night, never to return.

Whatever the truth, whatever the year, and whatever her reasons, by the time she may or may not have invoked the storms, while bent on self-destruction, it had become clear that emancipation did not mean equality or true freedom for her or her people. It had come to mean institutionalized terror, armed militias, lynchings, rape, and Jim Crow, with no end in sight. No one can ride a raft, charting their own course through a hurricane, forever—might as well pick the time and the place one takes you under.

What historians do know for sure is that during "the hottest spell for half a century," Marie Laveau, the Widow Paris, succumbed. There is no doubt about the date of her passing, June 15, 1881, or the cause, dehydration, likely brought on by some intestinal malady. By that time, the Widow Paris—already often credited as the lone Marie Laveau and the embodiment of both her own legend and that of her somewhat chimeric daughter—had become an American celebrity. Even in the post-Reconstruction South, when an American celebrity's body, regardless of color or if they served the devil, got laid into a carriage and paraded through the streets to St. Louis Cemetery No. 1, the crowds grew so large a person couldn't get within three blocks of the procession. They might as well have been returning a Goddess to Olympus.

Obituaries for Marie Laveau appeared in all the New Orleans dailies and even in the *New York Times*, a rarity for any woman of the era, particularly one of color. While the write-ups were all paeans to her power, they took two distinct roads. Some painted her as "the prime mover and soul of the indecent orgies of the ignoble Voudous," to whose "influence may be attributed the fall of many a virtuous woman." Others described a woman who "spent her life doing good for the sake of doing good alone," who "enjoyed the respect and affection of thousands who knew her, of numbers whom she befriended in times of dire distress, of sick folks snatched from the shadow of death and nursed by her to health and strength."

Philomène, who would cross over last in 1897, chose to feed this binary of good or evil, avoiding all references to Voodoo when speaking about her pious Catholic mother's sainted life to white reporters. This left the Voodoo side of Marie's legacy entirely up to the racist publications to spin. But whatever the reality of the powers and lives of the Marie Laveaus, one thing stands as verifiable fact: one week after the Widow Paris's death, on the first summer solstice in half a century with no Marie Laveau reigning over the city, for the first time in years, it rained on Saint John's Eve.

3

And Then the Floods

After the rain came the floods.

In 1893, the city of New Orleans officially renamed what remained of Congo Square for Confederate General P. G. T. Beauregard. That same year, a Creole man of color named Homer Plessy appealed his arrest for refusing to leave the "whites only" section of a New Orleans train. His resolve resulted in the 1896 Supreme Court case *Plessy v. Ferguson*, which established the doctrine of "separate but equal"—a mythical title, but nevertheless the legal precedent for segregation and Jim Crow in an entrenched white-male-supremacist America.

On August 29, 2005, Hurricane Katrina hit New Orleans with 127-mile-per-hour winds. But it wasn't until the levees surrounding this city built below sea level burst, after decades of ever-expanding cracks, that the chaos started.

After the levees unleashed, 80 percent of the city flooded, with the waters over fifteen feet high and rising. More than fifteen hundred people died statewide, and four hundred thousand in the city alone faced displacement, many—largely people of color—never to return. In the Superdome, home to the New Orleans Saints, some thirty thousand residents, mostly people of color, sought sanctuary. Inside, without power or air-conditioning, temperatures passed ninety degrees daily, food ran out, potable water ran dry, and toilets overflowed. Images like those of "a wasteland," "a war zone," a "third-world country" filled TV screens nationwide, along with the footage of all those people, once again mostly of color, stranded in the deep waters, on roofs just above the flood line, or on makeshift rafts, fighting for survival, with little help from the government.

Basically everyone who didn't already know got it, at least for a moment, a flash: the legacy of our past and the parts of our foundation story that we, as a nation, had been doing our darndest to close our eyes to and bury, were on an endless loop on prime-time TV, with the waters continuing to rise. The forces of creation and destruction have never been polite—or subtle. Though what we do with them remains up to us—and at the present moment is to be determined.

When Marie Laveau II died sometime circa 1880, perhaps in a hurricane she conjured, her remains were allegedly laid to rest in an unmarked vault in St. Louis Cemetery No. 2. What is nearly certain is that, unlike the rest of her family—her father and mother and brothers and sisters—she did not find her final resting place in the high Glapion-Laveau crypt in St. Louis No. 1. She remained a pariah, even on the other side, at least to Philomène, who was by then running the show for the family. The story goes that eventually they demolished the cemetery wall containing the vault, which her admirers had come to call the Wishing Vault, in order to make way for an office. A construction crew moved the human remains across town to Girod, a Protestant cemetery.

Today, Girod Street Cemetery, too, is no more. In its place stands the Superdome and the surrounding commercial district. And when they built the stadium in the 1970s, bystanders reportedly watched construction workers laughing as they tossed about the bleached unburied bones. Then, thirty years after the stadium opened, to the month, the waters came—washing away much illusion.

People often say New Orleans is the least American city in America. I disagree. What could be more American than that place, the good and the bad—and the very, very ugly.

The Saint John's Eve festivals out on Lake Pontchartrain died around the time Congo Square became a Confederate general, at least the actual ones presided over by actual Voodoo priestesses and priests; however, minstrel mock-ups of the once-holy rite persisted to at least the turn of the twentieth century. In these, "a huge Negro clad in breechcloth" boiled and ate a black cat while "impassioned black savages danced naked as islanders to the beating of ox skulls and tom-toms, the weird crooning of the hags, and the sharp ejaculations of bucks and wenches."

History may be written by the victors, but legend remains a free-for-all. Despite a calculated campaign to desecrate all things related to Voodoo and Marie Laveau—and the empowerment inherent in them—including attempts like the minstrel spectacles and an 1897 law outright outlawing "Voodoos," a religion (check your Bill of Rights), Voodoo Queens don't just go quietly into the night. They become spirits, myths, legends, something—for better or worse—no man can kill with pen, paper, or semiautomatics.

However, like her obituaries, the legend of Marie Laveau, a whole separate entity in death, and the third Marie Laveau in our story, took two distinctly forked roads—one that helped grease the wheels of power and the other a flaming pebble in their spokes. The first legend, forged in book after book written by white men (a few of them bestsellers), painted Marie Laveau and her "Voodoos" as powerful but satanic, a people prone to group sex and turning babies into black cats after "they took their terrible oaths" to the devil with their "lips smeared with the blood of freshly slaughtered animals and fowls."

At the same time that those white authors were cashing in on Marie's name, the second fork of the legend spread in predominantly black neighborhoods like the Ninth Ward, the Tremé, and Algiers, as an oral history, ever evolving—placing it firmly in the realm of myth, a creation of a collective mind, and a far more potent and immortal sphere than mere legend. However, this side of the bifurcated Marie Laveau remained largely underground and inaccessible outside those New Orleanian enclaves.

Then, in 1928, at the height of Jim Crow, a black woman in her midthirties with devastatingly cool eyes, a slanted broad-brim hat, and a sharply tailored skirt falling just below the knees arrived in the Big Easy. Zora Neale Hurston had come to learn of the local Hoodoo scene and considered herself something of a Hoodoo or African "folk-tradition" expert. But what she found, to her consternation, was that she had no idea who this Marie Laveau was whose name everyone kept dropping like she'd been a world-famous mahatma.

Soon enough, Hurston found herself at the door of a fading-pink stucco house in the Vieux Carré. It took a while for Luke Turner, the man who opened the door, to warm to the fast-talking lady down from New York City, but when he did, he led her right to his back altar. There, draping himself in a looping dried snakeskin he claimed belonged to a long-dead serpent named Le Grande Zombi, he attested that he himself was the directly descended nephew of that snake's Voodoo Queen master, Marie Laveau II.

"Time went around pointing out what God had already made. Moses had seen the Burning Bush. Solomon by magic knowed all wisdom. And Marie Laveau was a woman in New Orleans," as Luke put it. He also happened to have unique knowledge of Marie II's Hoodoo spells and wisdom, crafted with the input of the Good Mother and passed down from Marie to Luke to his visitor and, soon, apprentice.

Realizing what she had found, Hurston stayed and studied with Luke Turner for months, learning Marie II's ways along with more recent concoctions for conjuring love and luck and death. Voodoo, like life, must evolve or die. Then Luke told her she was ready. So Zora lay naked and prostrate on a snakeskin for three days and three nights, immobile and fasting, and eventually hallucinating, ecstatically, five times. On the fourth day, Luke Turner painted a lightning bolt from her right shoulder to her left hip, telling her the Great One was to speak to her in storms—just as the Great One did to Marie Laveau before her. Then, after a blood oath and some light feasting on Saint Joseph bread and spinach cakes, among other dishes, Luke, Zora, and five other members of his Hoodoo tribe headed to the swamp to sacrifice a sheep and formally baptize their initiate into their Hoodoo tradition.

First in the *Journal of American Folklore*, then her book *Mules and Men*, Zora Neale Hurston set out to record the Marie Laveau who served as a symbol of liberation, not Satan. "Marie Laveau is the great name of Negro conjure in America," wrote Zora. "It is probable she sums up traditionally a whole era of hoodoo; she was the great name in its Golden Age." "The loving ones find a boat and went out to where her house floats on one side and break a window to bring her out," Luke told Zora, of Marie II's rescue just before being drowned by that hurricane forever.

And Zora's own mission to rescue the Marie Laveau conjured by her own people from obscurity was soon bolstered by the Louisiana Writers' Project, part of the Depression-era WPA, which sent workers door-to-door asking almost every person of color old enough to remember what they thought of Marie Laveau. The field notes were never published in full. They were, however, exploited by the white writers to give a whiff of authenticity to their books about evil Marie and her demonic minions.

Still, try as it may, the white supremacist peine forte et dure could not press Voodoo to death. Like so many tributaries forced from the source, Voodoo instead squeezed out from the clutches of the powers that be into several distinct new practices. One faction slipped underground in the Jim Crow South, and there it morphed into a more purely Hoodoo variation of the original, into the tradition of Luke Turner—focused on spells and charms and mojo bags. The larger cosmology of the New Orleans Voodoo religion, never recorded on paper, now remains only in the ether, yet eternal, as I've been told that on the spirit side there is no time. However, the more religious aspects of the New Orleans Voodoo legacy, with its melding of two pious old worlds into something new, did not perish entirely in the flood either.

On a humid Sunday in September 2018, on the heels of Tropical Storm Gordon and the eve of Marie Laveau's birthday, a Black Spiritualist Church just off Abundance Street celebrated its eighty-eighth anniversary. The number eight signifies new beginnings. And this church had undergone many of those, surviving through Jim Crow and Katrina and into the second decade of the new millennium.

A few dozen worshippers, each exuding an ample Sunday-morning openheartedness, took seats inside the bright sanctuary in freshly polished pine pews stocked with both *Good News* and King James Bibles. On the high altars in the front, back, and at all four corners stood fogged plastic bottles, half filled with rainwater and blessed with nine Lord's Prayers—like some sacred moat protecting the aging statues of Saints Anthony, Peter, and Michael. The paint had flaked off from each saint's face and robes, leaving jagged puddles of exposed alabaster.

The ministers and bishops, both women and men, entered. The people rose. The clergy conjured the Holy Spirit with shouts set to gourd rattles and tambourines. The congregants shook with what they'd conjured, stomping. The gospel tunes, inflected with an African twang, as all gospel tunes are, brought on the climax, with everyone shouting and reaching out and up to the divine. Then the archbishop, cloaked in the color purple, invoked the number nine as all shouted "Money" into the four cardinal corners—manifesting there in a sector of the city where money, or more specifically its dearth, often seemed its own inexorable God-Force. In the end, everyone processed out so ecstatic they took to hugging the stranger, in from Brooklyn, sitting quietly in a pew toward the back.

Exactly one century before that Sunday service, in 1918, Mother Leafy Anderson first came to New Orleans on a mission from God. Anderson was a black woman from Chicago, a proper sort, thin with erect posture and a string of pearls. She learned of the Voodoo then still humming in the city's water—though deeper and deeper underground— and incorporated it into her self-made medley of Catholicism, African American Protestantism, and Spiritualism. As New Orleanians of color moved north during the Great Migration, they brought her vision with them. And when she died nine years later, at age forty, her divine inspiration had already manifested into the Black Spiritualist Churches of America, a loose national Christian confederation that placed extra weight on the Holy Ghost prong of the Trinity. In the final years before the Great Depression, Black Spiritualist Churches claimed a substantial portion of African American Christian congregants in most major US cities. However, the words *Marie Laveau* and *Voodoo* remained a taint, not a benediction, that hung over the religion, curtailing its expansion.

Still, many devout Christians have opted, and continue to opt, to attend Black Spiritualist services. Many have attested that the difference from other church services that struck them most, especially at first, does have to do with the legacy of Voodoo and Marie Laveau, though not in the way they'd been warned. It's the women who stand at the pulpit preaching the Good Word every Sunday. In fact, from the time the church was forged by Mother Anderson, in the spirit of its ancestor Marie Laveau, to the end of the twentieth century, women constituted 60 percent of the denomination's leaders in New Orleans—unprecedented for a mainstream branch of Christianity.

Many services are, indeed, rife with Voodoo-derived practices and symbology—healing spirit possession, manifesting, the sacred number nine, the color purple, blessed rain. But the Voodoo influence has grown increasingly covert and coded with the years. Back when Mother Catherine

Seals replaced Mother Anderson at her local congregation's helm, things were different. Mother Catherine's Temple of the Innocent Blood, a massive tent topped by a Greek cross and located in a muddy marsh out past the Industrial Canal, proudly featured a giant red, white, and blue serpent made of panels on its main wall. At the church's height, as the Jazz Age gave way to the Depression, some ten thousand congregants regularly gazed by the light of five hundred kerosene lamps at that paneled image of Creation snaking across the wall, and at Mother Catherine, dressed all in white save a red cape or blue bandana. She preached atop a simple chair perched on a high platform, the opposite of pretension.

Zora Neale Hurston recorded it all, having visited the sanctuary in addition to Luke Turner's pink stucco house during her prolonged research visits to the bayou.

Like Marie Laveau II, Zora Neale Hurston lived as a woman both of and before her time. Her detractors, who were legion, found her focus on Hoodoo and Voodoo and black spirituality unworthy of scholarly study, the realm of superstition and stereotypes (and women), not literature. And though she had been a leading light of the Harlem Renaissance who received two Guggenheim Fellowships, she fell out of fashion and into obscurity, her works forgotten, suppressed. Finally, in 1960, after years of working as a maid, she died alone and was buried in an unmarked grave in Florida.

It took another woman, a Pulitzer Prize–winning writer, and black second-wave feminist, or womanist, named Alice Walker to buy Zora a tombstone and pull her writings—including the Voodoo and Hoodoo tomes and *Their Eyes Were Watching God*, a novel now regularly listed as one of the best books of the twentieth century—from obscurity.

Back in the Jim Crow New Orleans of the turn of the twentieth century, another alchemic synthesis was taking place. That time and place has long been credited for birthing jazz. But historians have now further pinpointed the art form's origin to Congo Square. For one, the square had served as the first public forum for an often-improvised fusion of Voodoo-inspired African music with European, and later American, influences featuring drums and horns. But historians also cite the square, and even more so Marie Laveau, as the ultimate symbol and reminder of the power and beauty of African culture, even as the floods of white supremacy tried to drown all such pride. It's no coincidence that Louis Armstrong's grand-mother, who largely raised him, was a Voodooienne, or that, when growing up in the Marigny, Jelly Roll Morton, a man of Creole heritage, often lived with his godmother, Eulalie, believed to be a latter-day Voodoo Queen.

Jazz has been called the greatest American art form. Historians claim it helped birth the Modern (capital *M*) world. And without jazz, and by extension Congo Square, there might not be rock 'n' roll and that whole other branch of (lowercase *m*) modernity. Of course, Voodoo is only one string in a complex knot that makes up modern American culture, but it's a thick one. Yet most Americans have never heard of Marie Laveau—and they certainly didn't read about her in their high school history books.

There is one place, however, where her name still looms promi-nently—embossed all over the Voodoo dolls the Voodoo Queen likely never used, Florida water labels, craft beers, faux-antique store signs, and the local Voodoo Museum. Because, in the New Orleans French Quarter, the name *Marie Laveau* no longer conjures fear; instead, it conjures money.

Starting in the 1970s, as the Superdome rose from the cemetery, a new brand of more visible Voodoo began budding up, led by people—more often than not white—who didn't feel so threatened by the shun-ning and violence that practicing Voodoo often still incurred. With New Orleans's own centuries-old Voodoo cosmology fractured and indecipherable, those individuals fused what they could glean from the Haitian Vodou tradition, which remains unbroken, with New Age sen-sibilities and the legends and myths surrounding Marie Laveau.

Before Katrina, locals estimate that around three thousand self-iden-tified Voodooiennes resided in the city (though it's hard to know for sure without, say, a Voodoo box on the census form). Most of the practitioners still lived in and around the Lower Ninth Ward and other African American neighborhoods. Many may have even practiced lineages passed through the generations and, like Luke Turner's, directly linked to the Marie Laveaus. But after the waters departed, leaving the city's population halved—with the largest losses in African American neighborhoods—the estimation is that only some three hundred Voodooiennes remained, many of them of the newer, 1970s variety. And so, in the twenty-first century, New Orleans Voodoo has reemerged from the storm far whiter than before.

Some argue that Voodoo is a living tradition, and the current version is what it's lived to become. Many others are angry that the leading faces of Voodoo in the city are now white—as there are many black Voodooienne still active.

Despite the best efforts of Zora Neale Hurston, Mother Leafy Anderson, and others, we will never know the exact details of either of the Marie Laveaus' lives, their religion, or their fights to maintain their world as white Americans, bountiful and rapacious as locusts, descended. But just like so many religions' seminal male figures about whom we know few concrete facts—men like Jesus and Moses and Buddha—the final Marie Laveau, the mythic Marie Laveau, persists as a collectively created incantation. She's a product of a people's desires and needs, somehow truer than recorded fact can be—words that never apply to politicians or the news.

The combination of these three Marie Laveaus—the first, the second, and the legend—is the closest thing to the real Marie Laveau we have. This Marie Laveau made police fall to their knees and bark while dancing with a serpent. She conjured the storms and walked on water. She collected dirt on every official in the city worth blackmailing. She was also a teenage mother. She also felt small and unsure. She pulled back hundreds who'd fallen sick with fever from death's door and ministered to men condemned to die. She put death curses on others bringing misery on her people. Marie Laveau is neither a saint nor a boogeywoman, strength nor weakness, Madonna nor whore. She is their nexus—power and life, resiliency, art, resistance, a maelstrom of creation and destruction, a crucible. She is the mother of the American feminist mystic tradition, our nation's founding witch.

> Now there lived a conjure-lady, not long ago
> In New Orleans, Louisiana, named Marie Laveau
> Believe it or not, strange as it seem
> She made her fortune selling voodoo, and interpreting dreams
>
> She was known throughout the nation as the Voodoo Queen
> Folks come to her, from miles and miles around
> She show them how to put that voodoo down . . .
>
> Now Marie Laveau held 'em in her hand
> New Orleans was her promised land
> Quality folks, come from far and near
> This wonder woman, for to hear . . .
>
> Oh Marie Laveau, Oh Marie Laveau
> Oh Marie Laveau, Oh Marie Laveau
> The folks still believe, in the Voodoo Queen
> From way down yonder in New Orleans.

—Oscar "Papa" Celestin, 1954[3]

---

3   Oscar "Papa" Celestin was born in rural Louisiana in 1884 to a Creole family and a father who worked as a sugarcane cutter. Oscar moved to New Orleans in 1904, as Jim Crow law solidified and Voodoo was forced fully underground. He started playing music with legends raised under Voodoo's influence, including Louis Armstrong and Jelly Roll Morton, before becoming a legend in his own right. This song perpetuating the oral history of Marie Laveau was recorded shortly before his death, which occurred in December 1954. It is his last known recording.

PART II

Cora L. V. Scott, Rock Star Nineteenth-Century Spiritualist Medium

4

CROSSING THE VEIL

2017

As I made my way toward the back room, I just couldn't shake the ingrained idea that séances were somehow satanic. By "back room" I mean a not-so-converted garage, its concrete walls painted solid black and lacking in insulation against the November chill, the lone source of electric light a low-wattage bulb dangling from a wire like a condemned man just departed. All of which contributed to my nagging concern that the night could go horribly, cinematically awry.

I'd come alone to this séance in Brooklyn's Bushwick neighborhood in the back (or former garage) of an occult store, nestled at the previously industrial pulsing heart of the now-hipster-Disneyland swath of New York City. As such, its glass storefront, branded with images of a full lunar cycle, was surrounded by converted warehouse lofts, thrift stores, and art studios, not to mention the rugged-chic restaurants, with interiors made entirely of reclaimed wood, that touted extensive lists of local craft beers one can sip out of a mason jar while munching wasabi-spiced fish tacos before heading to one's first séance.

Prior to that moment, I hadn't hit up such a happening in years. The hipster, spirit-side confab marked my return to the mystic fold— and ultimately sparked my quest to connect with my ancestral spirit coven.

I couldn't say exactly why I decided to rejoin that night, one of the first cold nights of a late hot fall. I can, however, pinpoint the general genres of the inchoate uncertainties that gnawed at my chakra balance as I surveyed the room:

(a) My country seemed to be in free fall toward an unrecognizable hell dimension.

(b) I was recently single—again—and disturbed not because I was brokenhearted, but instead decidedly relieved at having concluded one more iteration of my personal destructive-relationship Groundhog Day.

(c) Amid all the flux, ghostly memories of childhood past were once again rearing up from their shallow graves and wreaking a bit of havoc on my mental stability.

Therapy is a widely recommended avenue for parsing this tangled yarn ball of discontent. But it seemed just too damned gradual. I wanted clarity and catharsis, and I wanted them now. And I was fully aware that may require divine intervention. Well, that, and one hell of a medium.

In the spring of 1840, outside the small town of Cuba, New York, on the border between a deep forest of shadows and rolling bright fields of carefully cultivated wheat, a small house sat on the fringes of a lumber mill lot. Inside, on the master bed, a woman screamed one final scream. She saw immediately that the baby was no ordinary baby. God himself had marked the girl-child as the bearer of a great cosmic gift, not just Eve's original weakness and sin. Over her head and face and eyes—deep set and the color of the sea—was a clear viscous membrane, blotched with red like splattered wine, that gave the baby a ghostly grayish-blue pallor. The scene of her birth also conjured one of death and the cycle of life itself. Therein lay the blessing. That veil, or "caul," portended spiritual greatness, psychic acuity, some kind of direct line to the other side.

Soon, talk among the adults turned to what to name the girl. The father, David, insisted she be named after the mother, Lodencia. Lodencia, however, objected, never having been particularly fond of the moniker. The attending physician, Dr. Washborne, offered a suggestion. Since the baby had been born with the mark, why not call her Cora, a name meaning poetess, priestess, and counselor.

David Scott considered it, recalling the way his baby had stared back at him from the other side of the veil—like someone who knew something he didn't. Yes, Cora it would be, but Lodencia too: Cora Lodencia Veronica Scott to be exact.

Cora L. V. Scott was definitely someone who was forever knowing something that everyone else didn't. The girl learned like lightning, flying past all her classmates, including the boys. One of her teachers later stated Cora had something akin to a photographic memory, an ability to retain anything she read.

But her schoolhouse lessons did not constitute the entirety of young Cora's education, far from it. The New York State of her youth was on fire, in a metaphorical leaping, licking, rapaciously contagious way, with the spirits of radical utopian change. Religious reform movements were popping up with such radical abundance in western and central New

York State during America's Second Great Awakening that it earned the region the epithet the Burned-Over District—it was said there was no spiritual "fuel" left to burn. The region produced religious hits including, but not limited to, Mormonism, Millerites (the seed from which Jehovah's Witnesses would sprout), the Oneida Community, and Spiritualism.

During the peak of that Burned-Over District blaze, in March 1848, one month before Cora turned eight, two adolescent girls, Kate and Maggie, popularly known as the Fox sisters, began communing with a farmhouse spirit via raps and knocks—a sort of "spiritual telegraph"—in Hydesville, New York. Their newly excavated ghost, whom they called Mr. Splitfoot, claimed to be a murder victim, killed in their cellar, haunting them in search of justice. Soon enough, neighbors, and then far-flung strangers, were flocking to their home, and the girls began knocking out messages from departed aunts, brothers, and lovers with far more mundane agendas. These remote farmhouse rappings turned out to be the spark that caught wind and set the whole of America aflame.

In 1848, a barely adolescent America—still parsing out its identity—was primed for blazes of radical change. Cemented norms and ways had begun cracking apart in recently industrialized East Coast cities and the new "wild" western towns. Just four years before the Fox sisters met Mr. Splitfoot, Samuel Morse had sent the first telegraph message from DC to Baltimore, collapsing time and space. Five years before that, Louis Daguerre had introduced the world to the photograph, and from that instant on, an image of any earthly thing could persist for eternity. Long-distance railroads had transformed the nation's conception of distance and national connection.

However, every light casts a shadow. Tuberculosis, smallpox, yellow fever, and cholera also spread like a blaze among the ever-more densely settled populace. Between 1790 and the start of the Civil War, the average American life expectancy decreased from fifty-six to forty-eight.

Still, with once immutable metaphysical mountains suddenly being moved one after another, anything felt possible in the New World. And it seemed only one small leap from the power of the human mind to transform such earthly experiences to that mind divining methods to commune directly with, and transfigure, our relationship with the denizens of the other side—beings who were then at the forefront of Americans' cerebral cortex.

By day, buttoned-up order and deductive reasoning ruled America's Victorian-era streets. By night, however, those same gaslit thoroughfares were awash in ghosts—phantoms of the newly obliterated past, the legion dearly departed, and all living who did not fit neatly within the strictly defined social confines of the time. These hauntings—and published tales of them—soon materialized into a national obsession.

A man of his time and place, David Scott spent hours reading Thomas Paine. He spent hours reading anything, really, that he thought might provide a spiritual alternative to the bleak Puritanical strictures of his youth. One day in 1850 as he flipped through the pages of avowed Spiritualist Horace Greeley's *New York Tribune*, God, or a spirit guide, coughed up a clue to the hereafter: an article about a place called Hopedale, located outside Milford, Massachusetts.

Started in 1842 by the Universalist reverend Adin Ballou, Hopedale was an oasis of nonviolent communal living and positive thinking. By 1850, when David Scott read about the commune, Spiritualism's ideology had also woven its way into Ballou's Christian teachings. David immediately took pen to inkpot and struck up a correspondence with the Universalist-Spiritualist reverend. A few months later, David loaded all his worldly possessions into a cart and relocated his young family—including Cora, then age ten, her brother and sister, and Lodencia—to Hopedale.

Situated on a verdant six-hundred-acre farm, Hopedale contained rows of glistening-new wooden homes and a small chapel for the 170 resident believers. It had a brown pond filled with green lily pads and gold-, yellow-, and bluegill fish—just as lovely as that pond called Walden, barely forty miles north, where Henry David Thoreau was channeling the same zeitgeist of change into a movement called transcendentalism.

Both of these very American ideologies could trace their roots to various spiritual and cultural traditions. One main road that led to Spiritualism traced back to European mesmerism, a philosophy centered on an idea of an all-connecting divine "fluid" that, when tapped, could heal or induce a trance state in which one could converse with the swirling divine. Quakers and Shakers also lent notions of a divine light found in all people that made them equal in the eyes of God. Another main root was the shamanic religious traditions of Native Americans and African Americans, in which the natural world stood as divine as anything in the sky, and any person could feel like they'd touched it by letting the spirits touch and take hold of them. And pretty soon these theological ideas of equal access to divinity begot radical notions of the equal right of all people to a decent life here on earth.

A man named Andrew Jackson Davis, known as the Poughkeepsie Seer, first wrote down much of the Spiritualist philosophy in *The Principles of Nature, Her Divine Revelations, and a Voice to Mankind*, published in 1847. However, no one paid much attention to it until the Fox sisters' debut.

Day after day in Hopedale, young Cora sat by her father's side as Adin Ballou, a handsome man with sharp features and calm, compassionate eyes, preached to his flock. Cora watched Ballou draw people in, build them up with his cadence and lyrical oratory toward a climactic bridge, and just as the congregants thought they couldn't bear it anymore, he provided spiritual release. Then he brought them gently back down to earth, like they were floating on a feather. Cora watched this, absorbed the power of having a throng dancing in the palm of your hand. She would never forget the then-radical words and ideas she first heard during that long fateful summer—about abolition, universal salvation, and, pivotally, female equality.

In July 1848, just four months after the Fox sisters' first rappings, and just twenty-five miles away from their home, in Seneca Falls, New York, sixty-eight women and thirty-two men signed "The Declaration of Sentiments," demanding recognition of women as equal members of society. From the earliest moments of these two parallel movements, born in tandem, some serious cross-pollination occurred. Many of the people at Seneca Falls would go on to become early subscribers to the Spiritualist movement—and nearly every Spiritualist supported women's suffrage.

More so than nearly any other reform Christian or mystical movement that arose during the Second Great Awakening, Spiritualism was rooted in ideals of equality and spiritual autonomy, eschewing the biblically ordained hierarchy of gender, race, and creed that had dominated the vision for America's future. As one speaker later put it at an 1858 Spiritualist convention, "The individual, the Church, or the State, that attempt to control the opinions and practices of any man or woman, by an authority or power outside of his or her own soul, is guilty of a flagrant wrong." Or, as it reads in *History of Woman Suffrage*, compiled by Susan B. Anthony, Elizabeth Cady Stanton, and other top-dog suffragists, "The only religious sect in the world . . . that has recognized the equality of woman, is Spiritualism."

In 1850, Cora was still young enough to roam free and untethered, though she knew soon enough that she, too, would endure the constraints put on womanhood. One August afternoon, Cora roamed into the reverend's garden to pick currants. Staring down at a berry in her palm, she heard a happy "hello." Looking up, she saw Ballou's oldest son, Adin Augustus, then eighteen and home for the summer from university. Suddenly, to the surprise of the politely smiling Augustus, this pretty girl with a halo of golden ringlets screamed and sprinted out of the garden. Cora and Augustus never spoke again that summer—in part because Cora assiduously avoided the young man, whose eyes she claimed "seemed to look right through her," and in part because David Scott had no plans to stay put in Hopedale.

The following spring, David moved his family to Lake Mills, Wisconsin, after convincing Adin Ballou to let him create a "Hopedale of the West." Lake Mills was a not yet formally incorporated community in a state that was not quite four years old. It was nestled among "virgin" land made farmland by Dutch immigrants newly arrived via the Erie Canal–Great Lakes route. When the Scotts rode into town on a horse-drawn cart through blankets of near ethereally green grass, dotted by barns with gently puckered roofs and by lolling spotted cows, it likely all seemed new enough to be magic—or at least a little enchanted by those American pastoral fantasies of endless possibility.

On a mild late-autumn day months after the Scotts' arrival, Cora sprawled beneath an arbor of trees behind their new home, planning to study. But, staring up at the bare branches, dark and jagged across the clear sky as black lightning, Cora drifted off to sleep. When she awoke, groggy and cold, the dusk was gathering. She wiped the dust from her petticoats and hurriedly gathered her belongings, only to see that while she'd slept her school slate had been covered in a strange looping script. The only other person in the garden was her four-year-old sister, whose literacy skills were, at best, questionable. Cora, perplexed, took the slate to her mother, who gasped. As the story goes, the looping script spelled out a message for Lodencia from her sister who had passed some time before, and of whom Cora had been told very little.

Quickly, Cora's divination advanced. Instead of writing out messages while in trance, she began to speak them in a steady, low tone that would become her signature style. But Cora still needed one key piece of her medium puzzle.

In 1852, back in Massachusetts, Augustus Ballou took fever and died. Days later, before news of his passing purportedly could have reached the Scott family in their rural outpost, Cora shuddered almost imperceptibly as the shadows of her face shifted. Cora had exited her body, and Augustus's "brilliant" spirit was speaking through her. From that day on, the two were inseparable. Dashing Augustus, who had been his father's ministerial heir apparent, became Cora's primary spirit guide, or "control." His spirit, not demure Cora's, was given credit for the eloquent, insightful extemporizing that would, nevertheless, make Cora L. V. one of the most famous people in America.

By this time, it seemed everyone everywhere in America wanted to chat up the angels. From Buffalo to St. Louis to Milwaukee, séance circles were forming. More often than not, women served as the mediums at their helm. Changing mid-nineteenth-century mores had promoted these ladies from mere sullied, weak descendants of Eve. But what they'd been promoted to, especially those of the more moneyed classes, was an ideal of delicate porcelain purity considered ill suited for the "real" world. And a pedestal is, indeed, just a different kind of cage. However, the ideal offered a loophole. By placing women in charge of their family's moral and spiritual well-being, they could claim a voice—albeit an at-first fairly quiet one—in certain public moral and spiritual causes.

Female Spiritualists in turn made that loophole a gaping portal, contending that it was their sex's very passivity and meekness that made women the perfect vessel for a spirit to take over and control. And that idea placed women front and center in the new spiritual craze taking the nation.

Still, in the early days, most mediums produced quotidian messages—missives about crop prices, birthdays, or personal grievances perhaps best left buried with the body in question. What Spiritualism had yet to find was a medium who could bridge these popular rituals with the movement's lofty progressive ideals.

Across the nation, adults wrung their hands as they debated the potential repercussions, benefits, and costs of the new phenomenon. But young Cora L. V. Scott wasn't bogged down with such compunctions. She was a delicate girl with exquisite features, abundant golden locks, and a demeanor of purity and patience, the very ideal of femininity itself—and, therefore, of a medium. She promptly but politely informed her parents that the spirits had told her to leave school. Her father, ever eager to follow signs from the beyond, immediately set his own ministering and commune-building aside to take Cora on a tour around the Midwest.

A father-daughter road montage rather like this then ensued: Cora and David rolled down dirt roads in their horse-drawn wagon. They ventured into a series of neighboring villages, each almost indistinguishable from the last, where locals trickled into the schoolhouse to see Cora. At first, the crowds were sparse. Soon though, Cora, or Augustus, began to master the craft, speaking at length and at ease on topics from science to theology, of things a young girl had "no way" of knowing—even one with a photographic memory. This hard fact lent Cora, and the many teenage girls who would take up the calling, considerable medium cred. Slowly, those small rural schoolhouses grew fuller, then packed, as news of the "Child Wonder" spread. The father-daughter duo then began to spread their itinerant mystic wings. They traveled as far away as Fond du Lac and Milwaukee, building momentum and the beginnings of a real name for young Cora. Then, in a breath, it all came to a screeching end.

In August 1853, David Scott suddenly took ill and died during a stay in their Wisconsin home. Cora later said that while standing at the foot of his deathbed, she watched as "a white, fleecy light, like luminous vapor," formed above her father's body, then consolidated into his likeness as he departed with a group of "spirit friends" happily welcoming him to the Summerland—as Spiritualists called the other side. However, with all the time on the road, he had not yet gotten around to establishing his "Hopedale of the West." He left behind a family with little income and far less comforting prospects on Earth. But they did have one asset, Cora, who at age thirteen was just starting to hit her stride.

2017
Brooklyn

Reverend Paul, our certified séance conductor, began, offering an overview of the mechanics of conjuring the dead. Our Brooklyn assembly of twenty women and four men—a fairly typical gender ratio at twenty-first-century urban mystical happenings—listened, some a bit apprehensively, others like this was all old hat. All of us except one, a woman of near-octogenarian status, were in our twenties or thirties and racially, ethnically, and sexual-orientationally diverse—a very Brooklyn crowd.

Paul, also a near octogenarian, informed us he would go at his own pace, which was often quite slow. This meant he may or may not have time to bequeath us all with missives from beyond the veil—as our crowd that night was unusually large. The ample attendance was little wonder, really, since the spirits had started to seem some elusive source of steadiness and wisdom in a world that had, every day since the presidential Inauguration Day ten months prior, felt anything but solid or stable—or even totally recognizable as nonfiction. This somehow put communing with the spirits on more equal footing with the rest of reality.

I looked around at the faces of my fellow séancers shifting in the flickering candlelight, each clear, expectant. Then, as if there was a line of spirits patiently waiting behind him, queued up for a payphone in purgatory, the reverend cycled through mystical communiques one by one.

"Do you have a female relative who recently passed away?"

"Well, last year."

"Are you drawn to animal energy healing work?"

"Yes."

"Great, the spirit is saying you should pursue that, take a class."

Smiles and nods.

"Are you thinking of changing jobs, going to a faraway land, buying property?"

He was, indeed, a slow and meandering talker, a rarity in New York City. What could be said in thirty seconds took, like, five whole minutes. Patience is not my strongest virtue, and I began to fret, a little testily, that I would not be given the missive I'd taken a bus then a train here to receive.

Then, just as my anxiety started to peak, the reverend's eyes connected with mine, before shifting, with a faint shudder, to someone or something else—a spirit of a young girl, maybe five or six, wearing a frilly dress and Mary Jane patent-leather shoes, "like they used to dress little girls in," he said.

Like they used to dress me in, against my tomboy will, I thought. As he talked, I felt a bit of buzz, a throbbing elevation, like a kitten lapping at my aura—as I have during other such confabs with the spirit side. "She has pigtails with bows," he continued. Do I know anyone who meets that description who has died?

Suddenly, as if it had been implanted there, I saw her image in my mind's eye—her face bluish, eyes like black holes, but her blonde pigtails perfect, not a hair astray, clutching an old-fashioned, worn-out cotton bunny. But no, I didn't know anyone who met said description. He nodded, getting it.

"The girl died in your home, some time ago, and wants your help passing to the spirit side."

"How?"

"Google it."

At that moment, I got something, myself: what had actually called me to join the good Spiritualist reverend's circle that night.

Ten years prior, after a late-night queer cabaret show, a burlesque performer I knew, still costumed as Liza Minnelli and trailing glitter about the bar, had invited me to come over sometime for a discount spiritual reading session. A few weeks later, I'd found myself mounting the hardwood stairs to Alexandra's spacious and strikingly furniture-free apartment on the top floor of a turreted old Victorian deep in Brooklyn. I entered highly dubious about all this communing with the other side. I did not exit that way.

Sitting on a blanket on her furniture-less floor, next to an altar covered in feathers, tarot cards, and lava rocks, I listened to her soothingly harmonic prognostications. My eyes wandered from our candlelit cross-legged circle of two to a dusty shard of light shooting across the dining room behind us—giving the tall, empty chamber a tranquil air of some slightly decayed old European church sanctuary. Then I heard, "So, were you abused as a child?" And like whiplash, I was back, eye to eye with this interlocutor to the other side who quickly added, "I mean that's just what the spirit guides said."

My memories of the events in question—which occurred when I was about the same age as that spirit girl Reverend Paul conjured—are themselves rather spectral, more ghostly cutouts and fadeaways than substance, the exact situation and facts hauntingly unclear. They were clear enough, though, to know that the details Alexandra then added, unprompted, were strikingly on point. At the time, I'd never been to therapy, didn't have a clue what to do with this fractal information. I'd just been running from it. The spirit guides had called out those ghosts I'd tried to lock in the back of my mind but that had instead been ceaselessly reverberating through my psyche, fucking with shit. It felt like some earth-splitting godsend; Moses descending from the mount but bearing tablets engraved with personal therapeutic revelation. And I, in turn, descended Alexandra's worn Victorian stairs a bit stunned and super converted.

A decade later, in the topsy-turvy late, hot fall of 2017, my need to stare the ghosts in my head in the eye and wrestle them had resurfaced with urgency. And to Reverend Paul's credit, the symbolism of that ghostly girl seemed, at first, to herald the sequel to those prior events that I'd probably actually been searching for when I hopped the train and bus to his séance.

However, it did not crack open my life. It did not provide transcendence, or a looking glass, or any other mystic or therapeutic buzzword I had felt all those years before and hoped to feel again.

But then, as I sailed home that night in a Lyft through Brooklyn back roads, I started to wax poetic, thinking how much both I and New York City had transformed during the past decade, for better or worse. It seemed little wonder that the city has stood as backdrop to so many of the nation's mystic greatest hits, past and present. More than any other American city, that city, my city, including each and every neighborhood from Bushwick to the North Bronx, is an ever-evolving entity, bigger than the sum of its parts and forever in flux with ceaseless cycles of creation and destruction, breakneck and ruthless in their speed, leaving ghosts of New Yorks past perpetually colliding and melding into New Yorks future, in some kind of mystical alchemy of some all-American hustle. Like a hot blue streak of divine lightning, I realized what I really wanted was a different kind of medium entirely—one who could connect me not just to personal catharsis but to something to reach for beyond the gathering clouds.

Later, knee-deep in out-of-print, leather-bound fin de siècle books on Spiritualism, I found myself staring down at a daguerreotype of Cora L. V. Scott. It occurred to me that her name not only bears a sonic similarity to my own—L. B. Scott—but that, like me, she had golden hair, pronounced cheekbones, a button nose, and blue eyes that were simultaneously skeptical and open minded. She had a look of having witnessed—and maybe even come out on top of—it all. It hit me then that I had found my inspiring badass medium to the past (the first, ultimately, of five). Because though she's been written out of history—as has Spiritualism itself for the most part—by age seventeen, Cora L. V. was basically Beyoncé.

5

The Line between a Diva and a Deity

Dr. Benjamin Franklin Hatch, or B. F., had tried everything. Mesmerism? He'd awarded himself a doctorate in it. He'd posted an advert in the *Spiritual Telegraph* informing the desperate and ailing that he could psychically diagnose and treat them sight unseen if they'd just send him ten dollars (approximately $300 today) in the mail. At the time, even the most devout Spiritualist would have readily admitted there were both real-deal mediums and frauds. So while little else is known about "Dr." Hatch prior to his meeting Cora, it's safe to say he was that infamous all-American archetype: the huckster, the snake-oil salesman, a natural showman who could, in fact, accurately diagnose one thing—a crowd's heart's desire.

Meanwhile, the Scott family had relocated back to the Burned-Over District, where Cora, now fourteen, had accepted a position as a full-time trance lecturer for the First Spiritual Society in Buffalo, New York. There, Cora could earn a comfortable-enough wage to help support her family at a time when few positions outside the home were open to women other than low-wage factory work. Her mother and siblings, however, had resettled more than a day's ride away in the family's hometown of Cuba.

While no one knows for sure (and Cora later had B. F. Hatch all but erased from her official biography), I imagine what happened next went something like this. One afternoon, B. F. found himself in his midforties and sick of the nickel-and-dime life of moving from hustle to hustle and town to town, sick of feeling alone, sick of what he saw looking back at him in the mirror—and in search of one thing: one final great con.

One day he made his way through the crowded, loud Buffalo streets, which were fragrant with horse dung, and into a spacious, richly appointed lecture hall with high vaulted ceilings and ample air. Young Cora slowly mounted the stage, her long dress dragging on the stairs behind her, her eyes downcast. Suddenly, she turned toward the crowd and, with a flair that just can't be taught, lifted her angelic face and small arms to the heavens, and like lightning, he knew.

After, as the earnest social reformers of both sexes—mediums, socialists, vegetarians, suffragists—milled about politely discussing the marvelous girl and the moral afflictions of their time, B. F. twirled the tip of his goatee, painted on his best smile, shiny and slimy as ectoplasm, and approached what he knew he'd found: solid gold.

From the start, 1857 seemed a time of some great, irrevocable falling apart. In March, James Buchanan was sworn in as America's fifteenth president, after carrying every slaveholding state but one and very few free ones. The Supreme Court issued the *Dred Scott* decision, ruling that black people were not citizens and that the federal government had no right to regulate slavery in federal territories. If that act had not made the American Civil War a foregone conclusion in and of itself, that fall, all the banks in New York and New England closed and didn't resume full operations for two months, causing panic and financial chaos across the nation. A severe snowstorm, which would remain the worst in known memory until the Blizzard of 1899 supplanted it, blanketed the East Coast, causing millions in damages. And an unprecedented 225-mile-long lip of terrain along California's San Andreas Fault opened up like a scream during the Fort Tejon earthquake, as if the earth herself was trying to reclaim the dysfunctional thing we'd so newly named the United States of America.

The year 1857 was also when Cora L. V. commandeered the bright (gas)lights of New York City, selling out "Great Halls" from Astor Place to Columbia University. Quickly, the city, and then the nation, sat up and took note of this seventeen-year-old prodigy—often somewhat breathlessly.

"A young girl, one that was but yesterday an untaught rustic maiden, blooming unnoticed in a country village, has been inspired by voices from the spirit world to become a medium of instruction to the seekers of truth." —Frank Leslie, in his *Illustrated Newspaper*, May 9, 1857

"And very curious it was to see a long-haired young woman standing alone in the pulpit, her face turned upwards, her delicate bare arms raised in a clergyman's attitude of devotion and a church full of people listening attentively! . . . I could detect no word that could be altered for the better—none indeed (and this surprised me still more) which was not used with strict fidelity to its derivative meaning . . . It would have astonished me in an extempore speech by the most accomplished orator in the world." —Nathaniel Parker Willis, editor of the *Home Journal*, October 1857

"[She made] my heart throb with sacred emotion." —Random male observer

Instead of just channeling mundane messages like most mediums before her, Cora L. V. gave Spiritualism what it had largely been lacking: a star.

Just months before the inaugurating flurry of press, in August 1856, Cora L. V. had signed away her father's name for her new master's.

Safely in legal possession of his prize, B. F. had promptly let his slick mask of charm, thin as a glamour spell, slide.

"Wife-beating" would not be outlawed nationwide until 1920 and marital rape until 1993. Incidents could receive case-by-case judicial consideration, but in 1857 folk wisdom still abided by the "rule of thumb"—that one should not beat one's wife with a stick broader than one's thumb. The courts rarely sided with a woman charging that her violent husband was dangerously ill suited to continuing on as "the head of the wife even as Christ is the head of the church" (Ephesians 5:23). Married women had little to no rights to property or income (the exact amount varying by state)—even their own—or their children, meaning they had few options for going it alone absent a judge's intervention.

Soon after arriving in New York City, Cora L. V. Hatch reportedly turned "pale as death and trembled like an aspen leaf" when her husband, B. F., entered a room. B. F. began forcing Cora to perform sexual acts that violated her "delicacy" and to entertain a prostitute he frequented. When winter 1857 came, with its blizzard of legend, B. F. refused to buy Cora flannel petticoats to keep her warm—despite the fact that the money man and wife lived on came from Cora and Cora alone.

The more perilous Cora's existence off the stage, the brighter her numinous light, that ineffable thumbprint of the angels, shined on the adoring mixed-sex crowds that gazed up with all the love and respect denied her when she dismounted the podium. All around her, a new cultural juggernaut, the celebrity industrial complex, was rising. As intuitively as a baby badger, Cora L. V. grabbed on and climbed.

Between 1835 and 1860, the number of newspapers in America near quadrupled, with many of the new "penny" rags chatting of celebrities and the latest fashions and fads. Spiritualist publications were among those proliferating throughout the nation. The devout and curious could read their favorite mediums' latest live lectures, typed up by a stenographer and printed in full, in addition to details of the lives of these illustrious ladies who brushed spirits with lesser deities daily.

Spiritualists could buy framed spirit daguerreotypes featuring their likeness with a phantasmagoric dearly departed placed over their shoulder via double exposure. There were bracelets made from locks of the departed's hair to facilitate summoning, and eventually Ouija boards. Meanwhile, the centerpiece of the movement—what really bound the people to it and one another—remained primal and old as human herstory. The ritual of public trance lectures and private séances left the—generally paying—attendees enraptured, touched, moved, cleaned out, and opened "toward freer thought."

By decade's end, Spiritualism claimed varying degrees of allegiance from approximately 10 percent of the American free adult populace. The movement's rapid growth prompted prominent theologian and abolitionist Theodore Parker to state, "In 1856, it seems more likely that Spiritualism would become the religion of America than [it seemed] in 156 that Christianity would become the religion of the Roman Empire, or in 756 that Mohammedanism would be that of the Arabian population." So why, instead, come the twentieth century would this movement be broadly denigrated as at worst malicious fraud, at best entertainment for impressionable bored housewives?

Spiritualism had three major marquee trance lecturers conjuring the divine in the late 1850s—Cora L. V. Hatch, Lizzie Doten, and Emma Hardinge Britten. None of the three were men. Americans could follow over two hundred female trance lecturers in the Spiritualist press, and there were doubtless many more not chronicled in those pages. Meanwhile, only twenty-one women not employed as trance mediums gave public speeches during the entirety of the decade. For many Americans, the first woman they witnessed talking in front of a mixed-sex crowd was a trance medium. And this channeled the most transcendent Spiritualist message of them all—that such a thing could be done.

Of those three de facto heads of the headless movement, Cora L. V. reigned supreme. Emma Hardinge Britten, who later wrote an exhaustive history of Spiritualism, described Cora's lectures as "crowded to suffocation" with throngs of men and women paying ten cents to hear this "mouthpiece of angels, who poured through her finely organized brain the melodies of the higher spheres."

B. F. was not in it for the angels. Ensuring Cora maximized the dimes flowing into his pocket required a whipmaster's pace. He joined her on trains, journeying from Baltimore to Ohio to Illinois to Wisconsin to Connecticut to Boston to Buffalo to New York City, and back again, without a break. He booked her in each city's largest hall, theater, or Universalist church, which she always packed. I envision her sitting before the hall's main entrance, finally alone, B. F. off collecting his dimes. The shadow lifts from her visage, as Augustus, with all his physical strength, takes over her thin adolescent form, and she flings open the doors.

Then the cancelations started. From March to June 1857, Cora disappeared altogether. In 1858, she made no public appearances for half a year. She left no firsthand explanations. Maybe the marks got too bad to cover with makeup or crossed over into broken bones. Some historians have speculated she had one or multiple abortions—back-alley at best. Later, Cora was said to suffer from hemorrhages of the lungs, attributed to her "delicate constitution." It's possible that affliction started during this time period.

Regardless, one summer night in 1858, in the middle of her prolonged public absence, Cora, by then eighteen, made a mad dash into a hotel lobby in New Haven, Connecticut—the type replete with black marble mantels and lush cabbage-rose carpets. Once inside, she begged the concierge for sanctuary, pleading, at volume, that death may befall her on the other side of his door. Offering lodgings to unaccompanied women remained verboten. And the concierge, dressed perhaps in a frock coat and single-breasted vest as fine as the interior design, began shuffling her, a depraved embarrassment, out the door.

Just as the hot gusts of fate greeted her tear-stained face, a doctor walked out of the adjoining reading room. Immediately, he recognized Cora, trembling like a sparrow and near nonsensical, seemingly on the verge of a breakdown. It was only then, with the male doctor intervening on her behalf, that the concierge would offer Cora L. V. Hatch, one of the most famous women in America, shelter—and even that was temporary.

2007
Brooklyn

Maybe it started with my emotional vomiting, which occurred four times in the course of a bad breakup. Or maybe the first tremors started later. Or earlier. I can't say for sure. What I can say is that the strangest thing about nervous breakdowns is that they are actually entirely confined to your mind.

The actual quaking came hard and fast, then departed. When it did, it deposited me, then age twenty-five, precariously on a ledge jutting out partway down the Cliffs of Insanity, able to see the sunlight above but also the chasm below.

Shortly before this cracking apart, I'd quit my full-time job as a journalist to pursue artistic endeavors. At first, this had seemed a wise move, but soon enough, it only increased my feelings of disconnection from all stable life structures possibly able to stop, or cushion, a free fall. I worked part-time and freelance. I felt like a cloud just passing through. I concocted a numbing cocktail of booze, meaningless sex, isolation from friends and family, and days that regularly ended well after 4:00 a.m., sometimes with me lying on my kitchen floor staring at the knives.

My inaugural Intuitive Reading, with Alexandra in the Brooklyn Victorian, had occurred a few months prior to the onset of all this. Not sure what else to do, I followed the spiritual thread that had, during that reading, felt like a lifeline. Suddenly, a pouch of crystals dangled from my clavicle daily and a deck of Goddess cards sat next to my desk. I did morning meditations followed by "spirit pages"—writing down whatever percolated up from my mental depths—and kundalini yoga by night. My two-bedroom Brooklyn apartment, which I lived in with a roommate of similarly mystic inclinations, filled with stones, lava rocks, seashells, Ganeshes, and antique pocket watches engraved with mystic sayings in Cyrillic script.

Some say purveyors of "woo-woo" prey on the weak and "muddle-headed," the damaged and desperate to heal. But what do these same naysayers say about the fact that, whether you believe the unconscious is tapped into the divine or is entirely unenchanted, going through these motions—crystals, Goddess cards, et al.—somehow works, for those who believe it might?

In the rare instances when I'd sustained a deep meditation, I'd felt I'd pierced something vaster than the surface chaos, touched some kind of stable ground. Even if fleeting, it felt like precedent, a place from which to rebuild.

In addition to a crystal collection, I also got a dog, an eleven-pound black-and-tan miniature pinscher named Vinni. Shortly before I met him, a hit-and-run had left Vinni's tiny body sprawled and bleeding on the side of a road in Queens, his pelvis shattered—down but not out.

Sometimes Alexandra—whom I continued to visit somewhat regularly—would contact Vinni's dog spirit during our sessions and report back.

"Has Vinni been doing work to try to open your heart chakra?"

"Well, when I wake up, he plops down on top of my chest, kind of like a furry snooze button, and I scratch his little ears for a minute." Alexandra gave me a knowing mystic nod. Turned out, my dog was a mini Reiki master.

Meanwhile, in the night, after yoga class, I started throwing myself more fully into the glittery wonders of New York City queer night-life. Though I was something approaching sullen, distant, and angsty most of the time, in those dingy dive bars and clubs you could always find me dancing, suddenly a creature of transcendent abandon—alive, if severely inebriated. Escaping, obliterating, self-medicating, sure, but also grounding my root chakra there in the honestly strange and strangely honest, where fluorescent jellyfish drag queens, aerialists, leather-clad-genderqueer-tastic "free spirits," shirtless tattooed men on psychedelic drugs screaming "I am Bacchus," and Goddesses sartorially crossing Minnie Mouse with Sid Vicious resided.

There among the denizens of the demimonde who grasp the liminal of the mystic as naturally as the fluidity of gender, I continued my occult training. I learned about rising and moon signs (Rising: Scorpio; Moon: Cancer; and Sun: Virgo), the benevolent will of the universe, the fun of uttering "God-dess yes" as an affirmative refrain. Vinni took to wearing two furiously spiked collars—a tiny queer mascot, barbed but with a gentle, cuddle-prone soul. And slowly, side by side, that little dog and I started to mend.

The day Cora L. V. Hatch met Walt Whitman she gave him very bad news. The scruffily bearded poet, his eyes pale to the point of trans-lucence, stood up in a packed, columned hall before the New York Spiritual Conference to ask his question. He'd taken Cora, the great teenage medium standing before him, as his "model." He'd worked at it assiduously for a year. So why, he implored, could he not connect with the spirit side and be made medium?

With a directness rare in those Victorian times, entranced Cora informed the young man it was not a matter of self-improvement or study. The angels simply had not designated him their mouthpiece. Crestfallen, Whitman returned home to Ryerson Street in Brooklyn, at the time still more farmland than city, and rededicated himself in full to channeling the Muse and the Muse alone—instead of frittering his energies attempting to connect with a larger pantheon of minor deities. He finished revising *Leaves of Grass* into the edition that made him world famous.

At the time, the wall between male and female roles was "radical and essential," designating two halves of the human whole who "neither think, feel, wish, purpose, will nor act alike." Spiritualism blurred, or queered, the stark boundary. A male spirit could possess a woman and vice versa. Plus, the importance of the corporeal, gendered plane dwindled when dealing with eternal spirits. This was summoning the not-so-heterosexual nationwide to the mystic fold. So it's little wonder that Whitman, clearly illuminated by his verse as both gay and a fan of the divine flow, longed to feel the full ecstatic force of that liberation.

Then there was Cora. Even for afternoon lectures, she always wore a provocative, or what some labeled "unseemly," off-the-shoulder evening dress with voluminous full-length skirts, a signature white rose, forever in bloom, peeking from her sash, and a large Gothic cross fastened about her neck. But on any given evening, out of that perfect portrait of femininity, haloed in golden curls and sweet as a Sistine Chapel cherub, truth, profound and articulate, came pouring forth in a surprisingly deep, melodic voice. At the time, these traits, from her deep voice to her self-possessed calm, qualified as "masculine," making Cora L. V. a sort of divine androgyne antecedent to David Bowie.

By September 1858, the gossip was everywhere. Headlines across the nation announced that Cora had fled B. F. and found alternate lodgings. B. F. had attempted to physically drag Cora from a New York street corner back to his dark Victorian home. Seeing no recourse, Cora had then stood before a judge—and in front of the entire press corps—to make her case for legal freedom. Her argument was bolstered by corroborating testimony of several prominent Spiritualist men, such as Judge John Edmonds and Professor James Mapes, and also Emma Hardinge Britten. Each testified to B. F.'s physical abuse and exploitation.

Even a few years before, these men might not have lent their respectability to Cora's corner. But Spiritualists were embracing a panoply of progressive causes, ranging from labor rights to environmental preservation, and at the apex stood a holy trinity: women's rights, abolition, and free love.

To Spiritualists, free love didn't mean free lust or abolishing marriage, as its legion critics claimed. It did mean reforming the institution of marriage so women had rights within it—and to leave it. Free lovers supported sexual bonds based in "soul affinities," not legal or physical force. Spiritualists contended that sex, like all nature, was divine, not sin incarnate. And understanding one's own sexuality, whatever its form, stood essential to self-respect and maximizing one's ability to help create divine order on earth. This proved controversial in nineteenth-century America. Due to the trial, Cora suddenly found herself the poster child of this lightning-rod cause—and a tabloid sensation.

Some press supported her:

"[Mrs. Hatch] has bolted from the arms of the Doctor, and, as it now appears, is making money on her own account, prophesying, preaching, going into trances, and coming out of them without putting a dollar into Dr. Hatch's personal and private pocket. Which seems to grieve him exceedingly."—New-York Daily Tribune, January 4, 1859

Others weren't so generous:

"I do not believe that there has, during the past five hundred years, arisen any class of people who were guilty of such a variety of crimes and indecencies as the Spiritualists of America . . . Women, thirty or forty years of age, with children growing up around them, and who have abandoned their husbands, of whom they were not worthy, and who are living in adultery with their paramours, produce abortion, and arise from their guilty couches and stand before large audiences as the medium for angels." —*Spiritualist Iniquities Unmasked,* 1859

The latter bitter tirade is from a windy pamphlet written and self-published by B. F. That fact didn't stop paper after paper from gleefully excerpting it when taking down Cora and her free-loving ilk.

Nevertheless, in March 1859, a New York City judge saw fit to give Cora an escape, if not full freedom. He granted her legal "separation from bed and board" and a restraining order from B. F., though the two remained legally wed. Suddenly, Cora L. V. was free from daily torment, and there was a very public precedent set for women across the nation. Then, just as suddenly, that national falling apart went from cracks to chasm as the first bullets flew at Fort Sumter.

The thing about a great falling apart is, no matter how complete the destruction, it can provide the chance to build something new, and potentially better, from the rubble—a phoenix. But if, and only if, someone does the hard work of actually restructuring, instead of just desperately trying to glue the pieces back together.

Before long, I turned away from the mystic. Amid all the turmoil, the ghostly memories of abuse had started hurling hatchets into my gray matter pretty constantly. My strategy reverted: don't look. Turns out that the thing about the shadows locked in your own basement is, they're fucking scary. And it's hard to delve too deeply into your mind to touch the divine without unlocking such demons' cages. Besides, I was functioning again. The quaking had stopped. I'd tried therapy for a bit—though it didn't so much take.

I felt stuck inside myself, but like I was looking out from a relatively geologically stable cave by this time, not the lip of a chasm. I was drinking way too much. Each romantic relationship I entered into was too unsustainably volatile to risk real vulnerability.

The thing about a great falling apart is . . . you might end up wondering if it's too late to do the hard work of burrowing in and restructuring since you didn't get around to it the first time you rebuilt.

Forever more comfortable onstage than off, and on the move than standing still, Cora kept up her grueling lecture pace across the North and Middle West, even without B. F. cracking a whip at her heels. As the ghosts of fallen soldiers and both literal and spiritual ruin proliferated across America, Cora and other mediums stood in high demand. In response to the desperate times, Cora amped up the star power. The deceased abolitionist Theodore Parker and late president Thomas Jefferson joined Cora and young Augustus on her tour. Via Cora, the team decried slavery as "a curse and a disgrace to a republican government," adding that "the spirit world was combining its forces to wipe it out." They outlined a practical "source of reconstructed [national] health, namely, the supremacy of just laws on earth, as in heaven."

Even after abolition became a done deal and the live rounds and cannon fire stopped, Cora and her ever-more-luminary spirit-side lineup kept on channeling the path of our better angels. In trance, she demanded a thorough reconstruction of the South, including legal repercussions for Confederate leaders and legal ballasts protecting, in addition to freeing, the formerly enslaved. She warned against just desperately trying to glue the pieces back together without doing the hard work of actually restructuring, addressing what had cracked the states apart.

She prognosticated that refusing to take these key steps would result in "the terrorizing and ultimate deprivation of the blacks of their political rights"—basically foretelling Jim Crow, the KKK, and exactly what ended up happening. However, America was ultimately less interested in her mission to help them forge a better nation than in a glittering distraction.

In January 1864, as Union soldiers retreated from the Battle of Dandridge in the rugged, bloodstained hills of Tennessee, Cora L. V. entered Manhattan's palatial Greek Revival Clinton Hall as a choir of medium trainees sang choral hymns, per usual. Per usual, Cora was already in trance, her arms crossed, her eyes looking to the heavens. And per usual, the gathered local swells agreed then and there on a topic for her, or her commanding spirit, to orate upon extemporaneously—the improvisation as thrilling to lecture-crazy Victorian Americans as jazz. The topic they chose was how impossible it is for man, as a finite creature, to comprehend deity, the infinite.

That's when things departed from the norm. When Cora reached the appointed Q and A hour, a distinguished gentleman stood to ask a polite, philosophical question. But just as he began to speak, a much younger man, around Cora's age, leapt up. "Do not let that man speak!" he shouted. "He is my father. He left his wife and children and is now living with Cora Hatch on East Broadway."

Lawsuits followed. And court dates, to which Cora, a consummate diva, failed to show—though her publicly disgraced paramour did. Unlike Cora, he could reclaim his good name by proving he paid his wife a generous alimony. Cora, meanwhile, had morphed from picture-perfect victim, and therefore picture-perfect free-love poster child, to something far murkier in the public eye—a sexual adult woman.

Always a moth to the limelight, B. F. showed up in the "densely packed" court too—despite not being invited—with his lawyers. At this point, both he and Cora desired a divorce, but divorces often required proof that there was one truly "innocent" party wronged. B. F.'s lawyers contended, without evidence, that Cora once visited a "house of assignation," or ill repute, three times in one day. The headlines, of course, went national—though this time without all the editorial commentary supporting Cora. In the end, no divorce proved forthcoming.

Nevertheless, the next Sunday, Cora did not cancel her Clinton Hall engagement. The crowd grew so large police were placed at every entrance to prevent another soul from entering. Whispers of *Will she really speak?* suffused the packed auditorium. The appointed hour of 7:00 p.m. came with a hush of uncertainty. Then the door opened, and Cora resolutely mounted the stage. Shame and/or B. F. would not silence or control her, it seemed. There were reports that B. F. was in the audience but left in a huff. Because Cora, as ever, triumphed. She didn't even falter during the Q and A when an audience member asked a barbed question about moral character. But no one really cared about B. F.'s comings and goings. All they cared about, all they'd ever cared about, was Cora. And the next day the press again displayed her, or Augustus's, or maybe Thomas Jefferson's, philosophical opinions on how to forge a more harmonious, free future for all Americans.

Finally, with little fanfare, in May 1865, seven years and countless newspaper articles after a teenage Cora had the temerity—or divine inspiration—to take her husband and master to court, a judge finally decreed their marriage officially rent asunder. By that August, she was once again lecturing as Cora L. V. Scott.

By then, the war and all its death had ended, but Spiritualism remained mainstream. Its stars remained some of the most famous people in America. The religion had rooted itself deep enough in the nation's psyche to shift a country recently broken and looking to rebuild. And the movement was growing increasingly radical.

"The experiment of masculine rule has been tried long enough," wrote the Spiritualist Thomas Hazard in 1868. "Six thousand years of war, bloodshed, hypocrisy and crime have pronounced it a gross failure. It is high time that the feminine element was called to its aid."

The system of "masculine rule," however, did not roll over so easily.

6

The Fall

In April 1863, President Abraham Lincoln attended a séance in the Red Room of the White House organized by his wife, Mary Todd. During the ritual, the august circle, which included the secretaries of both war and the navy, in addition to the spirits and the president, discussed matters of state and emancipation before contacting Willie, the Lincolns' son who'd passed in February 1862 at age eleven. Nine years later, in 1872, both the *Boston Herald* and the *New York Times* mocked Mary Todd, by then widowed after a shot rang out at Ford's Theatre, for seeking out the solace of those who could contact his spirit. Then, in 1875, the sole survivor of her four sons, Robert, had Mary committed to a sanitarium.

But when Cora L. V., newly rechristened Scott, determined to start over in the nation's capital in 1865, the system of "masculine rule" had yet to cut down the Spiritualist threat to their order. It remained much more the Washington, DC, of 1863 than 1872. You could still smell the blood in the soil. The air felt combustible. Consensus over what exactly defined America, that grand experiment, had been far from reached, despite the body count—and upstanding lawmakers kept their rapid-fire Henry rifles, soon to be patented as Winchester, close at hand just in case.

Several of those lawmakers also attended superstar Cora L. V. Scott's hot-ticket, near-nightly séances—including Michigan senator Jacob M. Howard and Indiana representative George W. Julian. During the confabs, Cora channeled the late, great President Lincoln, in addition to her usual lineup. Together, Cora and her controls would prescribe policies and laws for the attending bigwigs to champion in order to thoroughly reconstruct the South and ensure liberty and justice for all, regardless of skin tone.

There was an irony to it all: the allegedly dainty, fragile Cora inserting herself right there in the brutal bull's-eye of the struggle to shift the wounded mess of a nation back into a functioning body. Of course, in 1865, prominent male séancers would never have consulted Cora herself, but following the orders of their former captain, Abraham Lincoln, emanating forth from that angelic visage, well, that was a different story entirely.

"It is no secret that certain efforts were made to incorporate into national law some of the hints and suggestions received from spiritual séances," wrote a clerk in the Quartermaster General's Office.

Cora even met Andrew Johnson himself, upon invitation, in the Oval Office, where the-soon-to-be-impeached president of the United States offered her a bouquet of flowers. According to the *Baltimore Gazette*, she in turn channeled Lincoln—startling his former vice president with his exact "horse" laugh.

But by 1868, when Johnson skirted removal from office by one vote, Cora was spitting her progressive oratory against the wind. After years of chaos and war, the nation had swung from an age of radical reform and liberation to a conservative one of order, control, and greed. Capitalist empires, rampant inequality, and Jim Crow, not new philosophical and spiritual foundations, defined the times. And Spiritualism seemed fated to fade into the ether.

The first step, though, was to silence the women. Fast as a phantasmagoric flicker, female mediums nationwide were locked in cupboards placed on the outskirts of séance tables, instead of sitting at their head. The idea was that, shut in the cupboard, unseen and unheard as a woman should be, the medium could "produce" "manifestations"—hovering ectoplasmic ghosts, levitating trumpets, spinning clocks, raps on doors at pivotal moments—as opposed to stirring oratory. With the female mediums confined like so many bodiced cupcakes, their male managers ran the baroque shows—operated via steel wires and cheesecloth, not the hereafter. So denuded of its philosophical core, Spiritualism then grew easy to kill, ground into dust with a doctor's mortar and pestle.

During Spiritualism's heyday, "healing" mediums had begun setting out their own shingles nationwide. Like the fever nurses of New Orleans, they offered herbal and energetic remedies that often actually helped people—unlike the male medical establishment's prescriptions of leeches, rampant amputation, and confining women to their beds for months on end. Unable to beat the competition fair and square, the medical establishment cheated. They coined the term "mediomania," linking insanity to Spiritualism, and then redefined insanity's symptoms as the most common side effects of entrancement—rigidity, seizure, ecstasy.

In a stroke of "scientific" genius, the doctors then shifted their lexicon and broadened the attack by branding all women's reproductive systems not just the root of human sin and weakness but of insanity itself. They first declared the angle of a woman's uterus caused "utromania." Eventually they settled on the more widely employed "hysteria," derived from the Greek *hystera*, meaning uterus. "Tilt the [uterus] a little forward—introvert it, and immediately the patient forsakes her home, embraces some strong ultraism—Mormonism, Mesmerism, Fourierism, Socialism, oftener Spiritualism," spake New York's Dr. Frederic Marvin in 1874. Plus, such hysteria, they asserted, spread when women gathered in groups—so best to keep them house (or cupboard) bound.

In 1872, medium Victoria Woodhull became the first woman to run for president of the United States—garnering zero Electoral College votes. However, amid the backlash and conservative national turn, the Women's Movement began shunning the "kooky" radical Spiritualists who had been their former compatriots. The mainstream movement also no longer demanded a total reformation of women's societal role via equal pay for equal work and free love. And though they'd fought for abolition, most groups would not link their own cause with civil rights or labor rights, marginalizing many American women from the American Women's Movement. The Spiritualist path to "one common brotherhood, where angelic wisdom and order can freely unfold" had faded into the shadows. Instead, the Women's Movement increasingly focused on suffrage and suffrage alone—with some space for temperance.

Some historians assert the pivot saved the suffrage movement from the same fate as Spiritualism: being mocked out of existence. Others contend that if they'd held tight to the divine light and refused to capitulate to the powers that be, they could have upended the world at the end of the nineteenth century. It's hard to say. Revolutions rarely go the way the crow flies.

Regardless, Cora L. V. did not then, nor ever, try to hide her Spiritualist affiliations in a cupboard. This was in no small part because, unlike most American women, Cora had the elusive economic independence the Women's Movement no longer really sought. She also, for the first time, found a true "soul affinity," between souls presumed equal.

In March 1865, in the final fateful days of the Lincoln administration, Nathan W. Daniels, a dashing Union colonel, attended a séance in the White House's Green Room presided over solo by Mary Todd. There, in what must have felt like the small, stable iron core of a molten America, Colonel Daniels glimpsed Cora on the eve of her twenty-fifth birthday and in full possession of herself. She in turn glimpsed him back.

By year's end, the somewhat modern lovers had married. Nathan supported Cora's career, taking assiduous notes during her séances with senators and celebrating her achievements. And she desired for him the professional advancement and fulfillment he craved. The following fall they had a daughter, and in May 1867, the happy trio moved to New Orleans, where Nathan had received a Reconstruction post.

They would have arrived just in time for Cora to ride the city's open-air locomotive, Smoky Mary, through plantation and bayou out to Lake Pontchartrain for Marie Laveau II's annual Saint John's Eve ceremony. Perhaps the two great interlocutors with the other side even locked eyes as Cora stripped down to her underclothes and, for once, writhed—instead of placidly stood—with spirit, before she entered that deep, hot lake. However, regardless if America's greatest medium and its greatest Voodoo Queen ever in fact met, or swapped tips, or danced ecstatically till dawn amid the calls of cicadas, whooping cranes, and alligators, Cora did experience another defining aspect of the swamp city.

In October of that same year, Colonel Daniels died of yellow fever. A few months later, their daughter, barely one, followed him to the Summerland. Cora returned to DC, making little mention of her daughter publicly ever again. Instead, in her grief, she retreated first from herself and then, in 1873, to England.

It is estimated that Cora L. V. spent something like one-third to one-half of her life in trance—quite a high proportion. But in the aftermath of fall 1867, it seemed to constitute her primary residence. In trance, Cora's spirit could enter, as she put it, "through archways of perfect light, tinted with thousands of hues unknown to earth, or through cloudless ether—lighted by neither sun nor moon nor stars—but self-luminous, I ever pass, accompanied . . . by my little girl—my little girl! . . . never since she came and stamped her image upon my heart and life have I passed into or out of the spirit state without seeing her first and last . . ."

Trance lectures articulating a moral vision for America had made Cora a superstar. But personalized messages from those dearly departed had proved as critical to Spiritualism's mass appeal in its golden age—be they from one's own entranced visits to the Summerland or via mediums in private séances. As such, past those glowing opalescent gates of the promise land, Cora also always greeted a familiar spirit named Ouina.

Ouina, too, had died young. And since Cora's adolescent days in Buffalo, this departed "gentle Indian maiden" had often served as her control at private séances—which she conducted prior to moving to DC. Back then, Cora's life out of trance consisted of physical and sexual abuse by her middle-aged husband and keeper, and isolation, including from the surviving members of her family, who lived in a different part of the state. She'd been called a witch, a necromancer, and soon enough a trollop. Young Cora stated that Ouina, that innocent soul whose ghostly remnants dwelled within her, had been killed by men from her—unspecified—tribe who had proclaimed the young girl a witch, tied her to a hemlock tree, then felled her with arrows before burning her, essentially, at the stake. All spirit-side communiques, however legit, are filtered through a medium's own unconscious after all.

In addition to the darker regions of Cora's own interiority, the story of Ouina also illuminates a hypocritical or gaping blind spot in Spiritualism—a movement striving for the light but still firmly entrenched in its time and place. From the start, Native Americans frequented séance tables in spirit, though not flesh and blood—and Spiritualists viewed this spectral appropriation of another's religious bona fides as a boon to their own legitimacy. By Reconstruction, most earthbound Native Americans had been violently forced onto reservations or killed, all but vanishing from most other Americans' day-to-day. Their spirits then grew ever-more legion at séance tables.

Soon Native Americans supplanted dead loved ones as the stereotypical spirit guide. Spiritualists romanticized these guides as particularly connected to nature, the Summerland, and a bygone world many white Americans felt nostalgic for. They also demeaned them as a "primitive race" entirely antithetical to "civilization." Still, in thanks for their sage ghostly guidance, Spiritualists advocated for Native American rights—though the phrase "too little, too late" certainly hovers around this caveat. Eventually, even the Native American spirits vanished from view, along with Spiritualism, as steel trains, then skyscrapers, supplanted the herds of buffalo that had once defined the American horizon.

Spiritualism declined further into a punch line. But again and again, the American feminist mystic doesn't die when throttled. It evolves. The two most dominant new branches to sprout off from the Spiritualist source—and also, not coincidentally, from the minds of women—were New Thought, founded by suffragist Emma Curtis

Hopkins, and Theosophy, cofounded by Helena Blavatsky. New Thought-ians aimed to tap the spiritual divine within in order to perfect and heal themselves—both physically and mentally—and then society. Theosophy blended ancient, largely Eastern philosophies and religions with Spiritualist thought in an effort to fashion a "key" to a universal truth that, once revealed, would facilitate "universal brotherhood." While neither of these offshoots ever rose to Spiritualism's level of dominance, they would each eventually rejoin in the latter half of the twentieth century into a movement that certainly did: the New Age.

And though Spiritualism did not succeed in completely upturning American culture or politics, by the time the movement waned in the final years of the nineteenth century, a generation of women and men had grown up believing female trance mediums were part of the natural cultural order. As adults, those women no longer needed the excuse of being inhabited by a male spirit to take the stage or collect a paycheck—or even to join the medical establishment that cut down Spiritualism. Spiritualists, in fact, helped found one of the first official medical schools for women, the Woman's Medical College of Philadelphia.

In 1875, after over two years in England, that calcified Old World, and another marriage to an American colonel named Samuel Tappan, which ended in divorce, Cora returned to the American East Coast, only to find her homeland had become a calcified establishment itself. A creature forged by flux, she immediately lit off on the newly completed transcontinental railroad. Pulling back her cabin curtain to get a straight shot at the sky, she rode the train all the way to the recently established Golden State and its City of Angels. And she wasn't the only one. Many Spiritualists and radicals fleeing the conservative turn back east took that same train west to more temperate, undefined shores. Upon arrival, Cora even helped establish a Spiritualist commune after her spirit guides selected a twenty-four-acre plot of gently rolling wilderness on which to build it. The Societas Fraterna then grew into a pioneer in West Coast alternative living.

However, Cora eventually opted to resettle halfway in between the mystic past and future in the heartland, accepting a permanent position as pastor at the First Society of Spiritualists in Chicago—a position that she would hold for nigh fifty years, though she still continued to travel the nation. She was a grande dame, and her trance lecture services remained in demand for decades, despite having fallen out of fashion. Her one concession to the changing, manifestation-happy times: she would manifest lilies, which suddenly appeared about her person, as if from the ether, while she stood onstage channeling the angels. In Chicago, she married her fourth and final husband, William Richmond, a businessman.

Finally, on January 3, 1923, at age eighty-two, after persisting long enough to see the passage of women's suffrage, Cora L. V. Scott Hatch Daniels Tappan Richmond made her final trip to the Summerland.

I have three pictures of Cora L. V. Scott on my computer desktop. One is a promotional headshot of her as a teenager, already married and famous, with that large Gothic cross swinging from her long sparrow's neck. She is tilting her head up toward the spirits with preternatural confidence—despite the violence and death swarming around her on earth. In the second, she looks to be in her midtwenties, about the age she permanently freed herself from Hatch and moved to DC to mold the minds of senators. Her Pre-Raphaelite curls have grown unrestrained and magnificent, her clear blue eyes wider, more otherworldly, but also unresolved, forlorn, stuck.

In the final photo, she's in her mid to late thirties, around the time she took roots in Chicago. Her wild curls are pinned back, her neck covered with a polite ruffled collar, her face a little stouter but as beautiful as ever, the combined effect not so much serene as content, whole—as she stares forward, direct at the world—and possibly at some lilies levitating just beyond the frame. To me, these pictures say that despite it all, Cora L. V. Scott never broke. She never turned hard. She never turned mean. She never said, *Fuck it, I'll just join them. It's better to be a victor than a victim.*

Sometimes, I see the Cora of that last image, close to my age now, standing on the jutting bluffs of the Pacific coast, staring through the mist of the breakers at the vast bright-blue water. Her hair, which they say is among the most well-documented features of Spiritualism, swirls above and around her in the trade wind. She's standing on the edge of the New World staring down a future she's finally defining while remembering, with both fondness and grief, a past that she wasn't.

Cora L. V. Scott paved a path of contradictions, but a brand-new path nonetheless. She was the only person not explicitly associated with the Women's Movement mentioned in an 1871 overview of the first twenty years of that battle for equality. She inspired flocks of women to speak publicly for themselves; conversed with presidents and senators, living and dead; presented on Spiritualism at the first-ever Parliament of the World's Religions, held in Chicago in 1893; published over a dozen books; and unlike any of her four husbands, she remained a touchstone of American culture for half a century, making her own money and loving whom she pleased.

Cora L. V. Scott never lost faith in Spiritualism's larger revolution or in a future America that lived up to all she fought to conjure. Instead, she became the first person to publicly coin the now-ubiquitous term for what she foresaw on the horizon—the dawning of a *New Age.*

"Have you ever seen the sun rise on the ocean? The first gray lines tremble on the horizon. Streaks of gold and crimson slowly rise. A gray cloud moves across the path and then it turns a crimson cloud, moving across the sky. On the verge of the horizon trembles the pale morning star, and then the full bright orb Phoebus, in his golden chariot, ascends, and a flood of light spreads over the Universe. Even thus will dawn the New Age of humanity, and not only slavery, but fear, darkness and death will be conquered in the light of the new morning." —Cora L. V. Scott, 1897

PART III

Madame Blavatsky, Cofounder of the

Theosophical Society

7

Once Upon a Time, When East Met West

In a land where castles perched like birds' nests amid a dense forest canopy, along the border between the Hapsburg Empire and the Romanov and the European and Asian continents, lived a princess who married a commoner for love. The princess, a botanist fluent in five languages, remained happily joined with her working-class husband, despite the scathing society whispers that trailed the couple like curses.

However, when their daughter, who was renowned for her beauty, came of marrying age and spun the pistol chamber every young woman then must when choosing a husband, she ended up with a bullet, not a happy breeze. In 1830, at age sixteen, Helena Andreyevna married a dashing Russian artillery captain of noble birth. He turned out to be prone to violent rages, berating, belittling, and mocking her. Within a few months of their nuptials, the girl returned to the princess with a growing bulge above her cascading velvet skirt and a bone to pick with the options society presented her. Before long, with the princess's encouragement, Helena Andreyevna wrote protofeminist novels, chronicling the humiliations women endure in a man's world, which earned her accolades and renown across the empire.

Helena Andreyevna's daughter, Helena Petrovna, underwent multiple exorcisms in childhood. She had been born premature—in the midst of an 1831 cholera epidemic—on July 31, a date traditionally said to bestow the ability to control goblins and demons. The family ordered an emergency baptism, fearing the sickly child would die damned. Before the soul cleansing could conclude, however, the Orthodox priest's dark robes went up in flames, victim to an attending child's errant candle. As a girl baptized by fire, not by the Christian God, little Helena Petrovna was followed throughout her childhood by local serfs sprinkling holy water—or so it's said.

After a spell, the artillery captain again managed to make a tenuous peace with his skeptical wife, Helena Andreyevna, who returned to him, though more separations followed.

During one of these separations, when Helena was five, the three unusual women in this remarkable lineage resided together on the mouth of the Volga and the steppes of Asia, in Astrakhan. Backed by misty-blue snowcapped mountains, Astrakhan was inhabited by Russians, Persians, Armenians, and Tibetan monks in bright-saffron robes. Little Helena walked its narrow, ancient streets walled in white stone with her governess. She absorbed the incense and turmeric, the music and languages and religious symbols like truth itself.

Even when the family resided in one place, the captain remained largely absent, forever off with his troops fighting insurrection or drinking in the barracks. Still, the couple had another daughter, Vera, and later, a son named Leonid. On occasion, the captain brought young Helena into his rough-and-tumble first home. And Helena, every soldier's pet, felt more at ease in those barracks than back studying French and piano among the fine hand-carved birch furnishings.

Then came the deathbed prophecy. When her mother fell ill with tuberculosis in 1842, a series of bloodlettings offered by the "top" medical authorities did nothing to help. That June, Helena Andreyevna died at age twenty-eight. Her final words: "At least I shall be spared seeing what befalls Helene. Of one thing I am certain: her life will not be as that of other women, and she will have much to suffer."

That fall, Helena, who'd just turned eleven, and her younger siblings returned to live with the princess and their grandfather, then residing in a crumbling old castle in the river city of Saratov. Never a huge stickler for propriety, the princess had always tolerated Helena's odd proclivities—her frequent catatonic states, claims that eyes stared at her from inanimate objects, a habit of hypnotizing pigeons. Helena excelled at her studies—remarkably enough that many later attributed her abilities to a photographic memory. But she chafed at the limited curriculum, designed to ensure she could adequately entertain her future husband. She skipped school, preferring instead to play with "ragged street boys" or to run alone through the dark woods until she reached the home of Baranig Bouyak, a serf and holy man who lived deep within the forest's shadows and taught her his mystic ways.

Helena would boldly walk through her grandmother's gallery, past the frightening glass-paned cases filled with taxidermied alligators, silver seals, birds frozen midflight, and arachnids, all staring back at her, past the freestanding scarlet flamingo large enough for a child to ride, on her way to the family library. Her great-grandfather, a Rosicrucian Freemason, first compiled the library, where Helena softly ran her sometimes sticky fingers across shelf after shelf of books on alchemy, astrology, Hermeticism, and all things occult (and therefore secret), until one of the leather-bound volumes whispered to her—as inanimate things apparently did. Then she would pull the volume out to study its magic.

The Russia of Helena's childhood remained a Russia little changed by the centuries, one of feudal monarchs (largely brutal), lords (also often not so nice), and serfs (indentured, if not enslaved). There were also fairies and dragons and a Rapunzel in most every castle. From Rasputin to Raskolnikov, Russia idealized men who were "partly truth and partly fiction," as Kris Kristofferson later put it, those "walking contradictions" both holy and rascal, drunkard and poet, fraud and guru.

But according to her sister, Vera, Helena also embodied this mythic schism, as a girl one part "mischievous, combative, and obstinate," the other part "mystically and metaphysically inclined." And in addition to the forces she reported glaring at her ominously from chairs and wagon wheels, Helena also spoke of glimpsing powerful entities that were benevolent and filled with light.

A superb horsewoman, Helena regularly rode astride—a position also then generally limited to men—at full gallop along the Volga and through the fields of wheat and serfs toiling with scythes. During one such ride, her steed bolted, jolting Helena off his back. As she plummeted, one foot got tangled in its stirrup, leaving her trapped and her head dangling above the hard, rocky terrain as the horse lunged along like lightning. Helena listened to the clomp and crunch of the horse's flying hoofs and waited to die.

Instead, "a tall Indian in whole linen" materialized on another plane—one she would later come to call "astral"—a figure she'd seen before in her dreams. He cradled her head, holding it high until the horse came to a stop. Then, just as suddenly, he vanished.

Thanks to his efforts, Helena then grew older, soon passing the age when even the princess could abide her failure to follow the strict protocols of womanhood. Helena, however, would not relent. At age sixteen, after the princess ordered she start attending society dances, the resolute teen held her leg in a vat of boiling water until it grew raw. The resulting burns kept her lame and confined to her home for half a year but also achieved the desired effect.

"When I was young, if a young man had dared to speak to me of love, I would have shot him like a dog who bit me," she later said.

But when a governess taunted that Helena couldn't get a man to marry her, the then seventeen-year-old immediately accepted the proposal of one Nikifor Blavatsky, a man in his forties. Helena's petulant whim then set the fates in motion. While the princess may have flouted convention by taking up the biological sciences and marrying a commoner, retracting an engagement would not stand.

"I had engaged myself to spite the governess, never thinking I could no longer disengage myself."

And so, Helena Petrovna found herself escorted on horseback by jailers disguised as a wedding party, up and up and up, past valleys and streams and startlingly clear seas, to a mountain resort near the border of Persia. There, likely surrounded by native gladiolas and nobility wearing veils of gauzy gold and black fox furs, the vicar eventually got to the crux of it. "Thou shalt honor and obey thy husband."

"Surely, I shall not," the girl snapped back—or so she later said.

Regardless of whether she swore obedience or not, Helena still trotted away as the man's wife and property in a country where acceptable cause for divorce included exile to Siberia and excommunication. She was also a wife isolated high on the Armenian plateau in the Caucasus Mountains, with little means of flight—though she certainly did try. Blavatsky in turn tried to appease his reluctant teen bride—while simultaneously keeping her under the twenty-four-hour surveillance of armed Cossacks. Helena later said she mocked him, raged against him, and avoided him, never consummating their union. Some doubt the veracity of this statement, thinking not even obstinate Helena Blavatsky could have prevented a nineteenth-century man from claiming the prize he'd signed for.

Regardless, some months after their wedding, late in an inky Georgian night, Helena successfully bolted from Blavatsky's home on horseback, eluding several Cossack men. First, she sought refuge with her grandparents. To her dismay, they denied her plea for shelter, instead arranging to forcibly ship her to her father, who Helena believed would promptly return her to her groom. So Helena again absconded into the night, making her way to the Black Sea. There, she sneaked onto the SS *Commodore*, an English ship bound for Constantinople. Once aboard, she paid off the skipper with "a liberal outlay of rubles" to let her stay; then she settled in to watch the Russian Empire and her contractual conscription fade from view. Instead, she watched the harbor police board her vessel. Quickly, Helena commandeered the cabin boy's clothes and bunk, where she then curled up, feigning illness. The ruse worked, the police finished their inspection, and her journey soon resumed.

The facts of this escape to Constantinople are not contested. Neither is the fact that Helena, alone and running short on funds in this foreign city of minarets and lutes ruled by the Ottoman sultan, almost immediately took up with a Russian countess in her sixties. The countess requested Helena, then lanky with an attractive moon-shaped face and sand-colored, tightly curled hair, dress as a "gentlemen student." Helena did not decline.

Together, the countess and her dashing trousered "companion" made their way to Egypt. Traveling in a caravan of camels, HPB, as she preferred to be androgynously known, witnessed whirling dervishes—Sufi mystics—spinning through the desert so fast it seemed to her they'd gone airborne. She studied with renowned Coptic magician Paulos Metamon, an expert in all things occult. She scrutinized ancient mystic objects and texts. At some point, she stumbled upon a man in the middle of a dark road, bleeding out from three stab wounds. Ever the gallant gentleman, HPB stood over the gravely injured man for four hours, holding off pickpockets and ruffians, until the police arrived. The man, it turned out, was a Serbian-Italian opera singer of some renown named Agardi Metrovich. That story *is* contested. The fact that the two somehow met and struck up a deep bond is not.

After Egypt, there followed a string of wealthy Russian women to whom HPB served as "companion," as she made her way up the continent of Europe, by now feeling the first spectral pulses of the Spiritualist craze. HPB proved a natural medium. That's known for certain. The exact nature of her relationships with her female patrons, however, remains lost to the astral plane.

Then, on the threshold of her twenties, HPB found herself in London during the Great Exhibition of 1851, greatly dissatisfied. For unknown reasons, she walked out onto the Waterloo Bridge, prepared to jump.

However, just like before when death came calling, the same strange "Indian" man suddenly appeared before her. This time, though, he apparently arrived in the flesh, having traveled to London for the Great Exhibition as part of "the first Nepal Embassy."

You have a great destiny lying in wait if you choose to accept it, he told her. He introduced himself as Master Morya, or M for short. However, before she could enact or fully understand her grand fate, he added, she must spend three years in Tibet, home of the Dalai Lama, studying with mystic masters, members of a Great White Brotherhood of which he was a part. Helena Blavatsky then backed away from the edge.

Like a cloud isolated in the world's highest mountains, Tibet was then perhaps the most inaccessible place on Earth. Westerners who tried to reach it often perished on the road. The few who managed to reach its borders, after months scaling rock faces and skirting bandits in harsh, frigid winds, found themselves turned back by Chinese Qing dynasty patrols. As a result, European "adventurers"—then a bona fide profession—spoke of Tibet with a tone otherwise reserved for Shangri-la.

Forever one to hear the word "impossible" as "I dare you," HPB, nevertheless, set off to reach her promised land. Over the next two decades, HPB circumnavigated the globe, possibly twice. She met an infant, deep in the Caves of Bagh, who walked upright on his chubby legs and spoke in full sentences channeled through him by the Buddha.

She studied with mystic adepts who could change tin into a window or a mirror into a magic crystal that could subdue tigers. However, try as she might—and she did repeatedly—she failed to penetrate her holy grail.

Then, in the late 1860s, HPB tried to cross into Tibet one last time. At the behest of Master M, and possibly in his physical company at the outset of her trek, she traveled overland three thousand miles, from Constantinople across the plateaus of Central Asia, then up the Himalayas, where a "slip of the foot mean[t] certain death." Thanks to her childhood years where East meets West, in Astrakhan, HPB knew basic Tibetan words and ways. Her round cheeks and broad nose, described by some scholars as "Mongolian," further camouflaged her. After five months, she finally crossed the border into Tibet, then walked farther still, following primary-colored prayer flags fluttering up snowy peaks, past villages with rough huts and bright, polished lamaseries overlooking valleys of mist, all the way to a remote southern village near Shigatse.

There she discovered Master M and another master, Koot Hoomi, living with monastic simplicity in a house full of light by a pure mountain stream. For once, she sat still—on floor cushions—and listened. The masters told her the secrets of the universe, how to project her form on the astral plane, read thoughts, and de- and rematerialize inanimate objects. In addition, they taught her English, as that tongue, they explained, stood critical to her mission. She'd also likely learned the language, at least in part, from her family's English governess.

M's Great White Brotherhood was composed of adepts of multiple ethnicities strategically placed about the globe who had each reached a spiritual state so pure they could rejoin the Source pervading all and cease the ceaseless reincarnations of the mortal coil. The Brotherhood's members—all indeed men—had instead elected to stay on earth to assist the rest of us, struggling in our own journey out of the darkness into self-realization (making them basically bodhisattvas or prophets).

In short, the order, old as time—which was an illusion—fought mystically for the side of Light in an endless cosmic battle against the Dark forces.

HPB's mission was to spread their message to the West and prevent that culture from drowning in the deadening materialism and colonialist exploitation then fueling the Dark force's fight. The roiling center of this conflict then lay in a place with a young culture still deciding between its own dark shadows and divine sparks of light.

Or so the legend HPB created for herself goes. There is an alternate account of how she spent those twenty "lost years." It also all begins that day on that London Bridge where HPB stood staring at the dank industrial Thames while contemplating suicide.

2015–2016

I started with a road trip from Burundi, a country then teetering toward months of deadly internecine unrest, through Rwanda to the Democratic Republic of the Congo, a certified conflict zone since 1996—but really since 1874 when Belgians arrived to brutally harvest rubber. Violence begets violence, after all, even if just against oneself. I then journeyed by road across Cambodia (former French colony, rooted in violence)—learning the grisly details of its twentieth-century genocide—before crossing Burma/Myanmar (former British colony, rooted in violence), which at the time, late 2015, was trying to shake off the world's longest-extant dictatorship.

I'd traveled to these places for work, as I'd returned to full-time employment by then—writing about AIDS for a nonprofit. But work was not the reason I kept moving, using up all my salaried vacation days.

I'd started having "suicidal ideation" again. It wasn't that I was close to acting on said ideation, but it's still highly disconcerting to have regular flashes of yourself, killing yourself, interrupting the usual programming in your mind. And it seemed motion might be just the thing to override the broadcast.

In Rwanda, the ground is startlingly red due to all the iron in the soil. In the Congo—called "the rape capital of the world" because rape is a common tool of war there, but also everywhere, as bodies must be colonized too—I came eye to eye with an adult male silverback gorilla. He sat contentedly, just eight feet or so in the distance, with no barrier between us, casually munching broad-leafed jungle foliage—so regular yet so glamorous, like a celebrity at Starbucks. My human companions, one American, the rest Congolese, including several park rangers armed with semiautomatics, hung back. I drew closer.

Suddenly, the gorilla stood, shouting "Humph, humph," as he beat his strong, furry knuckles into the dirt. I heard the scuffle of everyone else fleeing farther behind me. But I stood my ground. I calmly watched the gorilla. He watched me. Mano a mano. No one moved, human or primate.

In a flash, I envisioned him submerging me in his deadly embrace as we tumbled together into the hot jungle mud. Then, looking at the gorilla, who was in reality still standing there looking back at me, I thought—something I'm not sure I'd really done in the moments prior—*if he jumps on me, the rangers will riddle his body with bullets.* I slowly retreated. But the thing is, I didn't want to die. I wanted to face that "brute" strength and, this time, come out the other side fully alive.

It turned out the motion wasn't enough. I remained numb and increasingly preferred the company of Vinni to humans. At some point during the preceding two years, I'd apparently given up on committed romantic relationships entirely. The cave I felt stuck inside seemed to be calcifying into bone, my permanent structure. If I wanted out, it felt like it might be now or never.

Again, I tried therapy. Again, it didn't take. After entering through a rusted-iron gate, I'd sit inside my therapist's home office each week, instinctively dodging her softly lobbed questions for the majority of the hour. I'd also silently construct various narratives for her life—as opposed to mine—based on her NPR-chic possessions and verbiage. Then I quit, feeling our progress had stalled out shortly after it started.

Not knowing what else to do, I considered doubling down on motion, heeding the voice that has always whispered, especially during full moons or after breakups, *Just go, quit your job, hit the American highway, bring your dog, live like some hipster-lesbian Willie Nelson, free as a bird.*

I argued back. I told the voice I couldn't really do such a thing. I was old enough to understand that growing up means accepting the consequences of your actions and circumstances, learning to settle for and enjoy the life that exists, not pining for the one of your dreams. *You can't just quit everything, risk all you do have to roam. You're not Jack fucking Kerouac. You're not some narcissistic ramblin', triflin' ass man. Not that I really have anything against Jack Kerouac.*

Then one Brooklyn night, in a dark, hopeless dirge, I fell to my knees—as one does. Though I hadn't reached out in years, I requested that God or the Goddesses or whatever term the universal divine prefers, take me, use me, point me down the path where I could most serve the light, do some good. There seemed no point anymore to anything I could come up with on my own. A very authoritative vibrato, not like the one I'd been arguing with at all, then rang out in my mind. *Go on the trip. You will be fine. You will not go broke. A road is a path.*

So what should a perfectly sane, albeit depressed, person do when they hear such a voice, the type defined as a symptom of "utromania" back in HPB's day?

Before I left Brooklyn, I bought a Taser. Because even if the voice insisted I would survive, it was 2016. The social fabric felt brittle and riddled daily with bullet holes—often literally. Every day, my Facebook feed offered up posts telling me the heartland hated me, was basically salivating for my blood—as a gay, a woman, someone with New York plates.

But I wanted to see for myself. I wanted to chat with people from all over America and find out which portrait of the nation was really out there: the dark dystopic one of rot and rage and violent division, or the one where some American light of ingenuity and generosity, optimistic perseverance and liberty, blazed on.

I should add, I didn't own a car—at least not until right before my departure—and hadn't really driven since age eighteen. I was rusty to say the least. But I didn't want to die. I wanted to find something to believe in.

Mile after mile, day in and out, driving and watching America unspool, with Vinni in shotgun, lying belly up and rhythmically wheezing like a tiny geriatric pig, I'd go into something like a meditative state, set to Hot 100 and classic rock radio. I'd finally stop thinking, *I want to drive until I find a freedom, a truth that is more than mere motion. I want to drive until I find a place to stand still.*

The Smoky Mountains. The Georgia swamps. Sunset. Pensacola. West Texas. Sunset. The Grand Canyon. The Mojave, hot as death in the sun. The Pacific Coast Highway. Big Sur. Mount Hood. The Badlands. Sunset. Buffalo, the animal, not the place. Endless cornfields conjuring idyllic yeoman and demon children, simultaneously. The New England coast. The places Americans still collectively go to find God.

The Waterloo Bridge, where HPB stood contemplating suicide, was situated just three blocks down Bow Street from the Royal Italian Opera House. The opera building, its auditorium domed, neoclassical, and latticed top to bottom like an ornate hamster wheel, proved key to an alternate theory of how HPB spent her "veiled years." This theory contends it was not a mystic master, but the opera singer Metrovich, who pulled her back from a fateful plunge into the Thames.

HPB and Metrovich, the theory goes, shared a carnal love. In this version of the story, Helena spent her "veiled" years traveling about Europe from grand opera house to grand opera house as his mistress. The theory stems largely from a memoir written by her cousin Count Sergei Witte. It's a text dripping with both factual inaccuracies and distaste for one Helena Petrovna Blavatsky.

According to Sergei, HPB was dependent on Metrovich but also occasionally earned a pound or franc or gram of silver playing piano, leading séances, or riding horses bareback for the local circus. Her main raisons d'être, however, remained Metrovich and raising her love child, a "hunchback" named Yuri. Amid her womanly duties, moneymaking endeavors, and drug-induced lounging—this theory also contends, with no real evidence, that she was addicted to opium and hashish—HPB found time to frequent every grand continental library containing books and scrolls on Egypt, India, Tibet, and so on, which by then, in this age of colonial empires, existed in most major European cities.

The masses, however, were enraptured by the imagined peril, spectacle, and exotic thrill of these far-flung locales, not by the scrolls, books, and esoterica explaining their cultures. This was the swashbuckling age of Jules Verne adventure novels, when the manliest European men dedicated their—often short—lives to "discovering" other peoples' rivers or lands, then claiming them, or plundering other peoples' monarchs' tombs and absconding with the gold, calling it divine right.

Basically, in her own account of these years, HPB out-manned the men. But the alternate story situates her fully in a woman's place, as a dependent mistress and mother—a convenient and more comfortable spot for her to be for many.

In both accounts, however, HPB showed up at her sister's grand Russian abode for Christmas 1858, to take a break from her travels either around Europe or the world, like a long-lost and unannounced ghost. In both accounts, witnesses reported that all around her strange phenomena had started occurring—heavy wood furniture moved, grand pianos played themselves, drawers jutted open on their own. She could not control these happenings, she said, any more than a magnet could its own cause and effect. She could, however, lead Spiritualist séances, titillating the mustachioed and powdered Russian elite arriving in fine carriages from kilometers around.

At some point during her roughly six-year-long stay in the empire, she may or may not have reconnected with Blavatsky. At some point, there may or may not have been a third male lover. Eventually, there definitely existed a disabled child named Yuri, of uncertain parentage, who died in 1867. According to theory two, when he died, his mother, Helena, always half-mad, had a full-fledged breakdown. She then resorted more and more to laudanum and other heavy opiates. In her drug-induced haze, she hallucinated a mythic life for her grief. A life she later presented as truth.

HPB never disputed she cared for Yuri after returning to Russia and before finally reaching Tibet. However, she attested he was the child of a dear friend, and her ward. She produced a certificate signed by a doctor stating, "I hereby certify that Mme Blavatsky has never been pregnant with child."

HPB also did not dispute that burying Yuri's small, misshapen body left her heartbroken. However, in her telling she fled not to an opium den but to Italy to dress as a male soldier and release her rage fighting in a battle for freedom against papal control. The battle ended with her shot, run through with a saber, and left for dead in a ditch. This could, of course, serve as an excellent metaphor for grief. Or maybe it was literal. Maybe she wanted to face what nearly destroyed her eye to eye—in this case death itself—and come out the other side fully alive.

HPB later attested that she took every precaution to wipe away all traces of her whereabouts during this period. She called all seeking answers "venomous mad-dogs who poke their noses under cover of the night into every family's and every individual's private lives." But there is some hearsay supporting her version of the story. Soldiers stated they met her in India. Others heard tell of a white lady trying to get from India to Tibet in 1854. Some talked of a European woman traveling through Tibet, past the "forbidden city" of Lhasa, on her way to a lamasery in 1867 or 1868—all of which aligns. Plus, considering HPB fled her native land at age seventeen, a stowaway to Constantinople, where she knew no one and no one knew her, the assertion that she spent the subsequent two decades defined only by the roles men permitted her seems equally as unbelievable as her traversing the world, utterly free, meeting babies possessed by prophets.

Either way, in July 1871, the SS *Eumonia*, bound for Alexandria, exploded just off the Greek isle of Spetsai when its cargo of gunpowder and fireworks combusted at sea. Listed among the sixteen survivors, out of four hundred aboard, was one Helena Petrovna Blavatsky. With that, HPB permanently emerged from her "veil," wet, bedraggled, baptized by fire for a second time, and ready to enact her fate. Again, these events remain uncontested. So again, I have to wonder, what else could be true?

The Greek government gave all sixteen survivors a pittance to cover immediate expenses and compensate them for their misfortune. HPB, it seems, promptly played roulette with her take—and won—using the windfall to travel to Cairo, before gradually making her way to Paris, where she ran out of funds. Then, a roll of cash arrived direct from the Brotherhood along with orders (at least as she told it). Despite her recent near-death experience at sea, she departed the next day on a steamer as instructed. Her destination: New York City.

8

The Famous Heathen of Eighth Avenue

2018

The Soul Oracle recommended a crystal dildo, informing me rose quartz is best. But I was more interested in her talk of my past life as Thoth, an Egyptian deity of writing symbolized by the moon. The oracle, an earnestly effusive black woman no older than twenty-five, her head expertly wrapped in a white tignon, then prophesied love—by the end of the year. It was March. This gave Cupid ample time to do Aphrodite's bidding. And I'd take love. But I came looking for other answers.

To my oracle's left, a sinewy middle-aged butch white woman wearing electric paisley offered an Astrological Karma reading to a very young woman in no-nonsense business casual attire. To her left, my Intuitive Reader Alexandra, petite and dark haired as a raven, performed a healing Reiki session, her hands fluttering with lepidopteran precision before a wall shelf sparsely covered in artfully displayed crystals, tinctures, and books on witches, self-care, and fermenting your own kombucha.

This "Full Moon Gathering," offering a variety pack of intuitive, psychic, and healing services at a reasonable price, occurred every month in this New Age store-cum-mystic workshop. The space, all openness and hanging plants and light, was located on the first floor of a luxury condominium complex that arose in 2013 from the ashes of Mars Bar, an establishment so dankly punk its bathroom had been labeled, by certain patrons, as the "most horrible" in New York City.

In the end, by summer 2016, I'd driven fourteen thousand miles across thirty-two states in a white MINI Cooper with black racing stripes. When I pulled back into Brooklyn—after talking with hundreds of Americans about the troubled state of the union—it seemed my #SoulJourney had, for the most part, restored my lapsed faith in humanity. People in the heartland had escorted me to a tire shop when I'd gotten a flat, instead of leaving me on the side of a desert highway with my tiny dog and New York plates in the bone-bleaching Texas sun. They bought me drinks and offered me egg-salad sandwiches while we chatted politely of our differing worldviews and our common values— something they, and I, very much wanted to find.

At least, it restored my faith until November. In the bleak aftermath of the election, I started to feel like I'd driven across the breadth of this continent and back and ended up right where I'd started—stuck in need of solid ground. But I also knew firsthand that out there in the rest of America, the majority remained decent, eager to connect, to cohere even, with the other side of the divide. And so, the feeling increasingly crept in that some swirling Dark cosmic force, not mere "red v. blue politics," but a conflict much more powerful and primordial, older than the fossil record, was preventing us from binding into one people in it together as Americans. Soon enough, I ended up at the séance helmed by Reverend Paul, my mind once again a torrent of disquietude. But I also knew I felt changed by my summer on the road, opened, but uncertain what that meant or how to extricate myself from the deep, hard grooves of my three-plus decades of living.

My young oracle concluded our session by telling me "they," as she referred to the spirits without further specification, said I'm trying too hard to be stable. I'm stifling my soul. I'm preventing myself from walking forward.

"What should I do?" I asked.

"Connect with the playful inner child within," she prescribed.

Somewhere in the astral plane I shrugged. We namaste goodbye.

Alexandra, who had just completed her own session, waved me over to her table. She'd been booked full, so even though I'd not seen her in some time, I'd had to opt for a new clairvoyant. Crossing the cheery honey-oak room, I missed the Goth gloom, that je ne sais subversiveness, of the occult stores of yore and Bushwick. I also asked myself how this mystic medley on display—of past lives and astrology and karma and energy work—came to be.

We hugged, Alexandra's flowing sheer white sleeves soft on my neck. Like me, she now wore glasses. She informed me she'd been working this event every month, that she loved the emergent state of mystic affairs in which she could publicly prognosticate without fear. What's more, she told me, she now had young apprentices, in their early to mid twenties, who had no irony or apology or urge to obfuscate their mystic tendencies—or, I'd wager, any snarky compunctions about inner-child work. Things had come a long way, we mused, since I first visited her furniture-free apartment, back when punk bars, secondhand shops, and boarded-up, graffitied former flophouses still populated the Bowery. It was a whole new New Age world for the kids, plus a whole new New York City.

I informed her I've been investigating feministic mystics. "Have you heard of Helena Blavatsky?" she asked.

I had.

"I've been channeling her spirit lately. Whoa. Talk about powerful," she offered.

I don't realize it at that moment, as I only asked myself and not her the question about the origin of the mystic medley on display that night, but Alexandra had just provided my answer. The answer also happened to double as a nomination for my ancestral spirit coven. Psychics.

We bid one another adieu, just an old-school see you later, and I exited into the cold night. Passing the Patagonia and John Varvatos stores that replaced the punk bar CBGB—previous haunt of Patti Smith, Blondie, the Ramones—then the new neighborhood Whole Foods, I gazed up past the tamed, aging Bowery, where almost no one making less than $200K a year could by then afford to live. The full moon's neon light called my inner wolf to roam. I decided to take the 6 train to the Brooklyn Bridge and walk across the frigid, slow New York Harbor to Brooklyn. *The gray March snow should keep the tourists at bay,* I thought, *leaving me nearly alone with Lady Liberty.*

She comes alive in the night, like a veil has been removed from her astral aura. *Communing with the copper harbinger of a New World tonight, especially, as she raises her torch to Luna, Diana, Thoth, or your full-moon deity of choice, might do my "stifled soul" a solid,* I thought.

Among the passengers crowded onto the steamer's deck, their fraying monochromatic frocks and flatcaps blurring into one, stood a large woman chain-smoking in a flowing red "Oriental" robe, its golden embroidery catching the morning light. She looked as if she'd been cut and pasted in from another story. As the ship passed through a cloud into New York Harbor, the assembled immigrants gazed out at a melee of clipper ships, steamships, ferries, barges, and tugboats floating in what was fast becoming the world's busiest port. In the rising heat, soot-covered men dangled from budding granite towers, the beginnings of the Brooklyn Bridge—an unprecedented suspension-wire marvel.

But Helena Blavatsky's intense azure eyes seemed to penetrate past this peculiarly American fantasia with "feelings not unlike those of a Mohammedan approaching the birthplace of his Prophet," as she later stated. Or at least it went something like that when HPB docked in New York Harbor in July 1873, one among a sea of immigrants filing through Castle Garden.

By then, she had become the creature of legend. The woman of whom the American press, both repulsed and magnetized, soon couldn't get enough. Sure, they mocked and debased her for her by then considerable girth, her odd Russian syntax, her loud guffaw, her penchant for wearing copious metallic rings and colorful androgyne robes, while chain-smoking, even in public—a practice then verboten for women. Nevertheless, write about her they did.

But upon her arrival, bad press was far from HPB's main issue. HPB may have gotten into Tibet, but she still couldn't get a hotel room in Manhattan as an unaccompanied woman in the early 1870s. She was also fast running out of her masters' funds. And so, HPB scoured the city for extremely cheap lodgings that would deign to have her.

On the Bowery and Lower East Side, the penniless yet striving huddled masses arriving daily packed into the muddy streets to avoid the stifling rot of their ramshackle tenement buildings, growing more dangerously overcrowded with each ship's disembarkation. Peering inside, HPB would have glimpsed bodies slumped over chairs after working sunup to sundown—half sleeping, half drunk, all often injured or lame—or lying in stairwells, or piled five to a bug-infested bed and coughing.

Walking just half a mile to Fifth Avenue, she would have spied men in shimmering top hats and women in spotless whalebone silk dresses parading together down an avenue lined by cavernous new French Gothic Revival and Beaux-Arts single-family mansions. HPB spied proof that the very condition her masters had sent her to combat, the dark "deadening materialism" of this Gilded Age, had grown critical.

Eventually, she found refuge at 222 Madison Street, a nice new tenement cooperative created for single women such as herself in need of the shelter denied them elsewhere. Even in that age of greed, there were groups of Americans still pushing—quite stridently—for a freer, more equal new world. HPB had found her target audience.

At forty-two, HPB felt her roaming days were over. It was high time she built something on which she could stand and enact her mission. However, as a loud, large, and the opposite of delicate and pure woman, she knew she put people off in this buttoned-up, industrious nation. But she also intuited that though Americans may have shunned the odd, they flocked toward the odd that was so big it'd grown spectacular.

Before her first month as a New Yorker was out, HPB had given her first self-branding interview to a reporter from the *New York Sun* interested in Russia. Chain-smoking tobacco she pulled from a fur pouch that still bore the original occupant's head, either rodent or weasel, while lounging in her tenement common room, Madame Blavatsky proclaimed into her hovering, clinging veil of smoke, "I have been to Tibet."

But this first profile in panache wasn't enough to make Manhattanites pause and ask for more. HPB knew she needed legitimacy, an in, a guide to these foreign, restrained people.

Henry Steel Olcott remained baffled by his perpetual dissatisfaction. Sipping tea in his private Lotos Club, he asked himself, as so many living amid "deadening materialism" do, *Is this all there is?* Though his firmly set features and heavy-lidded eyes made him appear forever drunk or bored, he was no one's definition of a malcontent or slouch. Before the age of twenty-five, Olcott, son of a Presbyterian gentleman farmer, had written a hit agricultural monograph on sorghum. He'd married a proper WASP woman and had four children, two of whom survived into adulthood. During the war, while serving in the Union Army as a special commissioner probing fraud allegations, he'd exposed a racket falsifying provision sales, prompting his appointment to a three-man team investigating the assassination of Abraham Lincoln. Ever indefatigable, he then passed the bar and set out a shingle for his own law practice specializing in insurance and customs, including cases of fraud.

At forty-two, he found himself separated from his wife, living in his club, drinking too much whiskey, and drawn to the night. He began moonlighting as a columnist covering spiritual manifestations. Unlike many such writers gleefully unmasking the levitating spirits vomiting ectoplasm as jerry-rigged fakes, Olcott offered a certain benefit of the doubt, a reverence. This professional fraud debunker—skilled enough to be called to investigate the assassination of a president—clearly still wanted something to believe in.

In late 1874, he read in the Spiritualist weekly the *Banner of Light* of the most fantastic phantasmagoria taking place in the farm community of Chittenden, Vermont. There, two brothers, the Eddy brothers, had discovered they could manifest all kinds of dueling, dancing, swashbuckling spirits. Titillated, Olcott convinced the *Sun* to send him north on assignment. After his piece was published that September, causing quite a stir, the *Daily Graphic* contracted him to pen a six-week series on the Chittenden happenings.

HPB picked up one of those very editions of the *Graphic*. After she put it down, she immediately purchased a train ticket to Vermont.

Just east of Union Square, the junction where the old Bowery Road transforms into Park Avenue, in an apartment HPB had rented on Irving Place, a group of seekers gathered on September 7, 1875, for a lecture on a mystic mathematical formula. As the orator concluded, Olcott rose from his seat with a proposal.

Instantaneously upon meeting in Vermont, Olcott and HPB had become inseparable "chums," as they called one another. And HPB had soon revealed her full mission to her newly acquired other half. Her masters had sent her to New York City to "spiritualize Spiritualism," provide that craze with history, a knowledge and craft, perfected by wise men over thousands of years but arrogantly dismissed by Westerners as superstition. This would give the fad—as she saw it—fuel to grow and deepen. But amid mounting incidents of manifesting scandals and fraud, it had quickly grown clear to all, even Olcott, that Spiritualism was undergoing a long death rattle. Faced with that foundering, HPB told her chum that new word had come from her adepts: Act fast. Build your own movement. The window is closing.

So that September night, one year after the chums first met, Olcott stood to request that all present come together to found their own society dedicated to applying scientific principles to the study of the divine. All agreed. Concurring on a name, however, eluded them. Then a bookseller named Charles Sotheran grabbed a dictionary, flipped it open, and proposed what he saw on the page before him: *theosophy*, a word meaning God, or divine wisdom.

The group appointed Olcott, a man, the new society's president, and HPB its corresponding secretary. Other inaugural Theosophical Society members included journalists, Freemasons, a Kabbalist doctor, an Italian sculptor, a New York judge and his wife, and Emma Hardinge Britten.

As a woman who was now able to control the phenomena swirling in the ether—moving objects with her mind, reading other people's minds, and the like—instead of the phenomena controlling her, HPB sought to flip the narrative of the passive medium on its head. While taking a definite feminist step forward, HPB went perhaps a bit far. She soon started insulting every Spiritualist in sight, often while cursing liberally. She condemned mediumship as base "necromancy," the "crude" tilling of "filthy weeds," produced by "weak and sick minds" who allowed the spirits to run the show. Olcott joined her in the disparagement. Even amid Spiritualism's long decline, this course of action made the duo few friends among the mystically inclined, and just as quickly as it had blossomed, the society's membership plummeted. No fated mission, even one ordained by a brotherhood of Tibetan adepts, is certain. The time had come for a Hail Mary.

The silver spoon levitated from its spot in the drawing room, then hovered past the mounted taxidermied crocodile and toy lizards, the potted palm, the mystic bric-a-brac, and Professor Fiske, a stuffed baboon outfitted in a collar and tie clutching a manuscript of a lecture on Darwin's *On the Origin of Species* beneath his furry bicep. Finally, the spoon plopped into HPB's morning tea, which she was having along with her favorite, fried eggs floating in butter. Across the table, Olcott, or Maloney as she affectionately called him, hardly looked up from his newspaper as the flatware made its splash entrance. By now, he'd grown accustomed to the peculiarities of living with "Jack"—as he in turn called her.

After dinner, the "Divine Hermaphrodite," as HPB would soon be called by many, might manifest a painting or a radiant orb of light languishing across the curve of the divan. But for the most part, since early 1876 when HPB and Olcott moved into a two-bedroom apartment they called the "Lamasery," on the corner of West Forty-Seventh Street and Eighth Avenue, HPB had been on lockdown in her room.

Olcott meanwhile continued with his law practice, supporting her mystic toil. At night, he'd read the pages she'd written that day, her edits cut and pasted atop one another like a patchwork quilt. He'd offer notes. He'd watch her curly blonde ewe's hair grow straight and black, as a "Hindu" adept she called her "lodger" took hold of her form, and the style of her handwriting transformed, or so he later attested.

"It is not I who talk and write; it is something within me, my higher and luminous self, that thinks and writes for me."

He'd watch HPB roll cigarettes with her left hand while furiously scribbling with her right, the words a torrent pouring, often quoting verbatim and at length from esoteric texts she reportedly had no access to. She claimed she transcribed these passages direct from the astral library. Fact-checkers later fact-checked. HPB's only real error, it seems, was that she sometimes inverted the page numbers of her references—as things appeared as their mirror image astrally, or so HPB said.

However, tension had started to percolate in Hell's Kitchen. Feeling the weight of looming failure, HPB took to frequently berating Olcott, even in front of guests. Her temper and tirades fell away as fast as they rose, and she'd return to boisterous belly laughs and good-natured ribbing. But the staid Yankee still balked at the verbal abuse. Thankfully, at key moments, letters inked in gold on green parchment, mystic missives, would appear to smooth the trouble. First, the letters arrived mysteriously in the post or fluttered down from the ceiling, but eventually the masters' messages apparently "precipitated" in full on formerly blank pages—like a Polaroid picture. Most were signed by Master M, Koot Hoomi, or a third master, Serapis Bey, but there were other adept signatories.

"Sister Helen is a valiant, trustworthy servant. Open thy Spirit to conviction, have faith and she will lead thee to the Golden Gate of truth," read one such memo, delivered to Olcott in a moment of doubt. Others dealt with far more practical matters, suggesting he, for example, borrow money from his in-laws to help finance the duo's lifestyle.

HPB had learned the hard way how America responded to a single woman. Before moving in with Olcott, she had married Michael Betanelly, a suicidal Georgian immigrant she barely knew, for reasons unknown, though she claimed she felt it was a way to stop her compatriot from killing himself. They separated not long after. Like with

Blavatsky, HPB insisted she and Betanelly never consummated their union.

"I had a volcano in constant eruption in my brain and—a glacier—at the foot of the mountain."

In Olcott, she'd found the truly platonic male partner she desired. The chums acquired two canaries named Jenny and Pip and a cat named Charles and shared similar ideas about interior design.

After six months of hermit-like living, HPB completed her manifesto. It clocked in at a rather astounding half a million words. Olcott went in search of a publisher. Against all odds, he found one.

On September 29, 1877, *Isis Unveiled* hit shelves. The *New York Sun* called it "discarded rubbish." The *New York Herald*: "One of the most remarkable productions of the century." The *New York Times* declined reviewing it altogether, stating they had "a holy horror of Madame Blavatsky." One might think a twelve-hundred-page two-volume book with meandering, dense content and mixed reviews would be a hard sell. The book sold out its first printing in ten days.

Isis was the first tome illuminating Theosophy. It outlined the teachings the masters had charged HPB with disseminating to the world. More books would follow, each a strange cultural medley of all HPB had seen and learned during her "veiled years."

Theosophy identified three founding goals:

1. To form the nucleus of a universal brotherhood of humanity, without distinction of race, creed, sex, caste, or color.
2. The study of ancient and modern religions, philosophies, and sciences, and the demonstration of the importance of such study.

3. The investigation of the unexplained laws of nature and the psychic powers latent in man.

HPB proclaimed that placing science and religion on two separate teams was utter "flapdoodle." It denoted either "tame subservience to the arrogance of science" or a fanatical relinquishing of critical thought. She had nothing against Jesus himself who, like the Buddha and other famed adepts of yore, she labeled a master. But she believed that what had evolved from his teachings of Love, the formal institution of Christianity, was the dark antithesis of the Brotherhood's side of light. She called it "a stepping-stone for ambition, a sinecure for wealth, sham, and power, and a convenient screen for hypocrisy" that encouraged blind faith in authority.

To find another way, a skeleton key for tapping our inner divinity and light, HPB surveyed Neoplatonism, Pythagoreanism, alchemy, astrology, Masonic symbolism, Hinduism, Zoroastrianism, Kabbalah, ancient Egyptian traditions, Western gnosis, and Buddhism, to name just a few. From each, she excised, according to her, the profound from superstition to produce one universal truth all could employ. In the process, she unveiled elite European occult wisdom to the masses— democratized it—and introduced unknown religious beliefs and ways from another hemisphere to Western popular culture and lore.

Critically for the feminist mystic, HPB's writings also resurrected the Goddess, the divine feminine force of many names and faces— including Isis. She wrote that Christianity pilfered the Triple Goddess, "the mother, the wife, and the daughter," transmuted her into "the Father, Son, and . . . Holy Ghost," and then killed her off. The Divine Hermaphrodite also took Spiritualism's queering of gender lines a step further via her talk of reincarnation—as a woman can be a man and a man a woman next time, or last time, around. Plus, HPB's astral plane remembers all that ever happened or ever will, obliterating time and space, so once a man, always a man, even if one is currently a woman.

Like the Spiritualists before her, HPB advocated re-creating the order of the heavens here on earth by ensuring all people have the rights, freedom, and material security needed to pursue spiritual heights, not just their next meal.

And though Theosophy emphatically moved away from a shamanic communing with the spirits, it maintained faith in "the liberation of the mind from its finite consciousness, becoming one and identified with the infinite." HPB deviated from Spiritualism when it came to the means, recommending one should achieve such an ecstatic state via meditation, Rāja yoga, and asceticism (e.g., chastity, sobriety, vegetarianism, and the like)—not through free love, trance, or the body's other unencumbered joys. However, none of this recommended abstaining constituted anything like a hard or fast rule—and HPB herself continued indulging in fried eggs and butter.

HPB brought the Western masses karma, astrology, reincarnation, yoga, meditation, and more. She provided the *philosophical* seeds of the New Age.

Theosophy quickly went from the verge of its last rites to a global phenomenon. Its ranks included disillusioned Spiritualists and occultists, and also suffragettes, socialists, progressives, innovators, intellectuals, queers, anticolonialists, and bohemians—then a new cultural force in New York City.

According to rumors, the bohemians' parties had dancing. They had peacock feathers, ironic uses of smoking jackets, and a natural affinity with both Theosophy's eternal truths of personal freedom and HPB's means of conveying these truths via something akin to theater of the absurd—a style so over-the-top fake it rang out profoundly true. Unlike most in the staid nation, the bohemians really got Madame Helena Petrovna Blavatsky.

"Camp is art that proposes itself seriously but cannot be taken altogether seriously because it is 'too much,'" Susan Sontag wrote in *Notes on "Camp."* "One should either be a work of art, or wear a work of art," stated Oscar Wilde, who is often pegged as the progenitor of the aesthetic and as a dabbler in Theosophy. Though subversively queer, camp is not arch or ironic. It is not self-loathing. It has a big heart, a joyful earnestness, a profound truth in its heightened artifice.

Shortly after *Isis* became the rage, HPB and her camp ways became the toast of literati and glitterati of the American Gilded Age. The bohemians, their patrons, and famed freethinkers like Thomas Edison entered the Lamasery night after night, greeted by Professor Fiske the baboon as they made their way to the living room. There, beneath a dangling taxidermied bat, sat Madame Blavatsky, shrouded in an ever-thickening haze of cigarette smoke. She'd absentmindedly put out the butts in plants, in glasses, or on a minor deity's bronze base, as her pet birds happily circled above. She titillated her guests with tidbits of transcendence and peril, read minds with stunning acuity, manifested mystic communiques from her masters, moved cutlery through walls, and caused jewelry to disappear and reappear on gasping women clutching at the buttons reaching their chins.

Accordingly, the fervor of the press, already enamored with the exploits of the odd Russian woman, intensified. "The Famous Heathen of Eighth Avenue," as the *Sun* called her, had fully arrived.

2018

Two swans with pale-blue feet rested, on loan, at the center of the divine white upward spiral at the heart of the Guggenheim Museum. They are mirror images across the canvas's horizontal axis, save the fact one is white, one black—one light, one shadow—the opposing dualities the painter, Hilma af Klint, felt fueled existence and time. "In alchemy, the swan symbolizes the union of opposites necessary for the creation of the philosopher's stone, a legendary substance capable of turning base metals into gold," the Guggenheim sign explained.

Turns out, though unheralded until recently, Hilma in fact invented abstract art years before the men who get the credit. She did so to represent the transcendent pulsing reality and realms we cannot observe with our senses, realms that her avowed Theosophical beliefs and the spirits she oft heard in her head had revealed to her. Unlike her male counterparts, she attributed her "genius" to the divine other side.

Today, the name "Theosophical Society" no longer conjures images of wild bohemian-chic parties or avant-garde creation but stuffy, dusty books and politely heated debates among corset-wearing women and bowler-hatted gents. As such, though still extant on five continents, the society is experiencing an international membership crisis.

The New York Theosophical Society continues to hold meetings every Wednesday in a stately gray stone structure next to Peking Duck sit-down, takeout, delivery on an otherwise rather bland stretch of Midtown East. The assembled partake in a twenty-minute meditation followed by a thoughtful talk, sometimes with slides, on how HPB's tomes describing the nexus of science and religion apply today. One evening, as I sat among about fifteen enthusiastic Theosophists, most age fifty-plus, an elderly white man wearing a navy-blue cardigan interrupted the presentation. In a nasal patrician trill, he told the room how, thanks to science, we now know electrons exist in one place, then another, but never in between—just like, he'd augur, how HPB said more complex beings reincarnate.

Electrons do not transition. Electrons do not go through the oft-painful process of change, I thought. *But maybe, in the end, I did drive far enough and make it to a place where I'm prepared to let go, fall inward.*

In addition to the tattoo of the Mississippi River snaking down my left side, I have two swans in the style found on ancient Grecian pottery etched on my right shoulder. Well, it's really one swan, two incarnations. First, the swan stands still. Then the swan takes flight. It was always aspirational. Two weeks after that Wednesday meeting, I discovered Hilma's mystic mirror swans in the Guggenheim. They momentarily arrested me—seemed some cosmic clue I'd not found by dissecting HPB's texts in Midtown East.

Swans symbolize transformation. Swans mate for life. Swans also sometimes murder their own kind by drowning.

My swans, inked in shades of gray, now cause me to think theosophically, in the way HPB intended. I think of the spiraling, violent creative-destructive revolution otherwise known as change, of Hilma, an artistic genius, and of HPB, whose own admittedly rather odd and refracted genius inspired her, of two women who harnessed the philosopher's stone to create and transform the world—for the better. Though history opted to forget about it or steal their ideas. The microcosm reflects the macrocosm, as the mystics say.

"Orders" had come: HPB and Olcott were to embark for India no later than December 17, 1878. Olcott demurred. How would they pay for passage and for living expenses once they arrived? How could he morally justify leaving behind his two sons, both just entering adulthood and not yet set up in proper careers, not to mention his former wife, who relied on his alimony for survival?

But despite her success, increasing fame, and Olcott's very practical concerns, HPB's leg had again gotten itchy. She told Olcott there was no better place to stop Western materialism from ravaging spiritual truth than in an India under the rule of the British Raj. They could fight a colonial regime bent on obliterating ancient divine revelations, one systematically denigrating the native Indian culture in an effort to make all the native peoples submit to the Christian faith culturally and spiritually.

This argument, however, failed to convince Olcott. Green letters ordering their departure then precipitated like leaves. Olcott still hemmed and hawed. Master M astrally manifested before him to assuage his concerns. Olcott failed to commit. Finally, connected Theosophists pulled strings to ensure his sons secured respectable positions. Olcott managed to obtain an open-ended post for himself as a US trade representative, plus a letter of introduction from President Hayes. Only then did he assent to his friend's demands.

It seemed HPB's American tale would only encompass five years, but it was a very American one nevertheless. She was an immigrant who rose from the tenement house to fame, a queen of self-branding, the original "there's no such thing as bad publicity" gal. She'd even become the first Russian woman to obtain US citizenship, calling her new nation the "only land of true freedom in the world."

One week before they were due to depart, Thomas Edison presented the chums with a going-away present: a hundred-pound brass phonograph, his latest invention, unveiled to the public just one year prior. That night, a group of boisterous Theosophical well-wishers who gathered in the Lamasery recorded their goodbyes on the technological marvel. Then, on the very day of her masters' deadline, HPB departed the way she came. As they sailed out of New York Harbor, the chums' ship would have passed below the new steel cables precariously joining the completed stone towers of the Brooklyn Bridge, grand as any cathedral, about to link once-separate shores into something new. Then America faded from view.

9

PROPHET OR FRAUD OR BOTH

The news arrived in a letter in spring 1883, and not one of gilded gold and empire green, but the regular sort, with postage. The treachery had worsened at the Theosophical Society's new global HQ, a small estate in Adyar overlooking the Bay of Bengal. Of course, HPB was no stranger to slander. She expected it.

"I am repeatedly reminded of the fact that as a public character, a woman who, instead of pursuing her womanly duties, sleeping with her husband, breeding children, wiping their noses, minding her kitchen, and consoling herself with matrimonial assistants on the sly and behind her husband's back, I have chosen a path that has led me to notoriety and fame; and that therefore I had to expect all that befell me. Very well, I admit it and I agree."

Still, it seemed surprising that after everything, HPB's private housekeeper, Emma Coulomb, could be the one to finally depose her.

The groundwork had been laid long before. Since HPB and Olcott had landed in Bombay five years prior, HPB's rages had grown more intense and less discriminating in their targets, her "phenomenon" more reckless and blustery. There was a scandal involving a Theosophist's lost brooch that HPB manifested in a hole in the woman's Bombay garden—a brooch, it was later uncovered, that HPB had every opportunity to acquire in advance of its disappearance. A similar outrage surrounded a teacup she located buried in a public park amid the roots of a cedar tree.

Many Theosophists had grown increasingly suspicious that HPB herself penned the Mahatmas' (as the masters were now known) letters, which manifested in a metalwork-covered lacquered cabinet called "the shrine," located in the Adyar estate "occult room." The "occult room" had been built into an alcove just off HPB's own private chambers. Others hedged their bets, contending that, on occasion, the Mahatmas beamed messages to HPB telepathically, and she then recorded that lot herself, but the rarefied guild "precipitated" others in full as advertised. Employed handwriting experts have never reached a consensus.

On top of that, HPB's health, never stellar, was deteriorating fast, leaving her "crumbling away like an old sea biscuit," as she put it. Still chain-smoking, she'd also developed dropsy, kidney disease, and ulcers.

Theosophy itself, however, had precipitated into her wildest dreams. In New York and even more so London, the chic bohemian set continued to embrace it; its lodge members included the likes of W. B. Yeats, George William Russell, and later Piet Mondrian. Soon enough, "Mahatma hats" would be sold in corner boutiques, "How's your karma today?" would become the "What's your sign?" of its generation, and dogs named Koot Hoomi would frolic in places like Hyde Park and New York's Central Park. But Theosophy had burrowed deepest in South and Southeast Asia—where 106 of Theosophy's 121 lodges were located.

Five months after arriving in India, the chums had launched the *Theosophist*. The monthly rag's cover displayed inked palm fronds, an Egyptian ankh, and a Kabbalist Star of David, and its interior featured articles on the wisdom of the continent's native religions—Buddhism and Hinduism in particular. With it, the chums aimed to unmask as colonial propaganda the rhetoric that besmirched these religions by calling them primitive superstition. The journal quickly developed a readership among the independence-minded in India large enough to fund the purchase of the grand new global HQ, with its airy arched promenades and banyan trees. And Theosophy's membership spiked accordingly.

With new recruits running much of the society's daily operations, Olcott, though still president, now spent more and more time on the road, preaching the virtues of Hinduism and Buddhism—and Theosophy—across the continent. Dressed in sandals and a pale dhoti that ballooned about his legs, his bushy beard grown white and wild, he traveled by oxcart through the mud roads of Burma (now Myanmar) and Ceylon (now Sri Lanka). He preached Buddhist teachings to cheering crowds. He convinced British authorities to permit public celebration of Buddhist holidays. He founded Buddhist schools. He competed directly with the Christian missionaries—causing these same British authorities to investigate him and HPB as potential spies bent on undermining their empire. They may have had a point. After its independence, the Sri Lankan government branded a postage stamp with Olcott's face and at least three streets with his name.

The Theosophical Society suddenly had much to lose. Its volcanic cofounder and visionary had always been skating some borderline between madness and sanity. She now seemed, to many, to be sliding off that thin wire toward nowhere good.

Enter Emma Coulomb. Emma and HPB's acquaintance dated back to 1871 in Cairo, where the two had presided over Spiritualist séances together. So, years later, when Emma and her husband washed up in Adyar penniless, HPB took them under her ornate cloak and gave them shelter and employment. Even given this generosity, one could imagine that life as housekeeper to HPB, who was prone to berating tirades, could provoke exasperation—or even, for a certain sort, vengeful wrath.

Patiently, Emma bided her time until her benefactor and Olcott sailed for England, where they'd been summoned to quell a power struggle brewing in the London lodge. Emma then led bigwig Theosophists, already suspect of their corresponding secretary, into HPB's private chambers, where she threw back a curtain.

She revealed a wall. But it was no ordinary wall. On it was a panel, which Emma slid open. There through the slit the Theosophists saw into the "occult room's" "shrine," plain as day. No one asked Emma to explain her contention. Her silence, she told them, had a price tag. The Theosophists, however, declined the blackmail.

With HPB off in England, and Emma and her husband free to do as they pleased, the couple certainly could have faked it all and constructed the panel themselves. But in the end, it came down to optics. Emma took her claim that HPB produced the letters herself, then slid them through a secret compartment into the lacquered Theosophical "shrine" to the Christian press, who, far from being fans of the Theosophists, were all too happy to publish Emma's allegations. The scandal ricocheted throughout Indian society and the Theosophical world, threatening to topple the movement. HPB stood firm, planning to take the case to court to clear her name. Olcott, however, issued an ultimatum. It was him or her, but someone had to go.

In March 1885, a crew hoisted HPB, by then too ill to walk, up a ship's gangplank in her wheelchair via an elaborate pully system—as HPB perhaps offered those ashore a jolly wave from her rolling perch. She would never return to Asia, where Theosophy had grown into its own, nor to North America, where she'd birthed it. Shortly before she set sail, her masters presented HPB, now fifty-three, with a choice: die now, or live until you complete one last manuscript, a map for humanity to reach the Source. And so Madame Blavatsky chose.

2018

Levitating azure eyes, glistening and beguiling as the disembodied red lips that open *The Rocky Horror Picture Show*, played before me. Alexandra shuddered. "I didn't know Madame Blavatsky was gay," she said, ending our joint meditation as she opened one eyelid.

"Unclear," I replied, as I opened both of mine. "But she totally seems to fall into the larger queer rubric somewhere."

"This is the first time I've actually seen her when I've channeled her, and I was like '*Ohh*' [Translation: Gay]."

It was half a year after Alexandra had offhandedly mentioned on a cold East Village night that she could contact HPB. It was eleven years after our inaugural reading. Alexandra and her wife now resided in a Brooklyn loft, converted from a former sugar factory, with ample furnishings. However, they were moving their ample furnishings, themselves, their cat, and their pit bull named Queens west to California, as mystics seem wont to do. That night would be our final reading. But, for some reason, even though I hadn't seen her much in years, I felt from here on out I was going to have to stand on my own two feet, mystically speaking.

"The line to her is unusually clear," said Alexandra, impressed with HPB, who apparently was sitting by a fire in a deep nineteenth-century lounge chair, smoking a hand-rolled cigarette with a small dog in her lap. HPB then motioned as if to say, "Well, what is it you'd like to know," or so Alexandra told me.

"Many people have accused her of fraud and of forging letters and things. Ask her how she responds to that," I offered.

HPB sat even farther back in her astral easy chair, her robe bunching slightly.

"I did things I kind of regret." She emphasized the "kind of." *"I did what I had to, to get people to pay attention to my ideas. I wouldn't have had to do it if I were a man."*

However, in her view, HPB told us, her tactics did have one main downside. All the spectacle muddled her message.

"I am not extraordinary. The point is we all have access to these powers. You do too. You just need to focus, develop them."

Then she suggested I read her books.

After disembarking in Naples, HPB again spent her days scribbling furiously, her words a torrent pouring. She shadowed her past, slowly making her way north up the continent of Europe in the care of wealthy women, writing all the while. In London, she found a city living in terror of Jack the Ripper and in the thrall of fictional monsters like Frankenstein's. She found a city primed for her cosmic battle against darkness.

Though stripped of her official position, HPB did not just relinquish all influence and quietly fade into the Theosophical night. Instead, she founded the Blavatsky Lodge. Essentially "Theosophy, the advanced course," the Blavatsky Lodge admitted only inner elites who worked directly with HPB to dig deeper into cosmic truths—sparking much mystique around the upstart lodge. This mystique quickly translated into influence, ballooning through London, then the world—returning HPB to her rightful place of Theosophical honor, at least culturally speaking. However, HPB's fall from grace did procure one concession: she swore off all phenomena, declaring Theosophy would be all philosophy, all the time. The spectacle had been retired. Besides, she had no time for such shenanigans.

She hauled her new manuscript—a more than three-foot-high and rising pile of single-spaced pages—in the carriage with her from posh residence to posh residence. At each temporary abode, during writing breaks, Theosophists and other well-wishers lined up to pay tribute to the grande dame.

During one such meet and greet in a swank Notting Hill home, a young Gandhi, then studying law in London, presented himself to HPB. He'd befriended some Theosophists at a vegetarian restaurant. In addition to taking him to meet their leader, they'd also introduced him to Hinduism's sacred Bhagavad Gita—which Gandhi had never read, having been taught to scorn it by British authorities. Gandhi then joined a Theosophical Lodge, albeit briefly. Later, the Bhagavad Gita inspired his "nonviolent" philosophy of revolution, and Gandhi continued to look favorably upon his short Theosophical tenure. "Theosophy . . . is Hinduism at its best. Theosophy is the brother-hood of man," he stated. "Whatever critics may say against Madame Blavatsky or Col. Olcott or Dr. Besant, their contribution to human-ity will always rank high."

Released in two volumes, the first in October 1888 and the sec-ond the subsequent January, HPB billed *The Secret Doctrine* as a "new Genesis," providing the real cosmic history of man and universe. It proved even harder to parse than *Isis Unveiled*. But it fast became—and remains—Theosophy's most revered text. In it, HPB outlined a dizzying cosmology, accounting for all that ever was or will be, including the lost city of Atlantis. She described seven spheres of consciousness (including the astral), seven supreme beings permeating all, seven forces in nature (earth, air, fire, water, ether, and two other imperceptible elements), and seven races—each confined to a specific epoch and more spiritually evolved than the last. We are living in the fifth. Eventually, if all goes according to plan, by the seventh root race, we will all have evolved to the level of her Mahatmas, into beings ready to return to the Source.

While reading through *The Secret Doctrine*, just as HPB had instructed, something occurred to me. The oral tradition, history, had made a myth of Marie Lazveau, but HPB chose to weave her own from the start, as naturally as a camp spider. By mythologizing herself, she didn't just grab people's attention. She freed herself from a host of shackling strictures, gender and otherwise. And standing there free, she indubitably altered the world.

Though a rabble-rousing socialist feminist, Annie Besant dressed properly and pinned her long hair in a sweeping updo with sharp waves that hardened her soft face. She'd helped organize the famed match-girl strikes, drafted union rules for striking dockworkers, and suffered arrest for publishing a pamphlet on contraception. However, by 1888, then in her forties, with years on the front lines under her sash, she'd begun to feel a creeping dread: true political reform, and revolution, would never occur without a deeper, spiritual shift. All she'd done was for naught without one. Or as HPB later put it:

"Foolish is the gardener who seeks to weed his flower-bed of poisonous plants by cutting them off from the surface of the soil, instead of tearing them out by the roots."

Annie Besant scoured London, sampling its mystic fads, in search of a way to grab the world by its roots and yank. Then, as luck or the fates would have it, the *Pall Mall Gazette* invited her to review *The Secret Doctrine*. After reading the tome, she sought out its author. And as she turned to go at the end of that first meeting, the author gnomically and beguilingly offered, "Oh my dear Mrs. Besant, if you would only come among us." Annie Besant obliged. Instantly, Annie and HPB seemed as inseparable as HPB and Olcott had previously—even cohabitating. Rumors of lesbianism ensued.

However, love or no, platonic or otherwise, HPB's masters had only granted her a small respite. In 1891, at age fifty-nine, she took ill with influenza. Then, on May 8, a date still celebrated by Theosophists as White Lotus Day, Madame Helena Petrovna Blavatsky passed on to another plane. Her final words, uttered to her attending Theosophist nursemaid, Isabel, with the wide eyes of one glimpsing the final reveal, were:

"Isabel, Isabel, keep the link unbroken, do not let my last incarnation be a failure."

Immediately, all hell broke loose. There were scandals and scrambles for power. The American branch of the society severed itself from the global operation entirely, becoming "The Theosophical Society in America" in perpetuity. Eventually, Besant, bearing HPB's cosmic imprint, took over in Europe, and then after Olcott passed away in 1907, as global leader, transplanting herself permanently to the Adyar HQ. After the dust settled stateside, a woman named Katherine Tingley, known as "the Purple Mother," took control of the rebel US operation.

Both female heirs had come to Theosophy via social reform work—"activism" in modern lingo. And under them, Theosophy's fight for "universal brotherhood" took a more overtly political tone. In India, Besant founded the Home Rule League, along with numerous Hindu schools and universities. In 1917, the Indian National Congress—created to spur independence from the Raj—elected her their president. In its early days, "all the top congressmen were Theosophists," stated Gandhi, who eventually replaced Besant at the congress's helm.

Though she started in the eastern US, like mystic manifest destiny, Katherine Tingley, too, headed west, creating the Point Loma Theosophical commune near San Diego in 1900. Known as the White City for its bright Islamic domes and Hindu temples, Point Loma's three hundred Theosophical residents joyfully performed Greek plays and Rāja yoga-ed away the day in lush gardens and orchards. But Point Loma wasn't all idyllic aesthetes in white linen pursuing self-circumscribed bliss to soft bell pings. They organized relief work for wounded soldiers, worked with "unfortunate women," and advocated for prison reform. They also added the avocado to the California diet (in and of itself a notable contribution to American posterity). However, no utopian surge lasts forever.

The Theosophical Society's popularity and membership numbers peaked with the passage of suffrage, achieved in the United States in 1920 and in England in 1918, for property-holding women over thirty, and then again in 1928, for all women. In the wake of this hard-won victory, feminism ebbed, too, giving way to the Great Depression, Freudian thought—which again offered "scientific" authority on women's inherent inferiority—and then, of course, global warfare. Besant died in 1933, Tingley in 1929, and Point Loma shuttered in 1942. However, though the society waned and would not have another female leader for forty years until the next wave of feminism, HPB's ideas continued to ricochet throughout the twentieth century.[4]

---

4   There is a notable exception to all the positive impacts HPB and Theosophy had on twentieth-century culture. HPB called our own "fifth race" of humans the Aryans, though she believed this race would reach its apex in the United States due to the intermarriage among nationalities taking place there. To her, the term had nothing to do with "racial purity" and blonde-haired, blue-eyed Germans. Theosophists also repopularized the swastika, an ancient Vedic symbol that, in Theosophy, represented karma, rebirth, and the unity of all faiths. Hitler was not a Theosophist. In fact, he violently oppressed them, but this symbol and term got appropriated by German occultists who were also not Theosophists. The occultists then put them through the dark bowels of white supremacy, and Hitler snapped them up on the other side and incorporated them into Nazism.

Einstein reportedly kept close a thumbed copy of *The Secret Doctrine*—which among other things outlined HPB's thoughts on the nonlinear nature of time and space in the astral plane. Plus, not just Hilma af Klint but Kandinsky—who has historically received the credit for inventing abstract art that Hilma apparently deserved—was inspired by Theosophy's ideas of color auras, vibrations, and floating forms. Gloria Steinem's mother was a Theosophist, as were any number of prime ministers and social reformers. Additionally, Waldorf schools and Method acting (or at least the Michael Chekhov school of it) stem from Theosophy and its offshoot, Anthroposophy.

L. Frank Baum, who wrote *The Wonderful Wizard of Oz*, subscribed, and Dorothy and Toto were basically astral travelers. In fact, Baum's mother-in-law, Matilda Joslyn Gage, a Theosophist and prominent US suffragist, inspired the character of Glinda the Good Witch. She did not mind the title. In 1888, the same year *The Secret Doctrine* manifested, Matilda stared forth from her ruffled collar with a thorny, self-aware magnetism, as she boldly opened a session at the International Council of Women with a prayer to a female deity. Picking up Goddess worship where HPB left off, Gage's 1893 book *Woman, Church, and State* explicitly linked Christianity, the witch burnings of the Middle Ages, and misogyny into one cause-and-effect package:

"Whatever the pretext made for witchcraft persecution we have abundant proof that the so-called 'witch' was among the most profoundly scientific persons of the age. The church having forbidden its offices and all external methods of knowledge to woman, was profoundly stirred with indignation at her having through her own wisdom, penetrated into some of the most deeply subtle secrets of nature," she wrote.

However, despite all this, after her death, society branded HPB a fraud and a joke and swept her under the carpet of history. At least there she could be controlled, they thought. Instead, like a glowing golden orb of divine revelation freed from a gout-ridden corporeal form, HPB suffused the modern world. HPB pioneered queer by blurring the false boundaries, once believed to be implacable steel walls, between male and female, science and religion, East and West, space and time, me and you, sage and charlatan. No one—including armed Cossacks—ever actually controlled Helena Petrovna Blavatsky.

PART IV

Zsuzsanna Budapest, Author, Activist, Lesbian

Witch, and Feminist Goddess Worshipper

10

WELCOME TO THE MACHINE

Later, she'd remember the lice, trading the family gold for lentils, eating the meat of emaciated horses who'd died on the narrow Budapest streets. She'd remember watching her favorite teddy bear shake on the floor of the cold cellar as a bomb reduced her fourth-floor home in the posh apartment building to rubble. She'd remember playing around the legs of a man sitting on a park bench, comforted by his woolen-trousered calm amid the blocks of decimation, only to look up to see that the man was a corpse. She couldn't forget her mother's and aunt's panicked scramble to hide each time the armed German, and later Russian, soldiers banged on their door. She couldn't forget her mother leaping from her paper-thin refuge to bite a soldier's nose as he dragged her Aunt Titi away. The bleeding soldier cracked her mother, Masika, with the butt of his rifle, but left both women behind.

Aunt Titi taught the girl, Zsuzsanna, born during a blizzard in January 1940, to pray to the ancient Hungarian Gladwoman, Boldogassznony. Zsuzsanna then determined that, though she was the smallest of them all, she could shield the entire family with her mystic might, seize control amid chaos.

Such power was her blood right. Her family could trace their line to 1270, and Zsuzsanna later counted four aunts who had been burned alive at the stake—witches all, they'd said. When her grandmother Ilona, a former suffragist, died of starvation during the war, her spirit appeared to the then three-year-old Zsuzsanna. The child, who could not yet formulate a complex sentence, took the sighting as an oath from Ilona, a vow of protection stronger than the violent earthly might closing in.

Masika, her mother, had been born wild as the Mecsek Mountains. She learned to read tarot cards and the winds from the family servants. She then dedicated her life to art and channeling the mystic flow. But when she'd married, at age twenty-two, her handsome thirty-five-year-old husband forbade her from working in her sculpture studio, demanding she devote herself in full to her role as his wife. Masika withdrew. In the only childhood picture Zsuzsanna has of her with her mother, she is nine months old and reaching for the nanny. Then the war came.

Still, Masika soon scooped up her daughter and fled to the countryside, somehow successfully evading the tanks and bullets as if shielded, it seemed to Zsuzsanna. There, life seemed more like living. Their country relatives had cows, and the cows still made milk. They had cheese to eat and even bread. Little Zsuzsanna watched the country people dance around a Maypole, holding bright swaths of cloth made magic in choreographed flight, an expression of an age-old Pagan fertility rite. She heard of herbal remedies, too, and healing incantations—the hushed talk of the Old Ways.

Zsuzsanna recalled playing in a barn among big, brown, fuzzy columns, unaware the horse's hooves could have proved fatal, until the adults found her there and scolded her. These legs, at least, belonged to the living. She recalled fluffy ducklings plodding to the pond, the differing songs of day and night birds, the rising and setting of the sun and moon, the calm constancy of the natural rhythms.

Then, when Zsuzsanna was six, Masika got cholera. She placed her daughter in the indefinite care of a country nunnery with a wrought-iron gate and halls lined with images of a wrathful God and his army of tortured, often maimed saints.

Long before Zsuzsanna first intuited the spiritual clashes that roiled through the Hungarian countryside of her youth, somewhere between 70,000 and 30,000 BCE, the Great Goddess who created the world began to shine, exalted above all other deities. It's a history recorded only in the bulbous bellies and breasts of opaque stone figurines, but one, blending both legend and fact, that would nevertheless make it through the millennia to Zsuzsanna.

The Great Goddess's human devotees, it's said, lived in clans organized like "chalices" of equality and personal autonomy, not "blades" of ranked regimented control. Inheritance was matrilineal, and women served as the high priestesses in the shamanic faith we now call Pagan. But men also occupied different sorts of leadership roles, and sex, nature, dancing, and everyday objects like pottery stood sacred, enchanted, and accessible by all.

Then, sometime circa 3000 BCE, organized war and its Gods emerged to turn men's bodies into weapons and reordered society to fuel military might. Sex became violence and control. Women, of course, bore the brunt. The new order aimed to permanently position them below men on the blade—where they'd then raise children, both female and male, who would blindly comply with the machinations of control. In fact, women's sole charge became replenishing and amplifying the army the machine ran on, then later, the labor force. They "alienated women from our bodies by incarcerating us in them."

Slowly, the Goddess—and the thousands of names that called her—faded. First, she was demoted from supreme creator to collaborator, then to a divine chorus member backing up Zeus or Odin or Ra. Then she disappeared altogether from ruling creeds—except in whispers and codes and sometimes in the form of a virgin—as a lone male Creator God born of nothing, and certainly not woman, spread across much of the earth. All humans' bodies became weakness and shame, suffering incarnate. The sacred, once enchanting all of life and nature, grew remoter than Mount Olympus, accessible only via death or the highest male authorities, cloaked in gold and silk and things the average person could not hold. Paradise was lost.

The serpent, as this story goes, didn't lure humans out of Eden. Instead, it's that ancient symbol of the Goddess and creation that could lead humans back to her gates. Some people say the Christian God—a war god—in particular feeds off death, like an aphid does a leaf. His followers worship and consume the flesh and blood of a dying man nailed to a cross of desiccated wood—formerly the tree of life—while also denigrating living, calling all its ecstasies sin. This, in turn, makes them good soldiers.

But in country glens and pastures, far from the center's control, the Old Ways persisted in shadows. Then after millennia, the Goddess, life's ecstatic birthright, started stepping back into the light. Men built cathedrals to Mary. Joan of Arc answered her call, referring to her as Saint Catherine, and electrifying all of France. However, we know how it ended for Joan.

And her burning at the stake, in 1431, was just the prelude. By the 1480s, the feudal and papal powers that be could not abide the Great Mother's—the divine feminine's—growing threat to their death cult. Previously, the Vatican had contended, officially at least, that witches did not exist. Suddenly, they decreed witches not just real but a boogeywoman responsible for society's every ill—a poor crop yield, the plague, a dead baby. The evil, lustful weakness named woman allegedly greased her body in the fat of infants to squeeze through keyholes in the dead of night and fly on a masturbatory broomstick into the woods, where she'd copulate ceaselessly with the horned devil.

Every woman who didn't conform to the order, submit to control—the healers and the midwives, the old and barren, the loud and freethinking—was burned, stoned, raped, flogged, tortured, hanged. Theosophist and suffragist Matilda Joslyn Gage estimated that by the time the "Age of Enlightenment" swept the European continent, nine million had been killed. More recent historians quibble. Some say that the number is closer to thirty thousand; some say a couple million. But counting is as futile now as resistance was then. The violence, more often than not, came from a mob that kept no records, not just the church or the state. And the point—even more than death—was the terror, enough blood in the soil and streets to ensure the message passed down from generation to generation: disorderly women die.

In the aftermath of these burning times, the Old Ways fell completely into the dark—save a song refrain here, a Maypole there, a poppet for protection hidden in a wall in Salem, Massachusetts. Just a collective dream fading over morning coffee, flashes of memory one can't quite fully hold. A collective shadow—the repressed "feminine," to speak in Jungian terms—then fell over the world. And here we are. Or so the story goes.

Finally, after something like seventy million people died—including six million European Jews—the global blitzkrieg ended. Like stunned woodland creatures after a tsunami, people worldwide peeked their heads out of doors to take stock. In Budapest, they saw the dark clouds remained, hovering.

In order to be a good comrade, the occupying Russians commanded that Masika work twelve hours a day, six days a week in a factory. With little time—and perhaps will—to care for Zsuzsanna, Masika removed her from the rural nunnery only to deposit her in a Budapest nunnery. The Russians soon seized control of the new convent's operations, replacing the Christian songs with Communist ones, the crosses with hammers and sickles, the sins against God with sins against the revolution—but still inculcating total obedience.

Nevertheless, like a bloodhound, Zsuzsanna sought succor, a whiff of the freedom she'd tasted in the country hills. She read *The Wonderful Wizard of Oz*—written by the American Theosophist L. Frank Baum. In this new bible, she learned that female witches could be both wicked and good—in short, fully human—that the all-powerful man behind the curtain was hype, and the ultimate truth, the "heart's desire," could be found in one's own backyard, or one's own mind and body. Zsuzsanna began dreaming of the United States, but she still managed to find magic amid her gray authoritarian monolith—in the smell of moss, the ancient stones, the hills of glistening green, then snowy white, within sight, just outside the city.

Masika had separated from her controlling husband and returned to her art. She'd begun sculpting busts for Communist officials and altars featuring the Gladwoman for the proles. She married a doctor and had a baby boy, and though Zsuzsanna came to live with them when she was eleven, Masika still had little free time for tending to her.

Instead, now a pretty adolescent with a "good figure," Zsuzsanna learned the lessons of being a woman in a man's world the hard way. When Zsuzsanna was sixteen, the janitor's wife caught her necking with a boy in the basement of their apartment building. Horrified, her mother banished her across the Danube, from Pest to Buda, to live with her father. Her father, in turn, took as sacred his charge to guard his daughter's virginity, confining Zsuzsanna to her room for all her idle hours—a Rapunzel shorn and daydreaming.

While Zsuzsanna whiled away time in her room, somewhere in the English woods six women and seven men sat naked in a nine-foot circle calling in the cardinal elements with a large, antique dagger. Among them were Gerald Gardner and Doreen Valiente.

In 1939, as Hitler marched into Poland, Gardner, a man with white hair like lightning-struck cotton candy and a brow so furrowed it perpetually shadowed his eyes, happened upon a coven of witches ritually dancing in a cool glen of green in southern England. They showed the interloper their *Book of Shadows* containing magic rituals and spells dating back to the medieval burning times, when the very soil they stood upon had been suffused with their ancestors' blood.

Evidence confirming such a coven existed has never emerged, and most contend Gardner made up the encounter to give his witchery and his own *Book of Shadows* the legitimacy that only comes with time. What can be confirmed is that Gardner frequented secretive occult societies—many with links to Theosophy—including Ordo Templis Orienti, headed by Aleister Crowley (aka Beast 666), a man infamous for his orgies and for first re-creating "ancient witchcraft" rituals at the turn of the twentieth century.

Most likely Gardner wove together the remnants and flashes that did remain of peaceful, nature-worshipping Paganism of old with the occult and with Theosophy. In doing so, he sought to give these Old Ways the form, theory, and ritual forever lost in the dark. Then, in 1951, Britain repealed its antiwitchcraft laws, on the books since the witch hunts. With the boot finally removed from their necks after half a millennium, witches, and the divine feminine, began percolating up from the underground. Many adopted Gardner's new Craft, which he called Wicca.

Witches contend the word comes not just from the Old English word *wicca*, meaning "sorcerer," but also *wiggle*, meaning "divination," and *wih*, meaning "holy," plus, perhaps, the Norse *vikja*, meaning "to shape, bend, or twist." A witch, therefore, is someone skilled in the craft of shaping, bending, and changing reality.

In Gardnerian Wicca the opposite charges of God and Goddess, the universal polarity of masculine and feminine—the anima and animus— spark the spiral of creation and magic itself. Wiccan rituals therefore require an equal quorum of men and women, plus a high priest or priestess. And Gardner soon found Doreen Valiente, the yang to his yin, the high priestess to his high priest—and, in many ways, the unsung source and author of his theology.

Valiente rewrote Gardner's *Book of Shadows* to augment the role and glory of the divine feminine. And it was only then, circa 1955, as the Goddess shook free her life-giving locks, thrilling hearts across a war-ravaged Europe, that Wicca took full-broomed flight.

Per usual, the devil had nothing to do with it. In Wicca, both the God and Goddess cycle through life, in conjunction with the phases of the sun and moon, taking many forms and names along their annual or monthly route from birth to death, or light to dark. The Horned God—eventually made Satan—is God of hunting, death, and magic, and connected to the sun, the forest, and the eight Sabbats, Pagan holidays linked to the seasons of the sun. The Great Mother is Goddess of regeneration, rebirth, and love for the living, and connected to the moon, stars, seas, and the twelve or thirteen Esbats, rituals held during each full moon.

Though both male and female stood divine, Gardnerian Wicca remained far from what one might call feminist. Gardner decreed each high priestess must recognize "that youth is necessary to the representative of the Goddess" and "gracefully retire in favour of a younger woman." Needless to say, this edict did not apply to high priests. He also proclaimed that "the Gods love the brethren of Wicca as a man loveth a woman, by mastering her." And so forth.

The movement, while not feminist or even particularly political, still had plenty of revolutionary verve, though.

For one, Wicca's only sacred commandment (the weird edicts don't count) is: "An it harm none, do what ye will." As such, the sole evil is violating someone else's free will or nature herself—as both are holy. The world is not a burden. Your flesh, your body, is not something to be escaped, not a prison blocking you from the spirit, not someone else's province or weapon or commodity or toy.

Zsuzsanna was running late to the protest. When she finally arrived, she saw limbs, tangled and intertwined, the blood flowing over them mingling until it blackened and dried. She looked up at the parliament and the other facades surrounding Kossuth Square, yesterday smooth, today pocked with bullet holes. The mouths of the fallen protestors— who she'd come to join—were still open in the shape of a scream. Only the brown waters of the Danube moved.

At first, the 1956 uprising of the Hungarian people had been peaceful. But the Russian tanks, steel invaders, took to roaming the streets, shooting at people who were often unarmed. Sometimes the tanks herded the resistance into the city's tightest medieval corridors, cordoned them off, then opened fire. Four of Zsuzsanna's classmates died that day in the square, and after a heroic battle, so did her country's revolution.

By the light of a full moon, Zsuzsanna ran, carrying only a change of clothes and some money she'd taken from her father without asking. She had told her mother of her plan. Though technically alone, the sixteen-year-old girl still felt her grandmother Ilona's spirit protecting her. She'd felt it slowing her legs as she made her way toward that square three weeks prior. She felt it as a divine spark of intuition, a knowing, the surest thing going in a world of upheaval and death that seemed interested in her primarily for her virginity. And she trusted that spirit to guide her, her personal North Star, as she illegally fled her country on foot through the machine gun–laden night. She knew she could likely never return to her homeland, had no idea when, or if, she would see everyone and everything she'd ever known again. Still, she ran.

Up ahead on a country road, a group of refugees hurriedly piled into the back of a truck. She watched them collapse with relief against the truck bed's railed walls, anticipating a smooth ride to the border. As the driver shut them in, she sprinted to catch up, but again her legs mysteriously grew heavy and slow. The truck started up but did not drive forward. It abruptly turned back toward Budapest. As it passed, she heard the people, now trapped, screaming.

She walked and walked. She slept alone at a desk in an abandoned office building, like the lone survivor of a man-made apocalypse. She met an elderly farmer, transporting sugar beets, who guided her where the tanks could not follow, through the soggy stagnant reed marshes smelling of ammonia rot and the occasional fresh winds off the grasslands. Then they crossed the foothills of the Alps, newly dusted with snow, and finally the Austrian border. She wondered, perhaps, what distinguished a rebel from a lemming or Russian mole who turned his truck back toward Budapest, and how to tell the difference. When they arrived on the other side, to her shock, the farmer intoned the Gladwoman's blessing, like a Jedi in faded broadcloth breeches muttering, "May the Force be with you."

In Austria, a middle-class family took her in and gave her a white fur hat and her first taste of the kind of family life she'd glimpsed in American movies. She learned German and enrolled in the University of Vienna. She struck up a correspondence with Tom, the boy with whom she'd been caught necking, who had since enrolled in university in America. They talked of the world lost to them behind an iron curtain.

The American Rockefeller and Ford Foundations were offering scholarships to Hungarian refugees in Austria, but while men's scholarships included a decent stipend to live on while studying, women received less money and had to take additional jobs. The message was clear: *Get married, young lady.* Zsuzsanna sent Tom Shakespearean sonnets. And when he sent her a ring in return, she accepted. In 1959, now age nineteen, Zsuzsanna got a visa and boarded a plane to Eisenhower's America, newly crowned the undisputed leader of the "free world." Gardnerian Wicca, too, made its way across the Atlantic at this time— the two like-fated passengers on the same ship destined to collide on the other side.

In Eisenhower's America, Zsuzsanna noted, one could buy Ivory soap, a panoply of facial creams, and a gallon of ice cream even in the middle of winter. Cities contained nothing old, but they did have diverse peoples, though it seemed the white people were fast fleeing the cities for the suburbs, in shiny boat-size Cadillacs and Pontiacs and Fords. Churches appeared to be concentrated in areas populated by the poor. TVs, however, were ubiquitous, found in most every household—a new type of pulpit. And in the condemned apartment building with rats where she and Tom lived on Chicago's South Side, Zsuzsanna learned English and of American culture by watching hit shows like *I Love Lucy*, about a zany, headstrong, but ultimately submissive housewife; *Lawman*, about rugged men in the Wild West shooting people; and *Bonanza*, about rugged men in the Wild West shooting people.

By age twenty-one, she had two sons, László and Gábor, to care for. Tom, meanwhile, worked for a professor at the University of Chicago— for a pittance. Zsuzsanna tried to take some classes there, but she soon dropped out. The course load felt incompatible with motherhood and household chores.

By then, it had started to seem that perhaps her and Tom's epistolary cross-continental romance had been based on a love of their lost country, as opposed to for one another. At Catholic confession, she informed the priest she'd had a couple of fleeting, unsatisfying affairs with men. Unperturbed, he prescribed several Hail Marys as penitence. She then added, believing it a minor aside, that she'd started using a diaphragm, as she was done having children. The priest's voice grew loud and wrathful. He decreed that she could have no absolution, no salvation, until she stopped using the offending circle. More and more, she stopped feeling the freedom promised in tales of her adopted nation, but instead felt the walls closing in.

She tried to block out the war and the past. She tried to find a way to keep moving—which can prove hard while housebound. Three words still held glittering allure, but when her family relocated there to New York City, after Tom found a teaching job at Brooklyn's Pratt Institute, Zsuzsanna didn't get to see much of that mythologized metropolis—at least not at first. They settled in Port Washington, a Long Island suburb of fenced-in backyards and women sequestered, with little to cling to save a stale, blinkered postwar belief in the transcendent possibility of conformity, electric household appliances, and processed foods. Tom took an apartment in the city and a lover for the weekdays.

He did, however, have one attribute his wife still found charming. He asked very few questions. Before too long, the couple lived like ships alternately docking in their town on the Manhasset Bay. Zsuzsanna spent weekdays with the kids while Tom lodged in the city; then she headed there on weekends. But instead of the electric, ever-evolving hustle she'd expected, she found the great Gotham pocked and scarred by blocks of rubble—formerly thriving working-class communities seized and decimated to build highways, skyscrapers, and bleak monolithic low-income housing projects. Zsuzsanna did not expect New York City to remind her of everything she left behind.

Now in her midtwenties, with platinum-blonde hair and cheekbones that could slice bread, she decided to serve the one thing Americans still seemed to collectively believe in: on television, she modeled refrigerators and other game-show appliance prizes. She landed a bit part as a maid in a whodunit starring Jane Russell. She started appearing in soft-core porn movies—never showing her pubes. She saw herself near naked and fifty feet long on a billboard advertising one of her films in Times Square. She had more unfulfilling affairs, with wealthy older men who'd give her $200 for cab fare home.

None of it worked, however. She felt she was just a "fuckable broad." She felt no more alive in the city than shut-in in Port Washington. So she headed downtown, to the Village, hub of bohemian artists and intellectuals and hippies. She befriended two gay Asian American artists, tried to avoid muggers, met Andy Warhol, briefly, and touched Bob Dylan's pants. Despite all the talk of revolution—a revolution in which women were told their position was "prone"—it was the Summer of Love, and she felt utterly alone.

Then came 1968. First they shot Martin. Then they shot Bobby. Then they bloodied up and gassed all those student protestors in Chicago. Zsuzsanna wondered why she'd bothered leaving her nation at all. At least it was home. At least there were old things and moss and stone.

That September, amid a slow dissolve shot from peace and love to fear and loathing, the light of liberty mounted a stand. A group of young women, with pastel sweater sets and a propensity for polite upspeak, unfurled a banner reading "Women's Liberation" over an Atlantic City balcony during the Miss America pageant—and onto TVs nationwide. With that, they officially cut the ribbon on American feminism's second wave. And the wave soon rocked the nation. All Zsuzsanna heard about the feminists those first couple of years, however, was that they were ugly, dykes, whiny middle-class white women complaining about nothing, hairy, immature, unfunny, unfun, prudish, bitchy, shrill, trolls.

While drinking gin first thing in the morning in her room at the Chelsea Hotel, the witch demanded Zsuzsanna's "cunt juice" and pubic hair. Zsuzsanna obliged. She felt certain that securing a new man and romantic partner was the only thing that could save her. So she'd come to this room in the Chelsea in the hopes the resident witch with matted red hair, a faint face tattoo, and a cocaine smile could make Zsuzsanna's lover, a mysterious and withholding cameraman, hers and hers alone.

Zsuzsanna had heard near nothing of Gardnerian Wicca and its American offshoots, which had begun embedding in the "counterculture," with the help of adherents like Jim Morrison of the Doors. But she had certainly heard of witches, and to her they connoted ancestors and the Gladwoman.

Using Zsuzsanna's vaginal sundries, the Chelsea witch created a charm, and like magic, after months of radio silence, the cameraman immediately called. But it seemed the witch cast more of a temporary glamour than a permanent love spell. After a weekend together, the man broke it off, this time with finality—and Zsuzsanna spiraled.

She found herself at a Crossroads. She attempted suicide unsuccessfully. She returned from the brink, however, with a new perspective on life. "I regained my true perspective of a Witch, how a Witch looks at life—as a challenge," she later said. "It is not going to last forever, and it's all right on the other side, so what are you going to do?"

Zsuzsanna tells a tale of omens and totems and fate—of intuition. While her kids were on a three-week vacation with her husband and his girlfriend, Zsuzsanna realized, in a hot blue streak, that she needed to take a trip of her own. She'd return to Port Washington when they did, she assured herself. Shortly before boarding a Greyhound bus to Toronto, she spied a book with a half-naked woman on the cover sitting on a shelf at Rockefeller Center. Believing it to be a salacious read, she snapped it up. It was *The Second Sex*, the seminal 1949 feminist text by Simone de Beauvoir, a bisexual French existentialist in an open relationship with Jean-Paul Sartre. Then she got on the bus, leaving home with little more than a change of clothes and a small wad of cash, for the second time.

In Toronto, on impulse, Zsuzsanna resorted to hitchhiking and secured a holy trinity of car rides. On the third leg of her exodus, she flew south from San Francisco down the Pacific Coast Highway, a winding road along cliffs jutting above wild endless blue, in the passenger seat of a bright-blue Camaro. The gregarious man driving it deposited her on the white sand beaches of Santa Monica, just north of the Venice line.

There, she watched two small girls settle quietly into the frothing lip of the vast deep water to play. Instinctively, though she was a stranger, the girls stuck close to Zsuzsanna, and she felt needed. She felt another sudden jolt of revelation, a deep sense of belonging and purpose there by the sea. She felt alive.

2018

Ketamine produces mind-bending, even spiritual effects in sensory deprivation tanks, or so the tattooed Asian man told me as he led me through a metallic door into his "float lab." The "futuristic" entryway was obscured by the Venice Beach boardwalk's throng of crystal shops, marijuana dispensaries, Egyptian-themed souvenir stores, and tanned tarot readers sitting in the sand behind hand-scrawled signs proclaiming their rates and services.

Floating naked in a sealed tank of body-temperature saltwater, constructed to mimic the womb, you lose all sense of time and place. The mind, with nothing else to do, not a sound or light to perceive, turns inward, like in a trance or waking dream. Timothy Leary loved it. So did Allen Ginsberg. Often while on LSD. Or perhaps ketamine. I, however, opted to embark sober.

I had to shower twice, both before and after, which gives it all a ceremonial feel. Between cleansings, I popped in orange-crush ear plugs—to keep the saltwater out—stepped into the chamber, and shut the red door.

I'd come to Venice to pursue the legacy of Zsuzsanna Budapest but also in pursuit of my own mind. Since that inaugural séance with Reverend Paul, the ghosts in the back of my head had continued to bludgeon about, complicating my mission to delve into the mystic, and by extension the depths of myself. I'd realized in order to find what I sought I needed to come to terms with those ghosts in some form or fashion. A confined, solid float tank, designed to feel safe as a womb, seemed as good a place as any to try—though part of me still hoped this realization would just grow so clear it'd turn invisible.

I lay in the silent darkness. At first, not much occurred. I think I even dozed off briefly. Then, *I'm watching Stephen King's* Firestarter, *a movie I saw at least twenty-five times around age six, before someone realized it was rated R and stopped me from renting it for the twenty-sixth time. In it, Drew Barrymore, a little blonde kid just like me, can set anything or anyone she looks at on fire, seize control amid chaos and violence, or cause it—though she's the smallest of them all.*

There are streaks of light like phosphorescence all around my hair when I move, or so it seems in my mind. Then there's a monster, or demon, made of flame, who morphs into a bloody flesh-eating flower. Suddenly, I can't scream, even though I'm trying as hard as I can to. I feel strangled. I think I'm going to die. The floor dissolves.

Then the images stopped. And I got out of the tank, my heart racing.

The mind is not now, nor has it ever been, literal.

I walked out onto the boardwalk across the white sand into the vast, steady, blue salt bath, with my clothes on. Surfers in bodysuits paddled on each side of me in the late afternoon sun—the fairy hour, when the deep golden shadows seem to reveal truths one can't see. *The sea birthed us all—the ultimate Goddess*—I thought, submerging myself just past the line of my shorts. I walked back out with seaweed dark as blood clinging to my wet legs, feeling primordial, like that first fish with lungs and feet, convincing myself I belonged here, and I belonged now, on solid ground—though my legs were shaking.

To the north and south, the Pacific Coast Highway was burning. It turned out to be the largest, deadliest, most destructive fire in the state's history, caused by drought from man-made climate change and human settlement encroaching on natural cycles that once kept such decimation at bay. Out on the highway, the smoke blended in with the breakers misting up the raw cliffs, totally evacuated, save the milling men in high-tech flame-retardant neon suits and reflective face masks. When the flames came, the neon rubber men retreated into the mist with the hoses to form a new perimeter. The only thing the fire can't touch is the sea.

Zsuzsanna took a bus from Santa Monica to Hollywood Boulevard. Just off that main thoroughfare, on Cherokee Avenue, she spotted a building with a banana tree and bright-red phlox flowers outside—an oasis amid shifting shades of soot-covered beige. She procured the keys to apartment number thirteen, long empty for obvious reasons. After paying one hundred and ten dollars for a month's rent, twenty-five dollars for security, and twenty-five dollars for some weed, she had twenty dollars left to get by on in a city where she knew no one and no one knew her—just another thirty-year-old "runaway housewife" with very few job skills.

But a hibiscus bush outside reached into her window, and she could see a blue frog climbing up a palm tree just beyond. Even the neon Max Factor makeup sign pulsing out on Hollywood felt vibrantly alluring. Sitting there in her rather rundown apartment, unsure what came next, Zsuzsanna finally got around to opening *The Second Sex*—and started to read.

11

THE COCOON

She appeared mysteriously. One day they persisted without her, the next, there she was, cast in plaster and sitting on a mantel at the new Women's Center on Crenshaw, protectively watching over the "casualties of the so-called gender war"—women with busted faces and trauma-scattered minds, pouring in the door of the shotgun duplex obscured from six lanes of LA traffic by a clanging industrial ice machine. Not everyone, however, was happy about the new Goddess statuary.

Charles Manson's cult, composed mostly of young middle-class women much like the center volunteers, had committed its nine grisly murders just two years prior. The metropolis still reeled from their misplaced faith and the blood it seemed somehow to leave on their collective hands. In fact, most of the feminist volunteers shunned God and religion entirely. All religions demanded some surrender. All served as the source, or at least as a justification, for the patriarchal oppression they spent every free moment organizing to expunge. But Z, as Zsuzsanna now called herself, countered that perhaps the sudden appearance of the Triple Goddess statue was a sign or signal alerting them to another road.

People forget, but at the start of the second major wave of feminism, American women couldn't serve on a jury in many states, attend Yale or Princeton, interview for most professional-level jobs, or, as often as not, receive the birth control pill. Abortion remained illegal. Married women couldn't secure credit cards or bank accounts without their husband's permission. Rape was rarely prosecuted—or mentioned. Domestic violence was barely even a phrase, much less a cause for a shelter. Sexual harassment was a boss's prerogative.

And so, the "personal was political"—as the Women's Liberation movement proclaimed. Z and the other volunteers at the center—among the first of its kind in the nation—organized rape squads, a rape hotline, linked women to divorce lawyers, birth control, employment, safe abortions, and safe lodgings in the wake of abuse. In their spare time they prowled the night, spray-painting feminist sayings on sexist billboards.

Across LA, feminists were launching womyn's banks, womyn's law offices, womyn's clinics, womyn's bookstores, womyn's coffee shops, womyn's music festivals, womyn's art galleries. If the man's commercial establishments would not cease and desist with the patronizing second-class treatment, they'd just create establishments of their own, thank you kindly. Z felt sure the next—and perhaps most—critical ingredient in creating a world apart, a cocoon where they could transform from having their worth decreed by men into whatever they really were, was a new feminist religion. One that did not worship a male God—for if "God is male, then male is God," as feminist theologian Mary Daly later put it—but a Goddess old as time.

For Z, and all Wiccans, the Triple Goddess represents the maiden, mother, and crone, and the cycles of the moon—waxing, full, and waning. She sacralizes the cycles of a woman's life, transmuting her body into the spiraling Source itself. But most of the other women at the center remained dubious. Most, that is, but not all.

Janet came from across the hall with her acoustic guitar and a pot from her porch that could serve as a cauldron. Susan and Joanie traveled from the Westside with goulash. Sherri, a Communist, arrived in a flannel shirt, work boots, and jeans. Dixie the cab driver grew concerned about Barbara. Barbara sat in the corner rhyming in trance dressed as a raccoon. Z, as hostess and high priestess, played Leonard Cohen's "Sisters of Mercy" on vinyl, as the seven members of the proto-coven prepared for their very first ritual: Winter Solstice, 1971.

They cast their circle by passing a kiss. Z brought out her red yarn and explained how to make a witch's girdle, a symbol of blood, fertility, and continuity with the past. They did not yet know any Goddess chants—as this was the first known ritual explicitly blending Pagan rites and American feminism—so they sang songs of political liberation. They cast spells to free Chile and win women control over their own bodies. After the circle had closed, and they sat about eating Goddess-blessed goulash, the women cast themselves the Susan B. Anthony Coven #1, believing that if you build it, covens #1, #2, #3 . . . #100 would come. Only time would tell if the Triple Goddess had been listening.

2018

On any given full moon, in all five boroughs of New York City, one can partake in any number of witch rituals. They occur in witchy and New Agey stores after closing, on rooftops, in parks, in empty session rooms in feminist houses of domination, in living rooms belonging to doctors and lawyers and business executives. Some consist only of women (or the women-identified). Others include men and all those in between and beyond. Most are explicitly feminist.

The full moon is the Goddess at peak power. Connecting to her then, at her most fecund, serves as an umbilical cord to healing, to change, to manifesting, to moving on.

I've watched an expert astrologer ritually pour water into her moon bowl before discussing the impact of the full moon's planetary arrangement on our day-to-day, as we listeners sat cross-legged in a candlelit circle studiously jotting notes. I've crouched in a veil of smoke while ritually descending into the depths of Hades to confront the destructive demons deep in my mind before eating pomegranate, the fruit of the underworld, from a cauldron. I've pulled back the purple velvet curtains between worlds and thrown cones of energy to the sky to heal the planet. I've sat with the Goddess incarnate, holding my head to her full bosom as her black veil tickles my neck and she whispers to me of transformation as someone beats an animal-skin gong in the dark behind me. I've watched a beautiful woman with wild, long platinum hair—her body covered in tattoos of serpents, skulls, and roses—dance naked, save some rhinestones, in front of an altar surrounded by flames while dragging an antique sacred dagger softly across her torso. I've circled and stomped in a packed dark room without windows before an intricate tableau of silk, fresh fruit, whole-grain bread, and animal skulls—a Pagan communion—thinking this is what it must have felt like to be an early Christian: radical, oppressed, fringe, devoted to Jesus and Love, not the War God, with no idea you, too, could become the oppressor, "the man," from whom you are hiding in a candlelit Roman catacomb.

I'd felt a ritual flash of clarity, ecstasy, transcendence during that last event in particular. Then I'd begun pondering the liturgy's exact historical provenance, accidentally snapping myself out of mystic bliss.

People say these spells and rituals derive from millennia of masters—occult, Pagan, witch, and otherwise—perfecting methods to transform how the mind communicates with itself and therefore the divine within it. The story goes, these cunning folk unearthed the language of the unconscious, a language older than time, that consists of colors and smells, symbols, incantations, and movements, that speaks to a deep, ancient, potentially collective part of the mind.

By speaking that ancient language, the conscious can induce the unconscious to act in specific ways, instead of just vice versa. The unconscious is a powerful thing, but properly commanded with the proper spell, also known as a prayer, it can manifest the love or money or health or revolution you petitioned your God(dess) for. Maybe it's the divine within that does it. Maybe it's just the mind. Either way—mystic power or placebo effect—the magic works, at least for those who believe.

For most witches, the Goddesses and Gods are not literal entities. They are the forces, ancient as human consciousness, that the spells reach. Archetypes that, when accessed, filter through your own culture and mind into myth and religion, magic and transcendence, healing and ecstasy—or their shadow, depending on who your God(dess) is.

Magic is moving energy. *Abracadabra* means "I create as I speak." Witches say magic includes art, which also channels the Goddess Muse, the flow, the unconscious. A witch feels and thinks that she or he or they are participating in the constant flow of life-energy emanating from nature. A witch is a shaman.

Shamanistic techniques take concentrated daily practice. I know because I read about all kinds of energetic exercises, designed by master practitioners, for aspiring shamans to undertake.

"Religion is the soil of culture," the source from which the belief systems, symbols, and stories that mold us grow—whether we think we subscribe to said theologies or not. The Craft is a religion of poetry and freedom, not doctrine or control. It seeks to touch the depths betwixt and beyond the five senses, the flow at the edge of being, beneath the chaos of any epoch—even the 1970s—that, when accessed, "evok[es] power-from-within."

Magic is "a liberation psychology."

That's what the books all said.

In the Craft, sex stands sacred, the ultimate rite. For more than most anything else, sex that results from mutual desire can open witches fully to themselves and the transformational energy of the universal divine and her many ecstasies.

Z identified as a nonpracticing heterosexual. One who had just driven to Juarez, Mexico, to file a quickie divorce in the heat beneath a rattling fan, and who thought it best to take some time away from coupling with her patriarchal oppressor to heal and grow. Her two sons remained back east with their father and stepmother, visiting Z in LA during the summer months. This left her, for most of the year, with nothing but time to get to know herself—something she felt she'd yet to really do during her thirty years of life dictated by the whims of men.

"I didn't have my twenties as a girl, I was already a mother. I didn't have any foolishness time," Z has said.

Z dropped the monikers that branded her a man's. Instead, she took a surname explaining her identity better than the names of her husband and father. She took the name of the place that molded her, for better or worse, in war and in peace. The move had the added bonus of preempting the question everyone forever asked her: *Where is your accent from?* She became Zsuzsanna Budapest.

When she'd arrived at the center, Z Budapest had felt immediately drawn to the lesbian volunteers—their parties, their coffee gatherings, their friendship. The lesbians just seemed freer, she thought. Lesbians could have fun without a man, leave town without a man, fix a car without a man. Lesbians asked her how she felt every thirty minutes. No one had ever really cared how she felt before, just how she looked and made them feel about themselves. Or at least that's how Z rationalized her affinity for the "women-identified women," as the lesbians called themselves.

On cue, Nancy, a dapper "women-identified woman," showed up at Z's apartment door, on the full moon, holding a bottle of brandy. Z invited her in. And that was that. Z had lesbian love triangles. She had an affair with a married straight woman. She muddled friendship with sex and regretted it. Then she kissed Janet. And on a night when the potency of the jasmine outside her bedroom window inexplicably amplified as did the beauty of the moon on their skin, Z fully discovered the power of sex magic.

Feminist Goddess worship takes magic's "liberation psychology" one step further than other Craft traditions, into something that resembles societal psychoanalysis. Feminist Goddess worship offers a refurbished soil—new symbols, stories, and rituals—that frees the repressed feminine from society's shadow, where it has been locked these five thousand years since the War Gods throttled the matriarchy and Paradise was lost. From that integrated place, we all—men, women, and those in between and beyond—can ride the Age of Aquarius to a balanced, peaceful world of true freedom, or so the witches say.

Witches have familiars, animals who serve as spiritual salve and guide. When I told Vinni about his new title, he stared at me, his pointy black bat ears cocking above his tiny spiked collar, smiled a knowing doggy smile, then hopped on my lap and farted.

Meditation, ideally at one's private altar, is a great way to start the process of connecting with the Goddesses who dwell in our mystic depths, I've read. Vinni barks at me when I meditate. Maybe he can sense my unease in traveling into the recesses of my mind. But witches are masters of change and flux. Of facing the stifling dark depths of Hades within, with the Goddesses' transcendent assistance.

Since setting out on my mystic quest to connect with my ancestral spirit coven, I'd attended a litany of rituals. I'd lived with my flatulent bat-like familiar and dabbled in many things Craft related, off and on, for over a decade. Connecting with my spirit coven had indeed done what I'd hoped it might: provided roots, context, and a new appreciation of the grace of a life lived in the liminal. But I still wanted something more.

I'd learned that in Z's day, many witches found their connection to Mother Gaia, that umbilical cord to healing, to change, to manifesting, to moving on, while standing on California hills and beaches. After I'd emerged from the sensory deprivation tank on the same Pacific shore, I'd felt both jittery with adrenaline and slow, like the air was thick with lava, not the light from the setting sun. I felt I needed to drink copious amounts of red wine to have a shot at equilibrium—an activity that, thankfully, my friend I was staying with was amenable to. I also knew one thing for certain. I wouldn't find what I wanted in California. I needed to go home. I needed to go to Kentucky. And as luck would have it, I already had a trip planned.

Quickly, word got around. *Witches throw the best parties.* With Z's small Hollywood apartment no longer able to contain all the new converts to the "dark arts"—otherwise known as the feminist arts—Z took the women to the water. There, standing by the black, rhythmic night sea, the witches—sometimes twenty, sometimes one hundred strong—placed the plaster Triple Goddess at their circle's center, then dug holes in the sand to block the copious candles from the salt-scented wind. Lit only by the moon and the stars and fire, they chanted and danced in the breakers, then lifted the swirling energy they conjured, the magic, into the night sky.

Soon the sea—a siren of rebirth—called Z even by the light of the sun. Z and her silver German shepherd, Ilona, moved from land-locked Hollywood to Venice Beach and Brooks Court, a narrow road of sculptured cacti and bright bungalows with picturesque porches and wind chimes, just across from the original Gold's Gym. The block's foot traffic soon became a medley of tanned musclemen in short shorts and witches, strolling together in the LA sun.

Anyone who knew Z during this time commented on her laugh—deep and soaring—her humor, and the spark of warmth in her pale-blue eyes. This was not the Z of New York City. This was not a woman longing for the Crossroads.

She got a tan. She joined her new city's enthusiastic embrace of all things New Age—an embrace unencumbered by the irony one often finds back east—including talk of the *I Ching*, the human potential movement, and Ram Dass. She became a vegetarian, drank wheatgrass, and let her hair go natural. She started wearing torn jeans and "peasant" blouses, though she found it odd that in this city of celebrity glitz and glamour the style was to look poor. But her personal ersatz salt-of-the-earth fashion had an authentic kick—Hungarian folk.

She started writing letters home to her mother, whom Z perhaps understood a little better, and even forgave, having left her own kids in the primary care of another, in the name of saving herself. She informed Masika she was concocting a new feminist religion, one brewing the modern New Age potpourri—and Gardnerian Wicca—in with her memories of the Old Ways and the Gladwoman. Her mother told her, "Folk Art, search those archives, it's all there." So Z looked, and further refined her Craft.

Empowered by her Goddess, she returned to Budapest for the first time in fifteen years, facing her family, city, and past distorted by trauma-infused memories of tanks and guns. Janet came too. Z relished bathing in the natural waters, showing Janet the countryside and the old houses made of stone dappled with moss. The trip became their honeymoon, the city their enchanted playground, forever after transformed for Z, fully reclaimed, not just in (last) name only. Then the two lovers returned home to California.

Diana: Goddess of female autonomy, the moon, the wild liberation of the natural world, a hunter. A triple deity contained unto herself who did not consort with men. Instead, she shot golden arrows into the eye of their machine. In her honor, Z named her Craft tradition Dianic.

The Dianic Susan B. Anthony Coven #1's manifesto states: "We are opposed to teaching our magic and our craft to men until the equality of the sexes is a reality." Unlike most other witches, Dianics do not recognize any male deity—as any so-called God-Force was birthed from the Goddess, like all the universe, and was therefore not her equal. In short, no men allowed.

From the beginning, Dianics were by and large lesbians, and lesbians were by and large shunned and ostracized as degenerate threats—even by other members of their Women's Lib movement who called them the "lavender menace." Therefore, lesbians and, by extension, Dianics, even more so than most second-wavers, fully embraced the creation of a separate culture, just one step left of the man's culture—but still fully of the world and the fight to change it, not isolated in some commune bemoaning its bleak state.

However, even if the patriarchal powers that be no longer built stakes and pyres, they did not just let women abscond in plain sight without a fight. And I don't just mean all the irate men who showed up at Dianic events shouting Bible quotes—though that occurred plenty.

On an April day in the early seventies, with the City of Angels newly in bloom, four men called Z's coven-mate Sharon a "dirty dyke," before dragging her off her motorcycle and into an abandoned building, where they gang-raped her. The police later found her unconscious on the sidewalk. But they took little action. The perpetrators remained at large.

Most witches don't take hexing lightly. Some don't do it at all, believing it violates another's free will and their lone commandment: "An it harm none, do what ye will." Plus, all magic one does returns on the caster of the spell tenfold, be the energy ill or good. But if sex is life at its most sacred, rape stands as the highest sacrilege. This, for many witches, makes rapists fair game for a blood hex.

The Susan B. Anthony witches set an altar with bones and black candles and menstrual blood. They chanted, held hands, and channeled their rage. Shortly thereafter, Sharon recognized the truck of one of her rapists. The truck, however, was newly beat up and battered. She asked around about the owner. No one had seen him in weeks, though they'd heard he'd been in the hospital. Then the truck was towed, the man never seen again. Or so the story goes.

More and more, Z craved privacy for her coven, a temple of nature where they could worship unthreatened and unencumbered, connect with the cycles of the moon and sun, birth and death, renewal and growth, the grand design—as opposed to with the perplexed stares of passersby.

One afternoon as Z, who worked as a gardener and housekeeper, pruned a manicured Malibu lawn, Ilona took off into the hills, a streak of silver dog lightning. Z followed her familiar. Ilona stopped in a clearing, a remote spot in the Red Rocks at the crossing of four fire roads, like the center of a compass. Standing there, one could hear the waves crashing past the horizon, smell the salt, and stare down from the unsullied peak at the kidney-shaped blue swimming pools dotting the scruffy hills of sage brush and red sand verbena. Good dog.

The circled Dianics invoked the four elements and corners of the universe, removed their clothes, and stood "skyclad" between worlds and before their Goddess—save maybe a few flowers in their hair. They drank (often quite a lot of) red wine. They hopped the cauldron. They chanted, "The Goddess is alive! Magic is afoot!" The chanting grew louder until it became a scream. They stretched their arms to the Malibu moon. They danced like banshees. They sang. Often someone cried. The energy felt like a spiral of golden light—i.e., freedom and power and peace and catharsis. They asked to win custody cases, get good jobs, banish their abusers, bless their children. They stood together to look deep inside, then seize control from chaos and disempowerment, to invoke solid ground from within—witches all.

2018
Lexington, Kentucky

Somewhere on my family's horse farm, a not-so-distant ancestor shot his brother dead while he was sitting on a fence.

I parked my parents' aging silver Volvo on a side road in a working-class subdivision, its roads lined with pickup trucks, shotgun houses, and young oak trees. The land had once been part of my family's horse farm. My family first came to Kentucky in the 1700s, just after the Revolutionary War—which included eight battles fought in the soon-to-be state, previously Shawnee territory.

Kentucky is the northernmost Southern state. A slaveholding state that didn't secede in the Civil War. A state about which Abraham Lincoln once said, "I hope to have God on my side, but I must have Kentucky." The place where both he and Jefferson Davis, president of the Confederacy, were born. A state divided, where brother truly fought brother. A state with a lot of blood in the soil.

I love the way the Kentucky countryside smells. I love the summer nights filled with fireflies, the wild moons, the natural rhythms decipherable only to its intimates.

I crossed a road without lane markers and hopped a weather-distorted wooden fence to what remained of the farm, though it was no longer in the family. After my grandfather's death in 2010, we sold our land. His was the last generation to want to live on it. Growing up, we lived in a residential neighborhood just outside downtown Lexington.

I am trespassing on my family land.

The fence deposited me in a back lot, out of sight of the main house and the barns, amid a defensive row of thick bramble brush that scratched my sweaty arm, clutching my tiny elderly dog, who was panting in the August heat. It'd been a week since I floated in a salty sensory deprivation tank in LA. My mind hadn't been able to settle, like it'd been blistered by getting too close to the flames. I felt back on the edge—literally teetering there.

In the middle of the pasture, I saw a tree, its full summer leaves cascading all the way to the ground—breathing cover. The sun was setting over where I knew the main house sat, the dimming light's rosy fingers waving at me from a past I couldn't quite see behind the hill. I lit a candle, sprinkled a circle of sea salt around Vinni and me for protection. I laid out a rose quartz, a pyrite, a tiger's eye; a sampling of Goddess cards, Lilith, Baba Yaga, the Sphinx, Artemis. I repeated the Wiccan sunset prayer: "A palette of colors fills the sky. With the beauty of the Gods. May I ever work to better myself. So that I may better reflect that beauty. Both inside and out. So mote it be."

I invoked the Goddesses, wondering what a farmhand might do if he found a witch in the back lot. I closed my eyes and meditated, hoping Vinni wouldn't bark at me and give us away. I asked for connection to my past, to the dirt clinging to my legs, damp with sweat, to a way through. The soil felt cool when I touched it. I came here to touch it. I wasn't totally sure why.

My mind wandered. *"Freedom is what you do with what's been done to you." "Freedom is just another word for nothing left to lose." "Freedom!" is "I don't belong to you and you don't belong to me." Freedom is "to be the girl with the most cake"? "Freedom is to be who you really are."*

Then, *I'm in my childhood room with pink walls. I stand up from my flowery-duvet-covered bed and flick my porcelain pink piggy bank from my antique wooden dresser, so it hits the floor and shatters. I'd wanted to see its body break. The floor starts to dissolve.*

But before the floor vaporized, I heard a loud snort. I opened my eyes. On a hill in the middle distance, as if emerging from the shifting pink clouds on either side of her form, stood a white mare.

The mare walked closer, stirring up dirt that hovered in the heat and the thickening shadows, the dark cloud making her white coat pop, luminescent as the soon-to-rise moon. I stared at her eyes, a sparkling shade of black. She stared at mine, a color I like to call "cathedral at dawn." There was no barrier between us, just grass. I wanted to touch the strip between her quarter-size nostrils. I've loved how soft that part of a horse is since I was a little kid burying myself in the farm oat bins, seeing if I was strong enough to toss a bale of hay (I wasn't).

I looked at my ten-pound familiar squiggling beneath my right arm, trying hard as he could to sniff the strange half-ton creature up close. I looked at the horse's hooves. As if on cue, the horse pawed at the dirt. I paused, fearing the worst for little Vin if we moved closer. I touched the dirt again with my left hand, then lifted my pointer finger to my tongue. The soil tasted mineral rich, like limestone, which is high in calcium, builds strong bones. This is why we breed superior racehorses in Kentucky. Our history, our soil makes us. But it charts no inevitable individual courses.

Tomorrow is the first day of September. Tomorrow the heat may break.

The mare turned and walked away before I'd stood up and walked forward to touch her. I realized I didn't have to touch everything. There are other ways of moving on. I watched her disappear into the falling darkness behind the gentle bluegrass hill she came in on, silently thanking her. Vinni relaxed. I blew out my candle and gathered my crystals and Goddess cards, leaving the salt where it fell. A waning gibbous moon rose, signaling the approach of a new lunar cycle. In the side-view mirror of my parents' slightly decrepit Volvo, I saw dirt streaked below my right eye. In the blue moonlight, the dirt looked like blood, but blood deliberately painted on in preparation for war. This time, my legs weren't shaking.

Z wanted to focus her third eye on battling the patriarchy. Annu wanted to be a feminist businesswoman. They realized these goals were in fact complementary. And in 1972, they got a loan from the Women's Bank in Westwood and rented a former laundry next to a Mexican restaurant on Venice Beach's Lincoln Boulevard.

The coven helped them paint the walls melon. Then, across the ceiling, they brushed as many of their Goddess's ten thousand names as could fit—Isis, Diana, Sarasvati, Pele, Inanna, Danu, Brigid, the Fates. They stocked up on candles, herbs, tinctures, oils, jewelry, and spell books, including some by Marie Laveau. They ordered custom vagina candles. Then they put their flag, a yellow one proclaiming "Feminist Wicca," out front and opened the door.

One day, seeing that flag waving in the Pacific breeze, a young woman named Miriam nearly ran her car off the road in her haste to park it. Z invited the enthusiastic, wild-haired young woman to their upcoming Spring Equinox ritual. After partaking in her first feminist Goddess-worship ritual, Miriam realized she had to embark on a vision quest, across the United States, on a bicycle. By the time she returned to California, her name, revealed to her in dreams, would be Starhawk. And Starhawk would go on to cast a different sort of circle.

But first, in 1973, Z and seven other Susan B. Anthony witches started convening every Sunday at Mama's Café in Malibu, sitting outdoors at a weather-beaten wooden table over piles of paper covered in hand-scrawled notes and sketches. They wanted to create a book to disseminate all they'd learned and fused and developed to women across the country—their invocations, love spells, hexes, their feminist Sabbat and Esbat rituals, their spiritual revolution.

The resulting tome, known first as the *Feminist Book of Lights and Shadows* and later as the *Holy Book of Women's Mysteries*, also included rituals for everything from menstruation to giving birth to menopause. In Dianic Wiccan, therefore, women's actual reproductive systems—decreed the root of evil and "hysteria" for millennia—stand as holy, their concerns as primal and powerful, not silly.

Unable to find a publisher, they printed 785 copies at the printshop where Z's new lover, Helen, worked after hours. The first volume featured a Goddess totem designed by Z's mother on its paprika cover, plus any number of Masika's Hungarian spells and folktales within. In this act of mother-daughter co-creation, Z felt a healing, a re-fusion of their relationship, a certain magic, if you will. Then, after the second volume, with a purple cover, came out, Masika died.

But their book remained. Women wrote Z from all over the country, telling her how much the book meant to them. How they fought over it in breakups, sprinted after pages that came loose on windy nights as if the breeze had absconded with their firstborn child.

But most of all, Z seemed to savor the freedom of the moment. A moment when she spent all day in women-run establishments, then drove out into the Malibu Hills on the back of Super Pat's Harley, the wind in her face, to stomp naked beneath a full moon at the center of a time and place finally built to lift her up, not cut her down to a manageable size. Z had spun a cocoon perfect for connecting with the Goddess and all the healing and power she could bestow. However, in nature, cocoons are temporary abodes.

Eventually, almost all the businesses by and for womyn closed. Eventually, Super Pat moved up north and changed her name to Sequoia. Still, Z tried to cling to the moment. But not even witches can suspend time forever. According to their Gaia's natural law, the only stasis is death. So it's little wonder, really, that that's when things started to go awry.

12

The Witch Trials

Outside the Los Angeles City Hall, in February 1975, a group of women in matching jaunty black capes assembled, brandishing protest signs and willow branches. **NO MORE WITCH TRIALS**, read one sign, lifted high by a young woman with neatly feathered bangs and a button-up shirt beneath her demon shawl. Not far away, inside a cement beige municipal courthouse, sat the witch on trial in question, Zsuzsanna Budapest.

Z had agreed to give a Feminist Wicca customer a tarot reading, just like on any other day. She'd sat down near the volcanic mounds of melted candle wax by the rotary cash register and pulled her deck from her hand-embroidered Hungarian cloth, with golden edges. Then things went sideways. First, Z discovered a stray cat had somehow shat beneath her reading chair. Next, the woman got "the Devil" as her signifier card—a definite hint. Finally, right after the woman walked out the Feminist Wicca door, two male police officers barged in it to proclaim Z under arrest for tarot reading. The woman had been a cop, too, sent in undercover on a sting mission.

The law itself was unremarkable, similar to those on the books in cities and states across the nation criminalizing magic, clairvoyance, palmistry, etc.—all dating back to panicked men stamping out Voodoo in New Orleans, or back further still to the burning times. However, Z refused to settle or accept her hundred-dollar fine as the cost of doing business.

The powers that be then increased the cost of Z's and the Feminist Wicca's return to normalcy to $500. Her lawyer advised paying up, instead of facing jail time. Undecided, Z went home and read her own tarot. She got the Tower of Revolution. The Tower of Revolution, mind you, is tall and phallic and on fire.

"I thought, I had the newfound integrity of Female Clergy at stake. I didn't want to pay a penny. I would rather go to jail," Z has said. "Hands off wimmin's religion." So she took the law—and the LAPD— to court. Turned out, it was her last revolutionary act.

For most everyone but the feminists, the ideals of peace and love, hope and change, had died with the 1960s. For most everyone but the feminists, the seventies were, from the start, a decade of chaos and cynicism, of gas lines, Watergate, urban blight and white flight, armed guerilla warfare, punk rock, acid rain, escapist orgies, and separatist communes for those who'd traded in changing the world for changing themselves alone. The feminists had missed the memo.

Then around 1975, they got it, with interest. Instead of following the nationwide cultural turn inward, the feminists blamed one another for their failure to completely upend the world—though they'd indubitably changed it. As a result, the Women's Movement fractured into a binary, that age-old patriarchal divide-and-conquer trap. The "politicos," those focused on legislative change, blamed the "culturos," as the Goddess worshippers were known, claiming they retreated into fantasies of a matriarchal past that never was, instead of focusing on the fight against all-too-real political inequality in the present.

The culturos countered that changing policies, while important, was a sprint and a palliative. The true revolution, changing hearts and minds, culture itself, was a marathon—the divine feminine the key to the long game.

In the midst of this cracking apart, Z lost her trial. Her feminist lawyers—the ranks of female lawyers in America having doubled immediately following the rise of feminism's second wave—appealed. She lost again. They appealed again—and again and again. But Z didn't see most of this. Because she'd left town.

The final straw had come when her German shepherd, Ilona, died of lung cancer. "I lost interest in staying in that town for many reasons, but the biggest was that the air died," Z told me from her rural Northern California home, her Hungarian-accented voice velvety as a steel harp.

So on All Hallows 1980, the day the veil between the living and dead diminishes to mere gauze the spirits can freely float through, Z passed her role as presiding Dianic Wiccan high priestess to Ruth Barrett—ritual name Rhiannon—along with fifty dollars and a cauldron.

In 1985, the news finally came that the decade of appeals had paid off. The state law outlawing "fortune telling" had been overturned by the California Supreme Court. Z, crouched in her Northern California garden, remembers looking at the soil on her hands while thinking "blessed be," then returning to her flower bed. She realized she didn't really care anymore. She no longer read cards. She no longer presided over a coven—though she did (and does) still preside over public Dianic rituals and their biannual Goddess Festival. She no longer plotted revolution.

Instead, she wrote books—*The Goddess in the Office*, *The Goddess in the Bedroom*, and others—some now published by major publishing houses instead of in her girlfriend's printshop after hours. Dianic, meanwhile, remained the same 1970s wimmin's religion, not budging in its separatist tenants and ways. Then times changed, as times do. And when they did, the feminist witchy past and future collided—and the furies came.

During the 2011 PantheaCon held in San Jose, several trans female devotees of Lilith—a rebel Goddess of the night often depicted androgynously—showed up at a ritual conducted by the Amazon Priestess Tribe, part of the Dianic Come as You Are Coven. The Dianics turned the trans witches away, telling them their rituals were for "women-born women" only—that "come as you are" did not include how they were—then shut the door and started their peace-loving chants.

Subsequent statements by Ruth, Z, and the brass made clarion this rule applied to all Z-aligned Dianic covens. Trans witches called Z transphobic. They protested at Dianic events. Each side made a case.

First, I'll present the defense. Z and Ruth attested that they maintained freedom of religion. They contended that presence of Y chromosomes in their circles could potentially trigger many witches who had been traumatized by men, sullying their safe sacred space apart. Besides, they said, Dianic rituals and rites focus on sacralizing female biology—menstruation, giving birth, et al.—things trans women don't understand, just as they don't understand the realities of growing up a woman in a man's world. Androgynous, third-gender deities and traditions abound. Trans men and women should create their own traditions focused on those, not intrude on theirs.

This is a sample of rebuttal testimony:

"How is a binary transsexual man, a binary transsexual woman, to see themselves reflected in such gods? We are not 'third gender'—we are men and women . . . I am tired of having to look for myself in your symbols."
—Foxfetch, trans man

"Unlike most Budapestian Dianics, I have actually circled with trans-women . . . Sometimes even in clothing-optional space. Sometimes with women in the circle who were sexual assault survivors. And guess what? We cast a circle, we called the quarters, we invoked the Goddess, we danced, we chanted, we worked magic . . . we affirmed that true sisterhood is powerful. Powerful, not fearful." —Ryiah Nevo, cis woman

"Take all the religious freedom you need. But if in so doing you are perpetuating bigotry, if you're perpetuating transphobia, think twice. Think hard." —Sarah Thompson, trans woman

"An it harm none, do what ye will." —Wiccan Rede

"This is a made-up fight," said Z of the trans women's protests against the policy. "They never come when I give lectures. They don't actually want to be part of [the Dianic tradition]. They have no respect for their elders. They just want the women to buckle and let them in. Because they are bullies. Because they are men." Z told me this in late 2018, a year that wound up one murder shy of tying 2017 for the most murders on record of trans women, who as a result of this violence and discrimination have a life expectancy of thirty-five years across the North and South American continents.

Starhawk began, her voice confident yet humble, and tinged by a high-pitched trill evoking both Minnesota, where she was born, and the Southern California valley where she spent her most formative years. The circle of activists, most middle-aged, listened attentively while snacking on organic cheese puffs and petting a skeletal elderly rescue dog with a terminal condition. We were there to learn how earth-based rituals can fuel environmental and social justice activism. It was one week after I had talked with Z.

As she turned from expectant face to expectant face, Starhawk's gray wavy hair grazed the shoulders of her outfit—palette witchy bruise,

shoes sensible orthopedic. She requested that we each introduce ourselves and include our preferred pronoun (which may or may not have
been the one assigned to us at birth), adding, "I like to ask that, not just
because it's what people are doing now in certain circles, but because it's
a reminder that people are not always what they seem. That we are like
pomegranates, slice us in half, and there are so many seeds."

As the 1970s gave way to the 1980s then the 1990s, many leading
"politicos," including Gloria Steinem, concluded it had never been an
either/or, politics or culture binary game. Starhawk, meanwhile, had
flown down that flowing unsegmented spiral long before.

After Starhawk, née Miriam, had screeched to the side of Lincoln
Boulevard all those years before, riveted by the idea of Feminist Wicca—
then set off cross-country on a bicycle—she conjured Reclaiming. Like
Dianic, Reclaiming is an explicitly feminist and political Craft tradition,
but unlike Z's tradition, it is a nonhierarchical one open to women and
men (cis and trans) and all those in between and beyond.

Starhawk's 1979 book *The Spiral Dance* codified Reclaiming, her
ideas of matriarchies past, and her theories on magic, including the role
of the conscious and unconscious mind. It expanded and formalized
the work of Z's ragtag bunch of feminists—then took it to the world.
Today, Starhawk's books, thirteen in total, have likely reached more
people than any other writer exploring the Pagan. She stands as the
high theologian of the Feminist Craft (though she'd probably not like
my hierarchical terminology).

Witches realign energy toward social justice, says Starhawk, who
has been arrested protesting twenty-plus times. And by the tenth-anni-
versary edition of *The Spiral Dance*, this realignment included casting
off the fundamental role of the masculine and feminine energetic polarity in her accounting of the cosmos:

*"Sexual reproduction is an elegant method of ensuring maximum bio-
logical diversity. Yet I would no longer describe the essential quality of the
erotic energy flow that sustains the universe as one of female/male polarity.*

To do so enshrines heterosexual human relationships as the basic pattern of all being, relegating other sorts of attraction and desire as deviant . . . it also cuts us all off, whatever our sexual preference, from the intricate dance of energy and attraction we share with trees, flowers, stone, the ocean, a good book or a painting, a sonnet or a sonata, a close friend or a faraway star. For erotic energy inherently generates and celebrates diversity."

I had first learned of Z by googling "lesbian witch," as I felt my ancestral spirit coven would not be complete without one. But though she's married to a cis man, Starhawk is the witch who fully queered the feminist Craft, blurring the patriarchy's favorite and most fundamental binary during the presidency of George Bush the first—before the majority of Americans would utter the word *gay*, much less *queer*, as anything but a slur.

Meanwhile, the explicitly feminist Triple Goddess, unleashed with Z's 1971 Winter Solstice ritual, circled the nation, then the world, morphing to fit ten-thousand-plus hearts and minds and spaces that had nothing to do with Dianic or Reclaiming. Feminist Christian women elevated the divine feminine in Mary. Black and brown second-wavers, who called themselves womanists, folded her, and the reclaimed title witch, back into Voodoo, Vodou, Hoodoo, Santeria, *Brujería*, and more—a full spiral, as these traditions had long elevated the Goddess and helped spark the entire American feminist mystic tradition.

"The original witch was undoubtedly black, bisexual, a warrior, a wise and strong woman, also a midwife, a leader of her tribe," wrote Monica Sjöö and Barbara Mor in *The Great Cosmic Mother*. The Goddess, in her guise as Gaia, stood central in Alice Walker's Pulitzer Prize–winning novel *The Color Purple*. And if you want to read the best treatise ever on how confining the erotic energy flow to sexual intercourse and gender binaries plays right into the hands of the patriarchal powers that be, I recommend womanist Audre Lorde's 1978 *Uses of the Erotic: The Erotic as Power*.

Today, the Feminist Wicca is a take-out BBQ restaurant that's been painted bright blue. Just after the lunch rush, a tall black woman in her twenties with Cleopatra hair and on-trend acid-washed jeans stood by the open door feeling the sea breeze. She'd never heard of the Feminist Wicca, though it used to stand here—but she'd definitely heard of the Goddess. "Girl, I could talk about the Goddess all day," she told me. "I read somewhere she's a gateway. A gateway with, like, really great hair. And I feel like she's just really getting started."

The divine spiral spirals on, with or without you. And like feminism, every generation must reinvent the American feminist mystic for itself, as the American feminist mystic must evolve or die trying.

The last sound Sarah Good ever heard was the sound of her own neck breaking. By then, she'd already heard her infant daughter, Mercy, die in their shared prison. She'd heard her four-year-old, Dorothy, also locked up there in the dark, crying and likely chattering, as her small bones grew ever-more visible beneath her jaundiced skin. In total, 150 people, mostly women, were arrested, tried, and shackled in a pitch-dark subterranean jail cell often no bigger than a coffin, surrounded by rats and their own waste and unable to move for months. Fourteen of the women and six of the men—implicated by association with an accused woman or for speaking out against the sham trials—would be executed outright for their alleged sin of witchcraft. More died either in that dungeon or later from the aftermath of the trauma. For nearly three hundred years, Salem tried to suppress its violent legacy, its shadow—to soldier on. One might think Salem, so cursed, would have shriveled. But no. For a time, it thrived. The town grew into one of the wealthiest places in the nation, thanks to its broad, shallow harbor and local sea captains blessed with rare knowledge of a direct route to the pepper farms of Sumatra—and also their exploitation of the supply of cheap or free labor (black people, recent immigrants, women, and anyone else below white male captains on the hierarchical blade). However, like anything fueled by PCP, or your chemical narcotic of choice—as opposed to natural rhythms—a crash followed the high.

As the nineteenth century became the twentieth, the local shipping industry, then the textile mills and tanneries that replaced it, declined. Blight followed—unemployment, crime, empty lots, heroin. This same fate has now befallen many an American small town—and our urban metropolises before them.

But in Salem, two witches flew into town—at the peak of both the blight and second-wave feminism. Laurie Cabot opened witch shops and publicly celebrated her Pagan faith, creating a flourishing witch community while also working extensively with special-needs children. This latter good deed prompted Massachusetts governor Michael Dukakis to issue a certificate dubbing her "the official witch of Salem." Almost in the same gust, a witch named Samantha arrived with a crew to shoot eight episodes of her hit sitcom, *Bewitched*. In the Salem series, as the episodes are known, the fun-loving, miniskirt-wearing Samantha, with her wiggling bunny nose and perfectly teased blonde bouffant, finds herself transported to the bleak hysteria of seventeenth-century Salem—thereby pulling the tragedy the town had fought to suppress back into the light of the American psyche.

Suddenly, instead of slowly fading toward the sepulchral, Salem reincarnated. Branding itself Witch City, the town built a thriving industry around its patron saint, and former shadow, in triple form: the actual Craft-practicing sort of modern witch who started flocking there; the falsely accused sort murdered in 1692; and the purely commercial variety with a green face and broomstick. Every October, this town of forty-three thousand now bloats with around one million visitors seeking the witch. Some visit the historical monuments, some just the witch-haunted houses, and some come mostly for the excellent witchy goth gear.

And though the locals do grow annoyed at the pervasive puddles of pumpkin-beer vomit and their inability to eat out for a large slice of autumn, the tourists' patronage sustains their economy. So they pay tribute. A stenciled witch-on-a-broomstick seal brands the town's police cars. She's the high school's mascot. Locals place straw broom heads on the backs of their fixed-gear bike seats. Though persecuted, tortured, slaughtered, and placed in unmarked graves in its soil, "the witch" did not smite, curse, or destroy Salem. Like her Goddess, she gave it a rebirth, a chance to redeem itself.

"Everyone I know in Salem practices, is in some way a witch—and also is just, like, kind of queer," explains a feminist witch of indeterminate gender identity dressed in an oversize army jacket, their hair shaved shorter than their faint brown mustache. They then playfully arch their eyebrows in faux annoyance at the suddenly commonplace of their once-weird world.

"This stuff just speaks to me. And to my generation. For people my age, this stuff is more normal," another young witch, with flowing long, honey-colored hair and a penchant for pendants, tells me. The young witch adds that the feminist millennial witches she knows, social justice warriors all, confine their Craft to their home altars and Instagram feeds. They may sometimes gather with an informal coven—especially on the full moon or for a voter registration drive—but not for tradition-based coven confabs, be they Dianic or Reclaiming or anything else.

"It's not like in the seventies, when everyone was just like, 'I am a Goddess, and I'm beautiful and powerful,'" adds the gender-nonconforming witch. "They needed that then. But it's a new moment now. And it's super queer and intersectional."

But even in Salem, all is not victorious bike-broom rides through clear October skies. Persecution persists. I'm told some landlords won't rent to explicitly witchy businesses. Some practicing witches hide their religious beliefs, for fear of losing jobs or custody of their children.

Standing before the town's central *Bewitched* statue—in which Samantha sits upon her broom and a crescent moon while wearing a fashionable circle-skirt dress—I ponder who exactly this archetype is, this cone-hatted black silhouette so powerful she can both resuscitate a dying town and conjure enough demon fear to destroy lives, even now in the twenty-first century. Ask a tattooed, altar-building, crystal-carrying, Resistance-leading millennial witch in Salem looking to #HexThePatriarchy, the one with blue sodalite around her neck, and you may hear, "WITCH: Woman in Total Control of Herself."

I agree. But now what?

PART V

MARIANNE WILLIAMSON, NEW AGE SAGE AND

PRESIDENTIAL CANDIDATE

13

A New Age of What Exactly?

Marianne Williamson offers tough love. Marianne Williamson offers a source of strength. Marianne Williamson offers what, as Joan Didion said, "used to be called character." Marianne Williamson talks about God, and her God is a He. Marianne Williamson also talks a lot about Jesus, and like Jesus she is a Jew.

On the 176th anniversary of the first reading of the Declaration of Independence, July 8, 1952, Marianne was born in Texas to Sophie Ann and Sam Williamson. Growing up in an upper-middle-class Houston suburb of identical ranch houses and spacious Bermuda-grass yards, young Marianne lived an active life of ballet and piano lessons, Girl Scouts, and wild blackberry picking. She loved Clark Gable, playing make-believe Eleanor Roosevelt, and attending synagogue with her grandfather, who in his advanced years often cried in the presence of his God. An empathy powerhouse even at age five, Marianne teared up right along with him. She also enjoyed "talking to God" each night on her knees.

In "The Girl in the Patchwork Dress," young Marianne's favorite "fairy tale," the eponymous working-class girl does not in fact rely on a fairy but on her own two hands when it comes to transforming into a princess. She sews a dress for the ball out of the motley scraps strewn about her sewing table. However, upon arrival at the dashing prince's palace, she feels shame among the girls in smooth, contiguous silk and lace. So she hides in the closet. The prince, of course, happens upon her there and marries her because she is the most interesting—marrying the prince still constitutes the heroine's lone life goal in this otherwise more feminist take on the classic.

To any outcast, however, out in the night looking in at the Williamsons' soft-white-lit dining room as the family of five gathered around a roast, Marianne looked the part of the perfect—as opposed to patchwork—princess. She was popular, gregarious, beautiful, a top student, a "real firecracker"—the esprit heir apparent to her dashing father, Sam, a passionate, charismatic human rights lawyer.

Yet her childhood world highlighted and then underlined that her father's esprit was all she could be heir to. In the 1950s, women married younger and enrolled in college less often than they had in 1920, the year suffrage was ratified. After two decades of chaos, breadlines, and atomic bombs, Americans reclung to rigid norms, gendered and otherwise, like they were Victorian. Now isolated in suburbs, many middle-class women had little to do all day with the kids at school, other than perhaps pop "a mother's little helper"—as Valium and other "minor tranquilizers" were known—or two and listen to the hum of their electric appliances. Like zoo animals grown listless, many suffered from "the problem that has no name," as feminist Betty Friedan put it.

Precocious from go, Marianne sussed out the hierarchy. She deemed her mother's life, dedicated to making a house a home, unimportant. Instead, Marianne wanted to join the rooms where men contentedly smoked cigars after dinner as they talked about the "real world" only they had access to. Later, she'd point to the moment she learned to disdain and deny certain "feminine" parts of her whole as a first turn down a dangerous and dead-end road.

Meanwhile, Sophie Ann, understanding all too well what happens to women who don't learn their place, tried to force her headstrong daughter into the 1950s mold called "girl"—often with combustible effect.

One night, a teenage boy broke into Marianne's suburban room and physically overpowered her. Somehow, Marianne managed to talk him out her door, or so her mother told an interviewer in the early 1990s. Marianne learned early that order, and obedience to it, didn't necessarily equal safety.

But Sam and Sophie Ann did not obscure the world, nor one's personal responsibility in shaping it, from their three children. In 1965, Marianne came home from school and repeated what her teacher had taught her that day: that the United States had to bomb the Vietcong or they'd be fighting Communists on the shores of Hawaii. Sam—the son of a socialist Russian Jewish immigrant—didn't miss a beat. He booked the family tickets to Vietnam for spring break. He told his children one should always investigate reality for oneself, not blindly trust propaganda.

And Marianne believed. She believed in 1960s liberal politics. She believed in the ability of men like her father to edge America toward achieving its lofty founding ideals through its established systems and laws. She just wanted the chance to join the fight.

Then the 1960s edged toward the 1970s. And not even Sam—blazer-wearing, newspaper-reading master of his domain that he was—could stanch the reality that the American system suddenly seemed to be failing entirely. That the center, along with consensus on what it even was or should be, had given way, then melted off the edges of the continent. Or that all across the country, people needed something new to hold on to.

Helen Schucman sat in a New York City subway car annoyed. It was 1938. Her husband, Louis, had insisted they take public transit to the party, despite the blizzard raging outside. The noise and grime, not to mention the man repeatedly sneezing just to the left of her face, agitated her further. The chic Manhattanite closed her eyes, hoping that like magic the scene would vanish. Shockingly, it worked.

Helen walks into a blazing light. She kneels, maybe before it, maybe within it. She touches the ground with her elbows then wrists then forehead. Prostrate, she is overcome.

Helen opened her eyes. The subway car remained, overcrowded and loud as before, yet somehow transformed. Looking at its puke-green walls and sagging wicker seats, she felt overwhelming love for every coughing, curmudgeonly New Yorker. She felt love even for the gale winds blowing snow into the metal doors at each stop on this aboveground line.

Then she promptly pushed her walk into the light to the back of her mind. Because she was very busy. After decades of helping to support her husband's bookselling business, Helen set out to become Dr. Helen Schucman. By 1965, when the Williamsons went to Vietnam, she was working as chief psychologist at Columbia University Medical School—no small accomplishment for a woman born in 1909. And that June, she got in an argument with her boss, a gay man fourteen years her junior named Dr. William Thetford.

The two worked closely in an intense, contentious relationship. In and of itself, the afternoon tiff was rather rote; however, on that day Bill shouted something that would alter the course of both their lives—and soon enough Marianne's life—forever. He shouted there must be "a better way"—an alternative to lurching through life at the mercy of one's own darker impulses. Helen and Bill then set out to find the path.

They traveled to Virginia Beach in pursuit of perhaps the most famous psychic medium of the twentieth century, a Kentucky-born man named Edgar Cayce. Though he'd died twenty years prior, the world had preserved and celebrated Mr. Cayce's legacy, unlike that of his pioneering nineteenth-century Spiritualist foremothers. The Cayce Association for Research and Enlightenment still stood in a sea-green mansion compound just up the road from the Virginia Beach boardwalk—a veritable Venice Beach of the South, with shops selling crystals, beads, and psychic services, thanks to Cayce's influence. There, Helen and Bill read the great man's works.

In addition to the Spiritualists, Cayce was heavily influenced by New Thought theologian Emma Curtis Hopkins. In New Thought, the spirit, or God-Force, doesn't just flow through our reality; it is reality. Matter, the material world we perceive as real, is in fact a false product of a flawed but correctable mind. Like Emma, Cayce believed, with can-do American verve, that anyone could touch the God-Force that dwells within, then channel that energy toward transforming the dark ego-based material plane into a divine one of peace and light. All it takes is a little mental elbow grease and practice. Helen remembered her subway moment. She remembered that divine light within, a light she could only call Love.

Upon their return to Columbia, the duo embarked on a joint daily meditation practice they learned of on their pilgrimage south. Helen, her mind thus cleared of conscious static, started hearing a voice—at first faint, but increasingly, as she calibrated her medium antennae, cutting through clear as glass. The Voice instructed her to take notes, telling her, "This is a course in miracles." Fearing an incipient nervous breakdown, she asked Bill what she should do.

"If I were you, I'd take notes," he replied.

That is how it came to pass that in October 1965, the words of Jesus Christ himself—as the Voice eventually revealed he was indeed the lone son of Mary and God—began flooding out of Helen, as Bill dutifully sat next to her, writing down every word Jesus said. Why had Jesus chosen to speak via Helen in the latter half of the twentieth century since his physical appearance on earth? People had gotten off track. Missed the point. And he was there in Helen's head to rectify the multitudinous misinterpretations of his word, his gospel of Love, twisted by the War God.

However, despite Jesus's wish to take his truth global, Bill and Helen told no one. They were professors. They knew how it sounded. But Jesus, a chatty sort, kept right on talking. Helen later said the most depressing day of her life was the day the Voice said, "Volume II."

Marianne's surface remained perfection: good grades, great hair—long, brown, and billowing—the right clothes, the right friends. Drawn to acting from a young age, she crossed paths with fellow Texans Randy and Dennis Quaid in high school. At Pomona College, Lynda Obst, who produced many a hit movie in the 1980s and 1990s, like *Flashdance* and *Sleepless in Seattle*, quickly became Marianne's best friend, regularly driving the duo to Big Boy for fast food in her red Camaro.

Marianne studied philosophy, running around Pomona's Southern California campus with Kant or Hegel clutched beneath her toned, tanned arm. She proclaimed God a crutch—including to the much older male professors she tended to date. What kind of God would allow the Holocaust, she wondered? Or children to starve? We are but random molecules colliding.

Maybe Marianne got the memo about the bleak 1970s on time, or even a little early. Maybe she needed her perfect exterior to finally align with the tumultuous patchwork and "feminine" interior it had learned to hide. After two years at Pomona, Marianne, daughter of Sam and Sophie Ann and the upper-middle-class Houston suburbs, a pretty, proper young woman with "it all," dropped out of college and moved to a geodesic dome in New Mexico.

After a season of back-to-the-land living, she moved to Austin, then New York City, then San Francisco. Almost every move she made was tethered to a boyfriend's personal and/or professional agenda, not her own, leaving the vast nagging uncertainty beneath the perfect wallpaper uncharted. "By my midtwenties I was a total mess," she later said.

She tried Ouija boards and meditation. She tried therapy. She tried drugs. She tried frolicking beneath a full moon wrapped in cut velvet, invoking the Goddess. She even tried disco. All to no avail. Every day, the five-foot-two ball of burning charisma and smarts felt the thin strip of rock between her and the abyss crumbling. *What else is left to try,* she wondered.

In 1972, Jesus told Helen they were finished. Their two-thousand-page tome stood complete. The message was clear. There are only two states, Love and Fear. And only one of them is real. Love is God. God is truth. Fear exists only in your conscious mind. The Fall had nothing to do with women's weakness. It was a metaphor, a parable, for how humanity disconnected from this Love and God-Force by putting its faith in the conscious mind, the devil ego. But that Fear, and the world it produced, the hell we live in, can still be escaped—by reconnecting with the light of Love within. But how?

Unlike Jesus of Nazareth, Helen Schucman had a PhD in post-Freudian psychology. This gave her collaboration with Jesus an added twist. Through their voluminous chats, Helen had come to believe psychotherapy and religion, at their peak, were one and the same road to understanding consciousness and, by extension, existence.

And really, long before Jung talked of "the shadow," Jesus did—at least according to the mystic Gnostic Gospels: "If you bring forth what is within you, what you bring forth will save you. If you do not bring forth what is within you, what you do not bring forth will destroy you," spake the son of God circa 30 CE.

Nearly two thousand years later, with Helen's help, he updated his language and tactics. Both psychotherapy and spirituality could strip away the hellish plaque painted on by the ego to expose the essential self, one with God and Love. The lifting of that ego fog is what is called "a miracle." The two then devised steps, a curriculum of sorts anyone could use to perform this miracle—with just a little hard work.

The resulting book, *A Course in Miracles*, is a psychotherapeutic how-to guide to enlightenment. It has three parts: the philosophical text, a workbook for students, and a manual for teachers. The text explains things biblically. Moses freeing the slaves is in fact a metaphor for us freeing our mind from our ego. The Resurrection is the great "aha!"—the enlightenment that comes from remelding with the Love force. The Crucifixion is what fear does to invalidate love. The workbook offers 365 daily lessons to retrain your mind to see all this for yourself.

There are no gurus, only fallible guides, teachers ever so slightly ahead on the path. The *Course* declares itself just one road map of many to the same ultimate truth. However, still a reluctant prophet, Helen demanded Bill lock the Great Work in a drawer.

Marianne watched transfixed. The musical duo, one with hair blond and feathered, the other with hair black and Jheri curled, danced bare chested and harmonized of things "Bigger Than Both of Us" and man-eaters in love with Jaguar cars. Standing before them, feeling the intimate crowd united in "a single heartbeat," Marianne had an epiphany. Hall & Oates were shamans, priests. And she knew in a flash what she could try next in an effort to stanch her existential dread. She'd become a cabaret singer.

After a two-year stint in San Francisco, Marianne returned to New York City. And as the entire borough of the Bronx burned north of her, bankruptcy loomed citywide, and her fellow residents reported six murders and fifteen rapes daily, Marianne sang show tunes. She sang originals. She sang the blues. She sang Judy Garland. Often, she appeared in small performance venues and piano bars in one part of the city where, even in the late 1970s, liberation reigned—as did Judy Garland's oeuvre. In the wake of the Stonewall protests, throughout the West Village, freedom, gay sexual abandon, and leather-clad, hard-hatted Village People fashion rained down like Quaaludes.

Still, Marianne was barely holding on. She worked as an assistant to a rock biographer who later described her as a girl "who cried all the time," "the last person in the world you'd think would have any success."

2011

I don't remember exactly what Marianne Williamson said the first time I saw her speak at New York City's Middle Collegiate Church. I do remember I sat transfixed in the compact East Village version of a sprawling stone Gothic cathedral. I do remember thinking she had fantastic hair, the type that looks professionally done without outside intervention, like all nature's most magnificent creatures, be they lions or peacocks or bonobos (who are matriarchal). I do remember she had a strong jaw, the kind Americans trust, and a voice like golden afternoon light on a gravel road, peppered with pauses and changes in cadence, in that way of all great speakers and most southerners.

That day, I remembered three years prior, November 2008, when I'd walked out of my Brooklyn apartment into clear blue skies and felt some imperceptible weight I'd never even known existed physically lift from my shoulders. Finally, we had a president and government that was actually on the side of my rights. Finally, the American system could do as it was meant to and usher in some better new age.

I remembered that day then, three years later to the month, because I'd just walked into the Financial District to protest the NYPD forcibly clearing the Occupy Wall Street encampment from Downtown Manhattan's Zuccotti Park. I'd immediately felt transported to an authoritarian showdown. Metal barricades lined the streets, empty except for the protestors and the battalion of police officers—some on horses, some on foot, all in riot gear.

I've been to many protests. That one will forever stand out. Police officers body-slammed a man who'd been politely walking next to me onto the concrete. Blood trickled up then started to pool down his face, before a circle of officers wearing insect helmets engulfed him. More and more people were taken away in handcuffs, many of them bloodied and sometimes crying. It felt like the government did not work for we the 99 percent, but only for that tiny human spire atop the hierarchical wealth juggernaut Occupy Wall Street had been protesting—like "the rich boys get their money back when the banks go belly up, but if you're downtown when the levees break, well, you're shit out of luck," to quote the band OK Go, who I'd say best encapsulated my mindset. It felt like we'd (democratically) deposed the head of our foe, what we'd pegged as the problem, but nothing much had really changed. It felt like the system itself had broken. It felt like we had little to hold on to.

Bill didn't listen to Helen's demand. Instead, he dragged the *Course in Miracles* out of the drawer where she had locked it, then recruited a nice Benedictine monk to edit the three volumes. First published in 1976, the *Course* gathered real mystic steam after the April 1977 issue of *New Realities* magazine featured it on its cover, flashing "You Are Entitled to Miracles" across a painted orb under a headline reading "The Buddha & Nuclear Physics."

Marianne first encountered the *Course* shortly thereafter, when she picked it up off a coffee table during an Upper West Side house party. Perhaps she went so far as to read Lesson 1: "Nothing I see in this room [on this street, from this window, in this place], means anything." However, she then promptly shut the Bible-blue cover with Bible-gold typewriter font. The last thing she wanted to read about was how Jesus could save her.

Then, in 1979, Marianne began a complete and total nervous breakdown—which, really, does not seem an entirely inappropriate response to the 1970s. "A nervous breakdown is a highly underrated vehicle for personal transformation," Marianne later wrote. "Until this happens, you keep trying all your old tricks, the ones that never did work but that you keep thinking might work this time."

Instead, as Marianne plummeted toward her bottom, she opened Helen and Jesus's book once again—and this time she kept reading.

Marianne's energy enwrapped us, comforting and warm, as she stood at Middle Collegiate's marble pulpit beneath the Tiffany stained glass and a painted golden arch. It was just two days after that brutal police crackdown. But Marianne did not offer platitudes. She broke it all down in a way I hadn't heard anyone else at the time really doing: the Fear and the Supreme Court decisions that had corroded our democracy until the 1 percent could rule we the people from their penthouses on high; the steps, spiritual and political, we must each take to counteract that dark magic and create a new way forward, as opposed to just more of the same. First things first, we had to learn the ropes for channeling Love, not fearful rage. For fearful rage could prove our national undoing.

I didn't actually know who Marianne Williamson was before that day, just that my friend Kara wanted me to accompany her to the lecture. But at the end, as the crowd rose to its feet and applauded, beaming—as crowds do after hearing Marianne—I turned to Kara and said, "She should be president."

Finally, Marianne understood. The God she'd turned away from didn't create starving children or the Holocaust. We did. We chose Fear, hell, the ego, over God and Love. If enough of us opted for the Love train, the world would immediately peg future Hitler types for what they were, one more small man behind the curtain, and promptly dismiss them.

However, the vast majority of Americans did not embark on these 365 lessons for enlightenment at the end of the 1970s. Instead, they welcomed an ersatz version of the light—of "morning in America." In January 1981, President Ronald Reagan took office, and with his paper-thin Hollywood smile, promised a return to the past—promised Americans they could stop looking at change they feared (instead of actually conquering that Fear, as the *Course* preached).

The same year, Helen Schucman died of pancreatic cancer. Only after her death was it revealed that she had been the one who channeled Jesus's word direct into the *Course*.

Marianne asked God to use her. She asked Love to use her. Marianne also enlisted a nice Jewish therapist in Houston—where she'd returned during her breakdown—in the reconstruction effort. As Helen said, when done properly, the spiritual and psychotherapeutic are one and the same and can augment each other. Slowly, God, the divine inside her, not the man she was romantically attached to, started serving as Marianne's compass through the world. She started to feel whole unto herself. Far from a mess, she even opened and operated her own mystically inclined bookstore.

Then, in 1983, Marianne received a flash, a reply regarding what God and Love wanted her to do. Without hesitation, she shut up her bookshop, put on her cowperson boots, crammed her belongings into the back of her mother's Oldsmobile, and with $1,000 to her name, headed west through that vast tumbleweed-strewn part of Texas formerly known as "the range."

Though I did not know of Marianne before that 2011 lecture, I did know of her *Course in Miracles*. A couple of years before, my mind a black hole trying to reassemble itself, I'd dabbled in the *Course* (among other mystic matters)—making it through thirty or so of the 365 lessons. But even so abbreviated, it helped. Completing the daily lessons kind of melted something in my brain. Each day when I shut the cover, the world around me briefly transformed into a pulsing thing, deeper and more complex than it had been—and I hadn't even smoked any weed. It felt revelatory and calming. And all I'd had to do was follow directions—IKEA for the soul.

Marianne had one key takeaway point that day in the East Village. The first step to the revolution is us. As someone somewhere once famously put it, "You are no good to anyone if you don't put on your own oxygen mask first." At the time, however, I just wanted to join the revolution. I was in no way ready to be it.

When she arrived in West Hollywood, the LA counterpart to New York's West Village, Marianne saw dead men walking beneath the palm trees. Only Love can vanquish hell on earth, according to the *Course*. Yet all over Ronald Reagan's America, people—especially those claiming the title Christian—wouldn't extend a hand to or touch the gay men dying of AIDS by the thousands. They couldn't even muster enough Love to demand their government do anything about it.

It is said that during the witch hunts in Europe, people would sometimes burn the village "sodomite" to get the fires hot enough for the women—and that's where the slur *faggot*, which initially meant "kindling," comes from. The only thing lower than a woman is a man who takes it like one.

By the early eighties, all across LA, sex-positive, Bentley-driving male gurus regularly hobnobbed with Hollywood heavyweights, and everyone who was anyone had crystals, a Native American dream catcher, and a swami. However, any ethos of collective, progressive change that had clung to the New Age at its inception had long since vanished into the Hollywood Hills, leaving behind a profit-driven "cult" of self-improvement. Those who were dying found this lacking.

Marianne remembers her first talk on the *Course* perfectly, down to her red pencil skirt, red stilettos, white cable-knit top, and cubic zirconia earrings. Though the event, fateful as it was, occurred almost by accident. Upon arrival in LA, she'd managed to get a part-time job—typing and filing and the like—at the Philosophical Research Society, a courtyard cluster of airy buildings hidden behind a high tan wall in Los Feliz. One day her boss told her they'd been looking for someone to give talks on the *Course*.

Marianne distributed flyers throughout the whole city in preparation, and a solid seventy-five people showed. So she started holding forth on Love and miracles every Tuesday. By and large, those who showed up were gay men dealing with AIDS. So like Jesus with those lepers, Marianne began leading *Course* groups that catered to these men in basements and chapels all over town. Every Saturday morning, she appeared at a Hollywood church located on Franklin Avenue and Highland, an unusually unattractive swath of multilaned asphalt, even for LA. But behind the church's high wrought-iron gate sits a placid rose garden where the beating fountain and notes of Chopin wafting from a back room blot out the engine roar of passing cars. Down an outdoor stone corridor is a small chapel with white folding chairs haphazardly assembled on a bloodred carpet made a rainbow by the diamond-paned stained glass that lines the walls.

There, Marianne and the gay men discussed how AIDS—four letters fast becoming synonymous with a radioactive curse, not a sickness—was just a word that no one's spirit could be touched by. They talked of self-love and forgiveness, of death as a transition, of the healing divine contact, faith, can infer—though Marianne always stated, "Pray but take your medicine."[5]

---

5   In New Thought's and *A Course in Miracles*' cosmology, disease is considered a product of a Fear-based mind, not of Love and God. Disease is therefore not considered real. As such, some of Marianne's spiritual contemporaries told people that their inability to cure themselves of diseases, including HIV and AIDS, was the result of a personal spiritual shortcoming, a failure to muster an enlightened shift in perception. Some also intimated medication was not needed at all to treat what ailed them. Marianne has considered HIV and AIDS to be a product of society's collective Fear-based mind and not the fault of any individual. She has said she believed the way to heal HIV and AIDS was to heal the nation. And when AZT, the first FDA-approved HIV treatment, hit the market, she reportedly drove people with the virus to the doctor, then paid for the pills. She has also pointed out that studies show meditation can boost immune function and contended that the spiritual and scientific work together in "holistic" tandem. But many people have claimed that Marianne's talk sometimes still deterred her fans from seeking out needed medical care or made them feel like a failure for not being able to Love their sickness away, even if she hasn't explicitly shamed them the way some New Thought-ians have. As of 2019, her take on disease remains the most controversial aspect of her rhetoric.

Unlike Marianne, after putting down the *Course*, I didn't pick it back up. Instead, as she once did with cabaret, I opted for turning to the Muse for answers or meaning or a connection to the God-Force. I wrote plays.

Both before and after this time as a dramatist, I often made a living writing about the AIDS epidemic. And I wrote a monologue basically explaining why. The play was set in 1996, the year the cocktail of drugs that can control, though not cure, HIV premiered. Those drugs hit shelves, despite all the societal inaction, because once-silenced gay men and others impacted by the virus determined to ACT UP, fight back. And when they did, they changed the world for the better against all odds—an outcome the *Course* asserts the way of Love can't help but bring forth. Still, despite the incipient breakthrough, the mood onstage during the scene was, I'd say, "desperate collective search for salvation." The crux of it is:

This virus, by who it most attacks, it thrives, literally feeds, on our deepest, most shameful injustices. The shit we refuse to look in the eye. And now half my friends are . . . The Dark forces of destruction are nothing if not adaptable. But maybe the forces of creation are just as cruel. Because, paradoxically, to have a prayer of stopping this virus we cannot yet cure with science, we're going to have to do something . . . good. Something we should have done eons ago. Empower all those people we try to bury in the shadows.

Soon, women began to join the gay men at Marianne's *Course* groups. Eventually, straight men—mostly actors—showed too. They came to hear Marianne talk of a Christian canon that actually lifted up and empowered them, to hear "this woman who look[ed] like one of [them], who you know could have been at Studio 54 or dancing at Fire Island Pines with a tambourine on her hip—and yet she's talking like Jesus

Christ. She's talking about the most fundamental precepts. She's talking about the Golden Rule."

Soon, Marianne's prayer groups evolved into Marianne's lectures, and the spaces where she held them grew into hotel ballrooms, auditoriums, and even the historic Fox Wilshire Theatre in Beverly Hills—which could easily pack twenty-five hundred. Marianne charged a seven-dollar suggested donation at the door, with no one turned away for lack of funds. Onstage, she honed her soon-to-be signature combo of tough love, personal anecdotes, and humor—first workshopped during her cabaret days.

To a woman who reported her youth in a "psychospiritual cult" had left a bad taste, Marianne quipped: "Go meditate. Charles Manson ate apples. That doesn't mean I'm not going to." To demonstrate the error of attempting to manifest the "shopping list" desired by one's ego, instead of just asking God to use you, she told the tale of her own misguided attempt to summon the perfect lover by making a list of attributes she'd like him to have: "The only trouble was, I forgot to say, 'Please God, he should not be a heroin addict.'"

Knowing that she had a lecture in the morning and that people were relying on her kept Marianne from staying out till all hours, acting unhinged, falling apart. In short, she'd finally found purpose—and something to believe in, not just to oppose.

One day, Marianne called up her devout Jewish mother in Texas to deliver the news.

"You're going to stay in California?"

"Yeah." Pause.

"And give talks."

"Yeah." Pause.

"About Jesus?"

"Well, yeah." Longer pause.

"What will you wear?"

14

The Bitch for God

The image is amber filtered and porous. Marianne, age thirty-nine and dressed in an early nineties power suit with the shoulder pads of a New Wave general, touches Oprah's arm as they face one another in matching accent chairs, patterned Rorschach taupe. The women in the studio audience stare rapt and nodding as Marianne tells them rapidly and with perfect elocution that a better, more harmonious America starts with them.

"That kind of spiritual transformation, that kind of healing inside us as individuals, which will then become a collective healing, begins with a lifestyle decision, 'We will spend time every day on healing our own hearts . . . My greatest gift to this nation can be to give up the places where I am prejudiced, where I am lacking in compassion,'" she says, the numinous glow emanating from her flawless skin seemingly a testament to her strategy.

Oprah concurs with her signature all-knowing and compassionate "uh-huh." She then informs her fourteen million viewers, "I've never been as moved by a book as I was by Marianne Williamson's *A Return to Love.*" In fact, she has experienced 157 miracles since reading it—so she's bought a copy for each and every studio audience member.

At the time, February 1992, *The Oprah Winfrey Show*—beaming healing and transcendence, empathy and connection, into America's living room at 4:00 p.m. every weekday—towered as the closest thing we had going to a national cathedral, at least for women. After Oprah's benediction of *A Return to Love*, the book, basically a quippy *A Course in Miracles* CliffsNotes employing an appealing pop medley of history, psychology, and Deepak Chopra, along with sex, drugs, and Hall & Oates, flew to number one on the *New York Times* bestseller list. Demand for the *Course* itself quintupled.

That is how it came to pass that Marianne Williamson, a latter-day Peter preaching a Gospel 2.0, was baptized an American New Age celebrity. By then, however, she'd been an exalted West Coast prophet of Love—"Hollywood's ticket to God"—for years. She'd officiated Elizabeth Taylor's eighth wedding at Michael Jackson's ranch. Cher, Barbra Streisand, David Hockney, Richard Gere, Kim Basinger, Steven Tyler, and Raquel Welch credited her with helping transform their lives—and also with improving support for those living with AIDS throughout LA.

In her early days in the city, Marianne Williamson had had another flash illuminating how Love wanted to use her, shortly after her sister was diagnosed with breast cancer. In America, a nation forever bent on pretending it was morning, a dignified death remained hard to come by. So Marianne found a house on Sierra Bonita in West Hollywood with a pool in the backyard and started the Center for Living, using a $50,000 gift from Hollywood producer David Geffen. At the center, the terminally ill—in particular those living with AIDS—could talk openly of the other side, sing, get massages, eat crudités. Shortly thereafter, she also founded Project Angel Food, which today delivers six hundred thousand meals annually to the ailing and housebound across the city.

Then Marianne went bicoastal, cutting the ribbon on a Manhattan branch of the Center for Living and regularly lecturing on the *Course* across the island. People on both coasts could pop in a cassette tape of Marianne's weekly lectures, with themes such as "Forgiving Your Parents" or "Death Does Not Exist"—all soon available for purchase on the newfangled World Wide Web, the best thing to happen to spreading the American feminist mystic since the proliferation of "penny" newspapers in the 1850s.

In July 1991, *Time* magazine published an article on this Love-espousing, charity-starting spiritual sage titled "Mother Teresa for the '90s?" Then Marianne's message suffused the heartland, not just "bicoastal elite" land, and everything changed—and not all for the better.

Four months before Marianne touched Oprah's arm and transformed the American New Age, a thirty-five-year-old black female lawyer named Anita Hill raised her hand before a panel of white male senators and swore to tell the whole truth. The all-male panel, however, didn't seem much interested in the truth she had to tell.

Instead, those august senators tore Anita Hill down from their mahogany perch, as she testified of the sexual harassment she'd experienced at the hands of her former boss, Clarence Thomas, then under the panel's consideration for lifetime appointment to the US Supreme Court. She was just another petty "scorned woman" with "a militant attitude," they said. One foolish enough to think her pain and rights weighed enough against a man's ambition to register on the scales of justice.

Anita did, however, tip another critical scale. Millions of American women tuned in live to their elected "representatives" mocking their daily workplace realities, while many of the men sitting next to them laughed right along that Professor Anita Hill was "a little bit nutty and a little bit slutty," and they got pissed. Then they got ballot petitions.

In 1992, more women ran for office than in any previous year—more than doubling the number of women in each congressional chamber and forcing the Senate to build a women's bathroom on the chamber's building level. But the subsequent third wave of American feminism—officially coined such by Rebecca Walker, daughter of second-waver Alice Walker, in an essay she published in Gloria Steinem's *Ms.* magazine—did not just laser in on electing women.

By the end of the nineties, vaginas had monologues, *Bitch* was a magazine, and a *Jagged Little Pill* of female rage clocked in as the decade's top-selling album. However, this flood of stories about women, in all their messy human glory, as told by women themselves, remained largely mocked and/or relegated to subgenres with pejorative names: chick lit, chick flick, "so Lilith Fair." But while women's realities could not yet officially qualify as serious art—any more than as worth a Senate panel's time—they could clearly qualify as big business.

> Our deepest fear is not that we are inadequate. Our deep-
> est fear is that we are powerful beyond measure . . . We ask
> ourselves, "Who am I to be brilliant, gorgeous, talented, fabu-
> lous?" Actually, who are you not to be? You are a child of God
> . . . And as we let our own light shine, we unconsciously give
> other people permission to do the same. As we're liberated
> from our own fear, our presence automatically liberates others.

Even if someone has never heard of Marianne Williamson before, there's a good chance they've heard the seminal quote from *A Return to Love.* It's often misattributed to Nelson Mandela—thereby rendering it profound as opposed to "woo-woo."

Still, despite her chromosomal makeup, Marianne, in collaboration with her cowriter Andrea Cagan, helped usher in the mainstreaming of the New Age. Soon enough, from yoga to mindfulness meditation to locating one's power center to organic probiotic yogurt and soy, the once "alternative" was thoroughly capitalized into the culturally commonplace. Women comprised roughly 75 percent of this new market, and Marianne was emerging as its Warren Buffett.

But unlike other top-selling "self-help" authors, Marianne Williamson did not just talk of "higher consciousness" and personal healing as vehicles to manifesting your dreams—like a new Mercedes. She talked of "higher consciousness" and personal healing as vehicles to defeating the Fear-based powers that be and transforming the world—often in catchy sound bites simultaneously ready-made for a somewhat cheesy needlepoint pillow and totally radical. Enter the inevitable backlash.

Marianne Williamson says humans are the only species to fault their women for getting pissed. The rest of the animal kingdom relies on female rage for survival. People say rage, like fire, can be cleansing and transformative, not just destructive, depending on how you use it. An ex-boyfriend called Marianne's rage "something out of Ibsen." A former coworker called it "like watching a three-year-old throw a tantrum." A national journalist wrote that it reduced her to "run-on sentences."

Sekhmet, an Egyptian warrior and sun Goddess who created the desert with her breath, is symbolized by the lioness. She was the greatest hunter in all of Egypt, with deadly stealth grace and claws. Eventually, though, she was supplanted entirely in the mind of her people by the sun God Ra. A male lion is often used as a metaphor for Christ, our single savior, in the Western canon. In *The Lion King*, lioness Nala serves as a helpmate for lion Simba to realize his own great destiny—not as a powerful creature with her own story and fate and her own cause to bare her teeth.

Sometimes I wonder what would have happened if the Boston Tea Party had been conducted by women—just a bunch of pissed-off ladies in bonnets and petticoats flinging overtaxed tea into the sea. Would we have even had a revolution, or would the male colonists have rolled their eyes, called the women "a little bit nutty and a little bit slutty," "like watching a three-year-old throw a tantrum," and returned to paying their taxes to the British Crown just to shut those ladies up?

I rarely feel rage. At least not at the people and things that actually do me harm. I kind of just wonder, *What's the point?* I do like to glare coldly at men who, say, cut the salad line at Chopt until they relent or look abashedly at their shoes. But Chopt rage aside, I find power, control, and a cold comfort in remoteness—not in unbridled release, or exposure, of whatever lays within, be it Goddess or Gorgon. But everyone knows stone walls are drafty, and life behind them, no matter how pretty or well put together, often doesn't feel much like living at all. I should get mad more. I should cry more. But what might happen if I step out and show my face, my underbelly?

Marianne Williamson sat in her modest two-bedroom in West Hollywood reading the news. *People*, the *Los Angeles Times*, and *Entertainment Weekly* informed her she was an "egomaniac," "tyrannical," a peddler of "woo-woo," "the epitome of a Southern snake oil salesman" preying on the desperate and weak with "platitudes gleaned from women's magazines." She was in it for the money and the adulation, and the money and adulation alone. Her bicoastal AIDS organizations—to which she had in fact donated her entire first *A Return to Love* royalty check—were mere vehicles to fortune and fame. Plus, she had been a cabaret singer. Did anyone need any more proof of all of the above than that?

Marianne Williamson was suddenly "America's latest Mary Magdalene," as *Psychology Today* aptly put it.

Sure, she yelled at her assistants and quite frequently fired them—but she also let them live with her if need be. Sure, she snapped at anyone who mucked up the AV at one of her lectures. She'd also spent a decade sitting in rooms talking of God's unconditional Love with people dying of AIDS when most Americans fled from them. She also gave away her lecture and private counseling services for free to those who couldn't afford the asking price.

But that was little matter. For women in America in 1992, it remained an either/or game. And the press, almost giddy at the prospect of swiping the ethereal pedestal from under "America's latest Mary Magdalene," had scraped any dirt they could from beneath the glitter. They'd settled on events they deemed suspect that had taken place at a September 1991 fundraiser Marianne had organized.

The corset Madonna wore during her Blond Ambition tour had fetched a hefty bid at the auction. Elizabeth Taylor, Anjelica Huston, and Daryl Hannah were among the glitterati mingling in the Santa Monica airplane hangar that had been decked out and transformed into a gala space for the occasion. In the end, the Marianne production had raised a cool $725,000 for the fight against AIDS. And at the time, it had seemed that was that. Then Marianne catapulted into national celebrity, and it turned out that it wasn't.

The press reported Marianne had talked of Love and forgiveness onstage that night, only to dismount and "bark" and "hiss" at everyone she saw. The fundraiser may have cleared three-quarters of a million dollars, but it was budgeted to raise twice that, they said. What went wrong? Marianne kneecapped the event planners with her outlandish demands. The lone example: she insisted on air-conditioning in the hangar. Never mind the fact that the average temperature in Los Angeles in September is eighty-three degrees and that airplane hangars aren't really known for their ventilation—even when not packed with people like sardines in black tie.

But that wasn't all. In addition to firing assistants, Marianne had fired the director at the LA Center for Living—then asked the entire New York board to resign. She felt the director had floundered as the organization grew larger. Tension among the trustees over whether Marianne should talk about God at center events and/or which side to take in a staff quarrel had boiled over into dysfunction. She had her reasons. The media still couldn't get enough.

"I'd do it again. Does Michael Eisner apologize for making policy at Disney?" Marianne told *Entertainment Weekly*. "The burning of the witches was based on the theory that she's powerful, therefore she must be evil."

Marianne never denied her imperfections, never claimed that after spending an unstable "lost decade" she'd suddenly become a Zen saint. In fact, being called a "guru" sparked a lightning flash of ire in her, before she'd calmly insist she was just a teacher, perhaps one step farther down the road but just as flawed as anyone else. And perhaps that defense could have passed muster. But Marianne was not just a bitch, she was a slut.

She found out she was pregnant during a John Denver seminar in Aspen. And on May 21, 1990, India Emmaline was born. Marianne never publicly identified Emma's father and was an unabashed single mom—or a disgrace "mocking the importance of fathers," as sitting vice president Dan Quayle put it when describing unmarried mothers in highly paid professions.

Knowing her reputation preceded her, she started referring to herself as a "Jewish unwed mother" and a "bitch for God." But her aim at levity, and full disclosure, did not quench the thirst for witch bitch slut blood. In fact, word on the street was that *People* had planned to publish something rather hagiographic in early 1992 until they heard word of the "illegitimate" child. Then they ordered a hatchet job.

Marianne was gorgeous, influential, and hitting her prime—like her actual prime, not the prime timeline given to a woman when her life's worth is pegged to her fertility. She had no husband around to control or neuter her. She talked openly of her free-loving (in the Spiritualist sense) dating and sex life. She had the audacity to invite six ex-boyfriends, reportedly all quite handsome, to one *A Return to Love* book party in 1992. Somehow despite being a venomous, erratic harpy, Marianne remained on good enough terms with the ex-boyfriends for each to show. Her writings clearly conveyed that she liked and respected men, viewed them as her equal. But this somehow made many men feel uneasy, "unimportant."

Though the book itself remained on the bestseller list for the better part of a year, the backlash still hit its mark. That spring, it was Marianne who had to resign from the boards of the organization she founded, both in New York and LA. Her city, too, went up in flames during five days of rage sparked by the acquittal of three white policemen charged with brutally beating an unarmed black man. Despite the attack being caught on a video watched round the world, Rodney King's pain and rights did not weigh enough on the scales of justice either. AIDS became the leading cause of death among all Americans ages twenty-four to forty-four—what with the decade-long refusal to act on behalf of gay men.

Marianne and Emma packed up and left LA, moving an hour-and-a-half north of the city to a remote estate in Montecito complete with an elevator, a pool, and a smattering of olive trees. It seemed the forces of Fear had managed to marshal this latest young avatar of Love into gilded seclusion, her female dog or serpent tail between her legs. There's more than one way to burn a witch.

2018

Upon arrival, I was handed a standard-issue tan cardboard journal and a purple wristband reading "A WOMAN'S WEEKEND: On Love, Work, and Power" by a smiling volunteer. I took a seat among about three hundred women. Directly to my left a shaggy-haired lesbian operated a camera that would livestream the talk to paying subscribers worldwide. I felt we would be two among a sea of straight, largely white, middle-aged women. I was very wrong. In 2018, the appeal of Marianne's call to Love stood broad.

Marianne entered in a fantastic Goddess-chic silver silk coat, emblazoned with pink and orange flowers, that draped down to her calves. She took her place at a plexiglass pulpit before a sprawling multihued floral backdrop connoting Gaia and the Goddess, not Jesus or her Christian He God. Marianne cites both the Father God-Force and the Divine Mother, a yin and a yang, as essential to the side of Love.

Speaking without notes, Marianne talked to us of the wild woman, the natural woman within us all. Unleashing her, that creature with both deep claws and tenderness whom society has menaced us into caging, was the reason we had gathered together in the basement ballroom of the LA Airport Marriott. Once we free her, the divine feminine within, we will use her strength to forge a better future, Marianne said. "Women can and must save the world, but broken women can't do it," she continued, adding that the Dalai Lama agrees. But the time for salvation was fast running out—it was now or never, ladies.

Marie Laveau built a mystic raft to ride atop the Fear-based torrent bent on forcing her to the bottom. But by 2018, it was clear to just about everyone, at least in some form or fashion, that societal system, our societal system, had a fatal design flaw. We no longer needed a raft but a portal everyone could use.

Then it began. The lights came up partway. Marianne ventured out among us. The ballroom shrank, sealed into something tighter, more covenly, as Marianne wove through the aisles, pouring her energy onto us like angel dust. Woman after woman stood for healing. Marianne came close to each, her deep-set auburn eyes absorbing their pain. Each woman, facing down that combo of strength and vulnerability, unfurled the most intimate details of her life—to a ballroom of a few hundred strangers and an untold number of unseen others tuning in online.

A middle-aged biker dyke stood and talked of childhood abuse. Marianne advised her. She cried. A young Asian American woman with a mother who escaped the Cambodian genocide spoke of the troubles in their relationship sparked by that past trauma. Marianne advised her. She cried. An undocumented immigrant told her story. A former prisoner reported how Marianne's talk of atonement transformed her life. All around me, sniffles. I didn't cry.

If the sharer didn't cop to their responsibility in whatever situation they had offered up, Marianne sniffed it out, held the mirror to their face. The *Course* says you pay a high price if you don't take 100 percent responsibility, if you don't ask "what part did I have to play," she told us. Only by subtracting what you must cop to can you see what you should fight to change. Remarkably, no one got defensive. Like magic, when Marianne touched the golden heart of the matter, they nodded, accepting their fault, purified.

Marianne does not suffer self-pity—nor the form of rage it sparks. And Marianne does not exempt herself from her program.

Marianne sat beneath her own private Montecito olive tree, pondering revolution and her mother. She took stock, as her *Course* instructs. The backlash had resulted, as she saw it, a little from column sexism—women can't be angry and/or powerful without being called a hysterical bitch and/or slut—and a little from column Marianne—she may have gone a bit far. In those early days of her career, she felt that as a woman she had to claw her way into the room. Then she forgot how to retract said claws.

"I realized they were cemented to my fingernails. They were not so easy to let go," Marianne now often says. Growing up, she'd devalued her mother's work and world. Now, she understood that devaluing and fearing parts of herself had made her hard. "Second-wave feminists said women are equal to men, but not feminine is equal to masculine," as she put it in that Marriott basement.

"Slowly but surely, generation after generation, over thousands of years, the feminine was made to seem ridiculous. She was debased in men as well as in women, all of us risking shame when we relate to her," she wrote in her next book, *A Woman's Worth*, aiming to rectify that age-old imbalance. After the world tried to "crucify her," Marianne Williamson didn't submit. She wrote a book aiming to dismantle the cross.

Marianne realized that to heal humanity and usher in an era of global Love, as her *Course* preached, the phrase "hit like a girl" needed to be reconstituted with images of, say, Serena Williams hitting better than pretty much any man alive, but also with those showing how a girl who really can't hit for shit but is fantastic at talking about feelings embodies human strength too.

However, Marianne wrote about this at a moment when—thanks to those second-wave feminists—barriers to women rising to become doctors and senators and factory forepeople were fast crumbling. Ensuring that women newly in proximity to real power still played by the man's rules grew increasingly critical to maintaining the status-quo system. Construing "feminine" as weak, muddleheaded, vain, silly, woo-woo, "chick-lit" constituted the clutch play.

After *A Woman's Worth*'s publication, members of the press debased Marianne for letting women "hear what they want to hear—how 'special' they are"; for talking of "Goddesses"; for being "a return to gibberish." But still, despite the mocking, the people—or, more specifically, the women—spoke.

A Woman's Worth, too, reached number one on the *New York Times* bestseller list—and remained atop it for nineteen weeks. "Women are at the forefront of the spiritual hunger march. Why? It's our only hope," as Marianne put it. But Marianne Williamson never planned to stop her Love revolution at the mere forefront.

The rumor had just started to circulate in the press. Three twenty-something women in from Denver arrived to the morning workshop segment themed "Power" wearing gray shirts that read "Keep Calm and Let Marianne Handle It." Marianne laughed gutturally, then snapped a pic with them—still available for view on Instagram. Knowing looks flashed all around.

Marianne's first-known brush with the presidency came in late 1994, when Bill and Hillary Clinton—taking a move from Abe and Mary Todd's book of shadows—invited her, along with some other leading mystics, to spend a weekend at Camp David. The main leak to the press: Hillary talked with the spirits of Eleanor Roosevelt and Mahatma Gandhi. The press mocked her mercilessly, of course, then later besmirched her as wooden and robotic when she tried to hide all they'd derided behind a wall to play by their rules.

In that movie *Firestarter* I watched twenty-odd times circa age six, the little blonde girl doesn't just have the power to set everything on fire, immolate anyone with the slightest glare; she bears the brunt of the repercussions, watches her power destroy her world. And she fears herself.

I don't get angry. I don't cry. Witches get angry. Witches don't just cry; they wail. So do Goddesses and Gorgons and people undergoing courses in therapeutic enlightenment.

I love watching Marianne. I find it thrilling, all that unrestrained life flashing about, whether it's her anger flaring when the lights fail to come up at the designated moment or when she's looking into my soul directly, her eyes saying, *You, too, can return to Love.*

I returned to my journal. Marianne told us to channel our inner Goddess, then to write a letter to God and jot down his reply. Our inner child also gets a turn to express herself. This time, I did not astrally shrug when told to contact her. I just did it. My inner Goddess told me, "I need to be unleashed. You are too controlled." God told me, "You have fought hard to be here today, alive and flourishing. Now you have to do the hardest part. You have to let go." And finally, my inner child weighed in, "You've done the work. You just need to stop doing what you learned to do long ago, lock up, go through the motions." I spotted a motif.

Around the time I returned to the mystic in late 2017, I also really committed to therapy. For the first time, I stuck with it, instead of remaining just long enough to stanch the active bleeding. The two paths worked in tandem, as the *Course* declares they can, and in that room full of journalers, I felt more fully equipped to do as Marianne counseled—take hard looks in brutally honest mirrors.

Still, in lieu of crying, I quickly downed two beers during the dinner break. When I returned, buzzed, a Grammy-winning New Age band called Opium Moon, led by a woman wearing electric purple, played some kind of punk Kamasutra tune. All around me wild women danced and swayed, some taking to the aisles, some shouting along. Women who just met hugged and jumped together, clasping hands. I kept largely still and largely to myself, wondering what it might be like to be someone who let go and swayed with strangers to punk Kamasutra music. Then I left early.

Marianne wanted me to embrace my inner "feminine." Marianne said she knows such things are currently "up for fluid review"; it's just what she has found has worked for her. Marianne wanted me to cry.

Marianne wanted me to deal with my shit, be less rigid, so I could devote myself more fully to being "an immune cell" in the fight for the soul of America. I would definitely have liked to be an immune cell in the fight for the soul of America. But I feared I may be more of a kidney stone.

After the workshop concluded, I met my friend Scout, and we drove to a sunset sound bath at a Malibu ranch for rescue farm animals in her Prius. Lying inside one of the dusty animal pens on a yoga mat beneath the Pacific Ocean sky, I listened to an orchestra of gongs—a Jupiter gong, a moon gong, a fire gong—and some medicine bowls harmonizing mystically, each tuned to a specific chakra.

The Californians that surrounded me smiled softly, their chakras singing. A black rescue pig named Einstein happily punctuated the symphony with soft resting snorts from a mud pit by the fence. A rescue goat, whose name I didn't catch, nestled in by my right shoulder and merrily twitched his ears. A deer named Daisy peed in a small patch of exposed ground amid our yoga mat constellation. As she then joyfully bounded over our defenseless supine bodies, the resident animal handlers watched serenely, trusting she would not misfire her hooves. Daisy safely cleared our perimeter. I exhaled, then closed my eyes, wondering why everyone including the goats seemed to be getting something from this that I wasn't. I felt a sensation of rushing toward something. It suddenly occurred to me. *I may have made this entire quest way too intellectual of an endeavor.*

By the late 1990s, Marianne Williamson had manifested two number one bestsellers (and two more would soon follow). Marianne Williamson no longer appeared in church basements. She appeared in packed grand halls nationwide. People traveled hundreds, sometimes thousands of miles to see her. She lived the rarefied, insulated life of a modern-day American celebrity, one at the very peak of the "Self-Help" and "New Age" markets that were then reaching new vertiginous heights.

Then, Marianne's father and sister and two uncles died in a close span of time. She felt in shock. She felt like she needed change—to get some "dirt under her fingernails again." She felt "if [she] saw one more beautiful pool and one more beautiful manicured lawn, [she] would scream." It was then Marianne Williamson got another call.

15

HEALER-IN-CHIEF

Once at a party, I heard a story about a lion who somehow escaped the Detroit Zoo. All golden muscles and powerful teeth, he strolled among the dilapidated mid-twentieth-century grandeur, the art deco downtown and brick Tudor homes sprouting vines through their cracking edifices. He ran through empty weed-filled lots, his mane streaking flat as he sped beneath traffic lights that forever blinked red, down roads in such disrepair they flooded out at the slightest rain. Those who encountered him wondered if they'd fallen asleep, or fast-forwarded to the end of American civilization. Then they backed away very, very slowly.

Once they made cars in Detroit. Once they made Motown. But by the turn of the millennium, they made headlines as "the murder capital" of America.

In 1997, Marianne published the first edition of *Healing the Soul of America*. America, she wrote, once offered "a light unto the world" via its aspirational founding principle "that there can be a land where all are free to be and to become their essential selves." But today,

Americans think only of "making things better for me" not "things better for us." That ideal was growing more, not less, remote—the word *free* set "to a note so high nobody [can] reach it," to quote the play *Angels in America*. Marianne warned that if we don't marshal our spiritual Love forces fast, there will be "a storm ahead" of Dark forces that could forever snuff out the light in America. The time to insert Love and the repressed "feminine" back into the body politic was now.

However, in the late 1990s, with the economy booming and the Cold War won, no one much wanted to listen to her prognostications that the time to choose Love was running out—that the prognosis in America was in fact dire. "It was a commercial failure compared to the other [books]," Marianne has said. Well, they didn't want to hear it in most of the country, that is.

It was then that Marianne got the call from a Unity Church—a Christian denomination spun out of Emma Hopkins's New Thought—on the fringes of Detroit, in Warren, Michigan. They needed a new senior minister and wanted to ask if she had some suggestions. Marianne, surprising even herself, replied, "How about me?"

In 1998, Marianne sold her Montecito estate for $2.65 million and moved with Emma, now age eight, to the yawning muddy mouth of the Detroit River and the upscale suburb of Grosse Pointe. She arrived to apply the principles of her new book, not in the newly gentrifying and economically thriving coastal cities she'd previously called home, but one floundering in their exhaust fumes. A place that was already looking for "a better way."

"Our political salvation will not come from our political system as it now exists. It will come from deep within us," Marianne wrote. "Yet where does one start?"

2019

My new girlfriend, Ellie, wanted to lie under a blanket and cry. I wanted to have an epiphany. We decided to do ayahuasca.

I entered the journey—and that is what the kids are calling it these days, not "trips"—through a gray metal door covered in band stickers and no visible street address. I found myself standing not in some punk rock basement, as I might have surmised, but in a posh two-story Brooklyn loft decked out in a rainbow of beige and cream, pleasantly earthen abstract art, and shelves of spiritual yet masculine books—no Marianne Williamson, I checked. After walking to the second floor, I put on comfortable pants and sat in a circle of ten women and men on a plush eggshell couch.

Our bespectacled, disheveled male guide arrived last, in a hoodie, sipping coffee, to tell us our intention: that January night, fully in the bowels of the season of dark, we were all to hallucinogenically travel into the shadows of our relationships, touch and release the things that keep us locked inside ourselves, the oil to the vinegar of the true intimacy we crave. I thought I forgot this assignment as soon as I was given the psychedelics—or the spirit drug, as my guide called it. I thought my girlfriend and I would just embark on our separate yet complementary agendas for the evening.

Marianne Williamson says salvation lies within you. But she also says that healing, spiritual transformation that allows us to access the Love that is God, is not a solo endeavor. It happens in relationship with others.

Hallucinogenic experiences boast a marked difference from dreams and other more mundane perambulations through the unconscious. Again and again, people emerge from the psychedelic depths stating, even years later, that their lives permanently changed there—that they saw God, peacefully faced down their most traumatic memories or retraveled the birth canal and emerged reborn.

Ellie and I had met a few months before this lofted journey, a couple weeks after I returned from Marianne's Women's Weekend. From the beginning, our love affair felt kinder, more tender, less combustible and depleting than any I'd had in over a decade, and possibly ever. But we remained at arm's length. We'd each been afflicted with chronic busyness—as is perpetually on trend in New York City. This excuse, however, just veiled the heart of the matter that Marianne would expose. We were two women suspect, tentatively peeking over our own walls at each other with a smile but cagey as fuck. And we each walked into that New Age, formerly industrial loft blind, unaware how on point the theme/intention of the night would be.

Ellie was kicking. On her back, on the floor, her arms and legs repeatedly thrusted into the air like an upturned turtle trying to right herself. "Kick," she shouted, again and again, all victorious rage, shaking her head, her long, wild, wheat-colored curls grazing my cheek. Then she proclaimed herself a mermaid and took to rolling in the glory of the exceptionally clean kitchen tile. I, meanwhile, saw Goddesses everywhere.

In the painted planked wooden ceiling, I saw a field of them, naked and of all races and shapes, their bare bodies peeking out from green leaves like ears of corn. In a flash of red, they all lay dead in a gray wasteland of ash, mass victims. Then another flash. They were Goddesses again. And on it went. Goddesses—most of all Mother Nature—cycles of life and death, rot and rebirth, vines and lush pomegranates suddenly ridden with worms, everywhere.

In a potted palm tree in the corner, I saw a witch—or a caricature of one with a green grimace and big nose, the green fronds serving as her Medusa hair. A bend in the trunk formed her ass, full and large. Suddenly, her ass was dancing. Then her face shifted, not changing so much as revealing itself. Her resting witch face was not angry, bitter, or mean, a shrew, but a face of dignity and strength.

A man explained to me how I felt and what my experiences were. His face morphed into Frankenstein's monster, glowing nuclear green, then faded out, as flowering vines, clovers, and more and more Mother Nature grew out of the eye sockets and ears and cracks in the edifice that had been his skin until the face went poof, like ash, and vanished.

I was literally on a feminist trip.

Ellie and I didn't talk much, lying together on the ground on parallel but separate journeys into the spaces in between. I knew one thing, however: I wanted to remain by her side. On the floor above us, the others chattered, listening to soothing spiritual music with the lights on. We'd somehow commandeered the entire bottom level of the loft for ourselves, leaving it dark except for the light from the night rain pouring against the giant picture windows behind us, the droplets fracturing the Brooklyn streetscape into its most essential parts.

"This woman has a direct line to God!" proclaimed Aerosmith's Steven Tyler joyfully, after showing up unannounced to lead Marianne's Michigan congregation in a chorus of "Amazing Grace." They stood together in the brick institutional church on a patchy twelve-acre grass lot that felt like it was on the remote fringes of America, though it was geographically at its heart. But that Sunday, a world-famous rock star had come to them, not vice versa—and he'd started singing, surprisingly angelically.

Even still, Marianne had conjured a rather bipartite reputation in the three years since she'd taken over the Church of Today ministry. Attendance had soared. The remote campus had become the second-largest Unity Church in America. Though the church was located in a nearly all-white pocket on the outskirts of a city that was 80 percent black, African American worshippers now constituted approximately a third of the congregation. With Marianne's guidance, over four hundred of the church's members had started flocking out, instead of just looking within. They regularly volunteered for Detroit-based tutoring programs, inner-city nursing homes, Habitat for Humanity, and the Humane Society.

But not everyone was pleased with their resident Left Coast Holy Roller. Marianne talked too much about liberal politics and Al Gore. Marianne had the choir sing gospel. Marianne was "an egomaniac control freak." And when Marianne pushed through changing the church's name to Renaissance Unity and breaking completely with the national Association of Unity Churches, the detractors saw an opening. They threatened to sue—even though the congregation had voted in favor of Marianne's proposal. The local press caught wind, and again the "bitch" part of Marianne's title began to distract from the "God" part. In 2002, she resigned the post.

Though she'd lost her flock, Marianne remained industriously based in Grosse Pointe, where Emma had friends and school and a life. Marianne toured, published more books—thirteen and counting—and remained a leading American itinerant mystic. In 2006, *Newsweek* listed her as one of the most influential baby boomers, along with her friend Oprah.

Then, in 2008, that bubble made of complex derivatives burst, and the financial crisis completely submerged the already struggling Detroit metropolitan area. Not even Marianne's head remained above the waterline. The banks foreclosed on the two Michigan houses she'd bought. "I got caught in the same unfortunate situation as millions of Americans," she's said. "I know the pain of a real estate investment that went south."

With Emma just turned eighteen, nothing was tying Marianne to the heartland. So she returned to the coast that had always called to her like a golden calf—the one that made her famous—to regroup. She retraced her steps all the way back to the start, to West Hollywood. Then she bought a condo and waited for her Love God to call again.

Standing by a wall of glass overlooking the Malibu sunset, wearing a sharply tailored dress, its black-and-white pattern mirroring the curve of shoreline visible just outside, Marianne talked about the state of the nation—and running for office to change it. Throughout the upscale living room, checkbooks fluttered like the tides around generously poured glasses of chardonnay. It was 2014, and Marianne, at sixty-one, still had it.

After her decade away from the glitz of Southern California, she'd grown even more viscerally aware and fretful of the brewing torrent she'd first charted in *Healing the Soul of America*. That torrent of diminished rights, apathy, and corporate greed all constituted what she now called "such a powerful force of darkness that it could put American democracy in a death spiral." In 1997, Marianne stood a Cassandra ahead of her time. By 2014, the Dark forces looming in everyone's peripheral vision were inching toward center stage.

"When I first started talking about metaphysical principles, it was news to a lot of people. That was thirty-five years ago. We've all read the same books now. We've all listened to the same tapes now," she's said. "This is no longer the era of data collection." Marianne believed the only thing that could save us from ourselves now was a "moral and spiritual awakening," not just en masse but in Congress. So she had decided to run for California's Thirty-Third District—stretching down the coast from Malibu to Rancho Palos Verdes.

Indeed, by then it seemed half the working actors in Hollywood had day jobs as intuitive healers, Reiki practitioners, and/or self-care counselors. Major corporations had meditation rooms. Police employed psychics. Harvard Medical School held seminars on the role of spirituality in healing. And our latest wave of feminism had just started percolating.

However, even in the greater Los Angeles area in 2014, a woman talking about the need for an angelic invasion of the boardroom at Monsanto could provoke a snickering sneer. "Martin Luther King said it was time to inject a new dimension of love into the veins of human civilization. I don't think anyone is calling Martin Luther King a New Age woo-woo," Marianne told the *Washington Post* at the time.

Though Kim Kardashian West, Sarah Silverman, and Katy Perry endorsed her, and Alanis Morissette recorded her campaign song, in the end, Marianne came in fourth in a field of seventeen. But she believed next time around, if there was one, she could do it all far better, listen more to her intuition, less to the experts bent on tailoring her message to meet the needs of data points, not divinity.

In 2016, as the zeitgeist grew frenzied, Marianne again left California, this time for New York City. The move put her a puddle-jump away from Emma, who'd enrolled in graduate school in London. Marianne had last called Gotham home in the late seventies, when it seemed the city might just self-destruct into the Hudson. Now, the median monthly rental price for a Manhattan one-bedroom was over $3,000. Citywide, average rent had spiked 75 percent since the turn of the millennium. And just like most everywhere else in the nation, people were pissed. Marianne knew as well as anyone that anger could be harnessed by either side of the great cosmic battle. But as that year lurched on, it grew increasingly clear which side currently controlled the rage's reins.

Coincidentally, or not, she rented a condo on the twentieth floor of a Midtown high-rise directly across from Trump Tower. Behind her TV, set to CNN, and her statue of Quan Yin, the Buddhist Triple Goddess, there the black tower stood. When watching footage of Hillary's Electoral College defeat, the victor's inaugural move banning Muslim immigrants, mass shooting after mass shooting, or the US withdrawal from the Paris Agreement on climate change, the tower's penthouse glared down like the Eye of Sauron. In her bedroom, adorned in black and white with pale-pink highlights and that photo of John Lennon wearing a "New York City" shirt, the black glass phallus of a building loomed so large not even the electric hustle of Fifth Avenue could blot it out of her mind. There in its dark shadow, Marianne Williamson got one more call.

Packed shoulder to shoulder in pews at Marble Collegiate Church,[6] a congregation first established by the Dutch in the 1600s and older than the idea of America, we waited. Since moving back to New York City, Marianne had lectured on the *Course* here in Manhattan's Murray Hill the first and third Tuesday of every month. But we all knew that this was not just a regular third Tuesday night.

Marianne strode to the pulpit wearing all white, the color of suffragettes, save a purple velvet jacket, the shade of both the Goddess and American commonality—red mixed with blue. Standing before the golden high proscenium arch, Marianne rasped, telling us she'd lost her voice, then immediately teared up. She'd cried all day. "It's grief," she said. She was mourning the end of her thirty-five-year career lecturing on the *Course*. However, "the call is clear." And one week from that Tuesday, on January 28, 2019, she planned to formally announce she was running for the 2020 Democratic nomination for president of the United States. Naturally, this earned a standing ovation in the church, filled full from nave to balcony.

At that moment, I recalled an astrological prophecy I'd been told by a feminist astrologer some months earlier: During the great American solar eclipse of August 2017, the dwarf planet Ceres began to oppose

---

6   Interestingly, the Trump family attended this church for a time, and its former minister, Norman Vincent Peale—author of *The Power of Positive Thinking*—officiated Donald and Ivana Trump's wedding in 1977.

Pluto, and after nearly 150 years of prophetic (and often musical) preparation, we entered the Age of Aquarius, leaving the dark, violent, highly patriarchal Piscean Age behind. However, things could get way worse before they get better—if they even got better at all. Because in 2020, the North Node will enter Cancer, unleashing the sacred feminine that has been shackled for millennia, and we as a human civilization will either begin transitioning into a two-thousand-year Aquarian Age of matriarchy or chaos, communal peace and love, or tribal fear and loathing. The choice is up to us.

As commentator after commentator soon pointed out, Marianne's policy positions seemed similar to those of other Democratic primary candidates who all had elected experience—including a record six women there in the latest feminist wave. So, the pundits soon asked her, *Why run? Why was she different than the, like, twenty-five others running for the nomination?*

Marianne Williamson ran not just on the shoulders of feminists and female politicians past but of feminist mystics—including the first woman to ever run for president, Spiritualist medium Victoria Woodhull. Like Marianne, each of these mystics had built a new path forward off those forged by the women who preceded her, forming an ever-evolving but contiguous religious and political tradition as fundamentally American as, well, American Christian fundamentalism. As such, unlike any other candidate, Marianne Williamson wanted to talk about, and tackle, what she, and basically every feminist mystic in my ancestral spirit coven, viewed as the roots of the disease, not just play "whack a mole," as she put it, with the symptoms—the shootings, the xenophobia, the buying of a fleet of new $500 million bombers while schools go without school supplies, the suicides.

"Today, we have a culture of death because that's what the ego is. Beastly," Marianne explained. Today, in America "all manner of goodness, truth, and life itself is sacrificed at the altar of the false God of short-term profit maximization—like Milton Friedman hooked up with Ayn Rand."

Marianne hoped that out on the campaign trail she could get a much broader swath of America to listen to these "principles of truth" she'd been talking about my whole life—get them to understand the policy wisdom of, for example, paying reparations to a council of African American leaders who would apply the funds toward economic and educational renewal projects of their choosing. It's called atonement, according to Marianne Williamson. It's called facing the nation's shadows and burning the bad karma with grace. "It stunts the collective psyche of the nation that we are so dishonest about our history," she's said. The only chance we stand of hitting that high note *free* is set to is through telling our true story.

Though Marianne focused her attack that night in Marble Collegiate on the Dark forces of Fear bearing down, she let no one off the hook for our national maelstrom: "You do not have time to finish your trauma work before you show up for your country. Do you think the people who were walking across the bridge at Selma were not traumatized? Do you think the suffragettes who were force-fed in prison didn't have anxiety?"

Still, she seemed vulnerable at that pulpit in a way she never had in all the times I'd seen her before, all exposed flesh, little Teflon, her voice a low naked whistle instead of its usual sonorous brass section. I felt closer to her somehow, though she was a vast, packed Reformed church nave away.

Marianne told us she knew there would be slings and arrows shot at her—as there have been at women taking a stand against Fear since before the burning times. She hoped to turn those slings and arrows into rose petals at her feet. Then we closed our eyes so we could collectively enter a golden temple together.

I'd come to this, Marianne's final *Course* lecture, not just to hear her talk about presidential politics, but because I wanted Marianne

Williamson to crack open my life. I wanted to stand up and ask Marianne Williamson a question. I wanted Marianne Williamson to make me cry. I wanted Marianne Williamson to free me from the tyranny of my mind, so the light poured through.

Marianne told us, in a soothing harmonic wheeze that sounded like the hiss of air from the tomb of some saint, that inside the golden temple we would see whatever divinity or God is to us. It may be an angel. It may be a light. I was only half focusing on the meditation at hand, caught in my reptile brain's looping desire for Marianne to crack me open. When I tried to focus, snap into my temple, I saw an image of my elderly dog smiling at me. I shook it off. Then I saw a stream. Then I realized I was right back where I started over a year ago, at that séance, wanting someone else to crack it all open. Had I gotten nowhere?

There in my golden temple, I realized that no, Marianne and the rest of my ancestral spirit coven, oracles all, along with some excellent therapy, had in fact given me what I sought—roots and depth and bones enough to trust I can plant my feet and let go without falling through the mud, fingers crossed. The rest, as Marianne would be the first to say, is all me.

That very weekend, during my "journey" in that loft, I saw water running in a stream, clear and clean as the Source. In it, and kind of *of* it, lay a woman, maybe a Goddess, maybe a human, maybe both. She emerged. All but her face was made of light. The water had healed her, cleansed her of the world's dirt, dark layers of plaque that blocked her now luminescent skin from the air and sun. Somehow, I felt the water too.

Then I was back in Brooklyn, fully, for the first time since ingesting the psychedelic substance. Also for the first time that night, I felt like speaking more than a simple declarative sentence. Ellie turned toward me at that moment, feeling the exact same thing. Then we began to talk.

Lying together on the floor beneath our blanket—which we had come to call our fort—Ellie told me the hard things to hear that she'd been holding back, about herself, her life, her role in how past relationships went sour. I felt only compassion and warmth, Love, not the anxiety or negativity produced by what Marianne Williamson says is my Fear-based ego mind. I talked of those things too—suddenly understanding and articulating them better than I ever had before. She offered me the same courtesy of nonjudgment.

"I feel like my mind is out of the way," I moaned. "My mind is always in the way."

"We are talking from our bodies," shouted Ellie.

"Yes!" I returned at volume. "Yes! Our bodies know so much more!"

"We may need to kick more!" Ellie proffered.

I went into the loft looking for an epiphany, a solo tête-à-tête with God. But suddenly it was 4:00 a.m., and Ellie and I were sitting cross-legged on the tile floor, forehead to forehead, eating cheese—rapturing on about how we tasted the grass the cow ate and the sunshine that grew that grass and probably a moonbeam. Everyone else was upstairs singing along to the Beatles.

Marianne Williamson says here in the Age of Aquarius, we, each and every one, are our only possible saviors—and we all have to walk outside and fight.

Today, the image that most sticks in my mind from the night is—mostly—nonhallucinatory. After Ellie's bout of cleansing rage-kicking, but before the soul-talking, she stood at the foot of the stairs leading up out of our lesbian sanctuary, still dark save the thick glisten of the night rain on the loft windowpanes. Her curly hair, in the moment looking like an august lion's mane, shined all chiaroscuro in the light from the floor above. I didn't want to go up there, to what felt like the outside world. I felt too exposed. All flesh, little Teflon. In my memory, Ellie was naked, totally free, though I know she was fully clothed. She lifted her hands up like paws, then cocked her neck to peer up the stairs like an inquisitive wild creature. She looked so pure and unencumbered, stripped or cleansed of whatever layers of worldly grime make people afraid to follow the call of their curiosity and drive, their heart. Sitting at a remove by the cold rain in an electric moonshine lounge chair, I found it just so beautiful. I couldn't help it. I cried. Then I followed her up the stairs.

In the end, I found that the feminist mystic isn't about the vocabulary, Matriarchy v. Patriarchy, Love v. Fear, Light v. Dark. But the fact that every time a bell rings, the feminist mystic helps someone, woman or man, or in between and beyond, realize their own worth and that they will not be silenced—despite an age-old system established to break them down until they zip themselves up.

"Mighty companions are gathering all over this country," says Marianne Williamson. "Mighty companions are rising all over this world. And it's giving us wings."

In spring 2019, Ellie and I invited our own mighty companions to start a queer coven. As is generationally appropriate, we have a very loose liturgy. Besides, in the course of investigating my ancestral spirit coven, I've learned a witch can be many things. Marie Laveau, Cora L. V., HPB, Z, and Marianne each forged their own mystic road against their era's particular pummeling headwinds. Only Z explicitly (re) claimed the title *witch*. But no matter their chosen epithet or mystic branch, my mighty spirit companions each bent and changed their America into a place they could fit into a little more freely, as witches do. And thanks to their collective magic, it's a place where I can too.

I've also learned, to me, the forces of creation and destruction are not cerebral. To me, the body, the flesh, the blood are not beside the point, a deterrent to higher truth, but part of the turning, frothing, universal, whatever you want to call the divine. To me, witches use graveyard dirt. Witches use bones and piss and roses and rose quartz. Witches use life and death. Witches use poetry. Witches stare into the chaotic void and come back laughing. Because witches stand on a lineage dating back to the dawn, on a strong spine of many vertebrae tapping straight to the core. Witches embrace the shadows as part of the whole. They don't banish them to fester into demons. The Craft provides the tools, the power, to surf the chaos, instead of feeling you'll likely drown in it. Patriarchy, fear, what have you, tries to build a dam, a wall of dead wooden control, to block the chaos surrounding us, pretend it's not there. But it is. And levees burst all the time.

"Woo-Woo 2020 hopeful Marianne Williamson to host event with Eckhart Tolle" . . . "Self-help author Marianne Williamson wants to be your healer in chief" . . . "Did presidential hopeful Marianne Williamson merit a cover story? Some readers had doubts" . . . "Marianne Williamson tells Iowa crowd America needs a 'moral and spiritual awakening'" . . . "Oprah's spiritual adviser Marianne Williamson wants U.S. to pay up to $100B in reparations for slavery" . . . "Democratic candidate Williamson says she has practical experience" . . . "Marianne Williamson: Can a presidential bid fueled by love transcend the politics of fear?"

In summer 2019, Marianne Williamson's talk of Love battling the forces of Fear ransacking the nation made her the most googled candidate during both the Democratic primary debates she participated in—and qualified for by both measures of popular support set by the Democratic National Committee. It was a claim some senators and governors who joined her on the stage could not make. Suddenly, she became a high-profile candidate. And, when she did, the real barrage of slings and arrows began.

Some criticism had merit, including backlash against a comment she made implying she opposed mandatory vaccinations of Americans. She promptly retracted the comment, stating she misspoke, then adding, "I am not anti-vaxx. I am pro-science & medicine." Most critics, however, didn't bother with such details or with details like addressing her policy proposals. They didn't debate her plan for reparations or her call to create a domestic Department of Peace aimed at addressing the undergirding causes of crime, from trauma to lack of opportunity, not only prosecuting it. Most critics just insisted she had no right to be there, that she was wasting America's time by speaking on the debate stage for an average of seven minutes a night—half that of the frontrunners. Heads, both wry and enraged, shook. Memes mocking her with sage and orbs abounded. People called her crazy left and right.

Nevertheless, each generation of American feminist mystics has persisted, from Marie to Cora to HPB to Z. Because they knew they had something to say worth hearing. And they knew, if necessary, they could get back up again.

"People are so invested in creating this false narrative about me as the 'crystal lady,' 'wacky new-age nutcase,'" Marianne Williamson said just before the second debate. "If you really think about it, I must be doing something right that they're so scared."

ACKNOWLEDGMENTS

I am deeply grateful to all the scholars and mystic-minded people whose previous work made this book possible, and to everyone who spoke with me and generously lent me their stories and points of view or invited me to mystic events. I am also deeply grateful to the leaders of the #MeToo movement for helping ignite the cultural moment that inspired this book. At TOPPLE, I would like to thank my editor Laura Van der Veer for her insight and Erin Calligan Mooney and Jill Soloway for believing in the book, as well as Zoe Norvell, Mya Spalter, Emma Reh, Steve Schul, Heather Rodino, James Gallagher, Merideth Mulroney, Robin O'Dell, and everyone else who contributed their time and efforts. I would also like to thank Jill for writing such a powerful introduction. I am grateful to Jane Dystel and Miriam Goderich for helping me develop the idea and making the book a reality. I would like to thank Bart Scott for his research guidance. I could not have written the book without Ellie Heyman's support and input. And finally, I would like to thank Vinni the dog for being one excellent familiar.

NOTES ON SOURCES

The Coven

The information about the number of Wiccans versus Presbyterians comes from Benjamin Fearnow's "Number of Witches Rises Dramatically Across U.S. as Millennials Reject Christianity," published on Newsweek.com, November 18, 2018.

The statistic that 27 percent of Americans identify as spiritual but not religious comes from the Pew Research Center, https://www.pewresearch.org/fact-tank/2017/09/06/more-americans-now-say-theyre-spiritual-but-not-religious.

PART I: Marie Laveau, the Voodoo Queen of New Orleans

The details of the life and times of Marie Laveau and her family come, by and large, from three books:

Fandrich, Ina Johanna. *The Mysterious Voodoo Queen, Marie Laveaux: A Study of Powerful Female Leadership in Nineteenth-Century New Orleans*. New York: Routledge, Taylor & Francis Group, 2016. First published in 2005.

Long, Carolyn Morrow. *A New Orleans Voudou Priestess: The Legend and Reality of Marie Laveau*. Gainesville: University Press of Florida, 2007.

Ward, Martha. *Voodoo Queen: The Spirited Lives of Marie Laveau*. Jackson: University Press of Mississippi, 2004.

I relied most heavily on Long's and Ward's books. Each takes a different approach to interpreting the scant historical record of both Marie Laveaus, with Ward giving more credence to the oral history and Long to documents. The latter approach might sound more factually accurate to many, but because the Laveaus were known to manipulate such official records, the "facts" that exist are not necessarily that cut-and-dried. I tried to incorporate both approaches in my recounting to present the most comprehensive account. Also, as the titles of these books demonstrate, there is no absolute consensus on the spelling of the religion in question. I opted for New Orleans Voodoo to distinguish it from its Haitian sibling and because it is the most recognized spelling in the United States.

Unless otherwise noted, all direct quotes from New Orleanians about the Marie Laveaus come from the Works Progress Administration's Federal Writers' Project and Louisiana Writers' Project interviews conducted between 1935 and 1943. Those who gave direct physical descriptions would have been speaking of Marie II, as there weren't any people living at that time who would have been old enough to recall the Widow Paris in her prime. The Federal Writers' Project documents are archived at Northwestern State University in Natchitoches, Louisiana, and the Louisiana Writers' Project documents at the State Library of Louisiana in Baton Rouge. I relied on excerpts found in the above three books.

Many descriptions regarding the ceremonies conducted by Marie Laveau II, and the legend surrounding her, come from:

Hurston, Zora Neale. "Hoodoo in America." *Journal of American Folklore* 44, no. 174 (Oct.–Dec. 1931): 317–417.

Hurston, Zora Neale. *Mules and Men.* New York: Harper Perennial, 1990. First published 1935 by J. B. Lippincott.

In addition to the above books and in-person conversations that occurred in New Orleans in September 2018, background information on Haitian Vodou and New Orleans Voodoo came from Kenaz Filan's *The New Orleans Voodoo Handbook* (Rochester, VT: Destiny Books, 2011).

Additional sources and specific citations are listed chapter by chapter below.

Chapter 1: Becoming American

Long offers the account of Marie's grandmother Marguerite potentially coming over on the slave ship *St. Ursin.* However, she states it's also possible that it was Marguerite's mother, Marie Laveau I's great-grandmother, who was forcibly brought from Africa, meaning Marguerite would have been born in Louisiana.

According to Long, in 1802, the year after Marie Laveau was born, her father, Charles Laveaux, married a free woman of color. Their relationship, as well as plaçage, likely placed a hindrance on Charles and Marguerite marrying.

The initiation presided over by Sanité Dédé is taken from descriptions of the ceremony found in both Long's and Ward's books. The original source is Marie Williams's "A Night with the Voudous" published in *Appleton's Journal* on March 27, 1875. Williams identifies the white man who recalled the ceremony only as "Professor D." Fandrich, Long, and Ward theorize what nineteenth-century white Americans might have meant by "orgies" and other salacious-sounding details when describing Voodoo rituals.

The mention that Marie would have fasted for three days and three nights before her initiation is taken from Hurston's account of her own Voodoo initiation at the hands of Marie II's nephew.

Both Ward and Fandrich provide accounts that Glapion started passing as "colored." The theory that he had the help of a half brother comes from Ward's book. She also cites the fact that he signed documents as colored. Long just refers to Glapion as white but comments that it was remarkable he and Marie were able to live together, even after the strict American laws against interracial cohabitation went into effect.

Approximately 46 percent of free Creoles of color in New Orleans enslaved people during the Widow Paris's time. While the legend and Ward contend Marie bought enslaved people only to free them, Long believes she, like most of that 46 percent, partook fully in the slave economy.

Chapter 2: A (Snake) Goddess Rising

The apartment on St. Ann's was listed for $1,800 on Realtor.com.

The account of Marie II and the Great Mother fusing, as well as the axiom about "Love," are taken from Hurston's "Hoodoo in America" (quote, p. 351). Hurston writes that Samuel Thompson, who claimed to be Marie II's nephew—and who she will later refer to as Luke Turner in *Mules and Men*—taught her many of Marie's Hoodoo incantations and rituals, which she then transcribed. His level of accuracy is unknown.

Long writes that Philomène's partner in plaçage was Emile Alexandre Legendre. Ward contends it was in fact his older brother George. Long cites an 1870 census report that Philomène was living with Alexandre on Dauphine Street, so I chose to use that account.

Because of this official 1862 date of death, Long is far less certain than Ward or Fandrich that Marie Eucharist was Marie II.

The account of Marie II's annual routine at the Saint John's Eve festival is based largely on Hurston's account that she attributes to Luke Turner/Samuel Thompson.

"Busted flat in Baton Rouge" is from the song "Me and Bobby McGee," written by Kris Kristofferson and best known through Janis Joplin's rendition.

"The hottest spell . . ." is excerpted from Long (p. 175). She states the weather was cited as such in local papers.

The obituary calling Marie the "soul of the indecent orgies of the igno-ble Voudous" was printed in the New Orleans *Times-Democrat* and excerpted from Ward (p. 15), who describes the publication as a "Protestant, Anglo-American newspaper." The write-up contend-ing Marie "spent her life doing good" was found in the *Picayune* and also found in Ward. She describes the *Picayune* as "favorable to Creoles and Catholics."

Chapter 3: And Then the Floods

The details about Hurricane Katrina are taken from multiple online news stories describing the hurricane and its aftermath.

"Impassioned black savages . . ." conducting Voodoo rituals is from a June 24, 1896, article in the New Orleans *Times-Democrat*. I excerpted it from Long (p. 129).

"Terrible oaths . . ." is from Robert Tallant's *Voodoo in New Orleans* (New York: Macmillan, 1946). I excerpted it from Ward (p. 60).

Luke Turner's quote that begins, "Time went around pointing out what God had already made . . ." is from Hurston's *Mules and Men* (p. 192). The account of her initiation is also from *Mules and Men*. "Marie Laveau is the great name of Negro conjure in America . . ." is from "Hoodoo in America" (p. 326). "The loving ones find a boat . . ." is from *Mules and Men* (p. 194).

The account of Mother Leafy Anderson and facts about the Black Spiritualist Churches are taken primarily from:

Estes, Davis C. "Ritual Validations of Clergywomen's Authority in the African American Spiritual Churches of New Orleans." In *Women's Leadership in Marginal Religions*, edited by Catherine Wessinger, 149–169. Champaign: University of Illinois Press, 1993.

With support from:

Albanese, Catherine L. *Republic of Mind and Spirit: A Cultural History of American Metaphysical Religion*. New Haven, CT: Yale University Press, 2008.

Jacobs, Claude F., and Andrew J. Kaslow. *The Spiritual Churches of New Orleans: Origins, Beliefs and Rituals of an African-American Religion*. Knoxville: University of Tennessee Press, 2001.

The description of Mother Catherine's Temple of the Innocent Blood is taken from Hurston's account of visiting the temple in the 1920s, entitled "Mother Catherine," published in *Negro: An Anthology*, edited by Nancy Cunard (New York: Bloomsbury Academic, 1996 [first published 1934]), and also Mark Sanders's article in *New Orleans Magazine*, "In Search of a Spiritualist: Digging to Learn More about Mother Catherine Seals," published online April 1, 2011.

Alice Walker recounted the process of locating Hurston's grave and buying her a tombstone in "In Search of Zora Neale Hurston," published in *Ms. Magazine* in 1975. I accessed it here: https://www.allisonbolah.com/site_resources/reading_list/Walker_In_Search_of_Zora.pdf.

For sources pointing to Congo Square as the origin point for jazz, beyond the three books about Marie cited above, I used Ann Powers's *Good Booty: Love and Sex, Black and White, Body and Soul in American Music* (New York: HarperCollins, 2017).

The account of Jelly Roll Morton comes from Stanford University's River Walk Jazz Collection, accessed here: http://riverwalkjazz.stanford.edu/program/mr-jelly-lord-tribute-jelly-roll-morton-and-his-red-hot-peppers.

The account of Louis Armstrong comes from Laurence Bergreen's *Louis Armstrong: An Extravagant Life* (New York: Broadway Books, 1997).

The estimates of practicing Voodooienne in New Orleans before and after Katrina are from Stacey Anderson's "Voodoo Is Rebounding in New Orleans After Hurricane Katrina," published on Newsweek. com, August 25, 2014.

The song "Marie Laveau" was recorded by Oscar "Papa" Celestin and his New Orleans Band in 1954. The song was rereleased by GHB Records in 1994.

PART II: Cora L. V. Scott, Rock Star Nineteenth-Century Spiritualist Medium

First, I would like to cite Ann Braude's *Radical Spirits: Spiritualism and Women's Rights in Nineteenth-Century America* (Bloomington: Indiana University Press, 2001 [first published 1989]). This book chronicles, in detail, how Spiritualism played a pivotal role in giving nineteenth-century women a public political and social voice, and her argument underpins part II. Details about Cora are peppered throughout *Radical Spirits* and employed throughout my account.

Molly McGarry's *Ghosts of Futures Past: Spiritualism and the Cultural Politics of Nineteenth-Century America* (Berkeley: University of California Press, 2008) served as my other primary source for the sociopolitical context and practices of Spiritualism, including everything from the movement's intersection with queer culture, to its appropriation of Native American spirits and religion, to how Spiritualism declined. The book also contains details about Cora's life.

For my account of Spiritualism's impact on first-wave feminism, I also relied on Mary Farrell Bednarowski's "Outside the Mainstream: Women's Religion and Women Religious Leaders in Nineteenth-Century America," *Journal of the American Academy of Religion* 48, no. 2 (June 1980): 207–232.

My main source for details on Cora's early life, including the stories of her early trances, is Harrison D. Barrett's *Life Work of Mrs. Cora L. V. Richmond* (Chicago: Hack and Anderson Printers, 1895). The total veracity of his work cannot be attested to. In addition, this biography is authorized and makes little mention of her private life, including any of her husbands other than her fourth one, William Richmond, to whom she was married when the book was published. Details are taken from it in all three chapters, but the account of her later life relies more on other sources.

Additional sources and specific citations are listed chapter by chapter below.

Chapter 4: Crossing the Veil

Many details about Hopedale and Cora's time there are from John B. Buescher's *The Other Side of Salvation: Spiritualism and the Nineteenth-Century Religious Tradition* (Boston: Skinner House Books, 2004). The flora and fauna listed in the description of the pond are indigenous to the area, not from historical accounts.

I relied on two other main sources, in addition to Braude and McGarry, to describe the origins and practices of Spiritualism:

Cox, Robert S. *Body and Soul: A Sympathetic History of American Spiritualism*. Charlottesville: University of Virginia Press, 2003.

Horowitz, Mitch. *Occult America: White House Seances, Ouija Circles, Masons, and the Secret Mystic History of Our Nation.* New York: Bantam Books, 2009.

"The individual, the Church, or the State . . ." is from "Reform Resolutions 1858, Free Convention at Rutland Vermont," reprinted in *Banner of Light,* July 3, 1858. I excerpted it from McGarry (p. 43).

"The only religious sect in the world . . ." is from Elizabeth Cady Stanton, Susan B. Anthony, and Matilda Joslyn Gage, eds., *History of Woman Suffrage, Vol. 3* (New York: Fowler & Wells, 1886), 514. It was also cited in McGarry (pp. 46–47). "Seemed to look right through her" is from the introduction of the second edition of *Life Work of Mrs. Cora L. V. Richmond,* published in 1991 and accessed here: http://www1.assumption.edu/WHW/Hatch/LifeWork.html.

"A white, fleecy light . . ." is from Barrett (p. 738).

Chapter 5: The Line between a Diva and a Deity

The account of B. F.'s exploits before meeting Cora is from John McClymer's "Who Is Mrs. Ada T. P. Foat? And Why Should Historians Care?: An Historical Reading of Henry James's 'The Bostonians'," published in *The Journal of the Gilded Age and Progressive Era* 2, no. 2 (2003): 191–217. This article also contains details of Cora and B. F.'s relationship and of Cora's trance lectures.

The financial crisis described is known as the Panic of 1857. I found details on it in Edward J. Renehan Jr.'s *Dark Genius of Wall Street: The Misunderstood Life of Jay Gould, King of Robber Barons* (New York: Basic Books, 2005).

I excerpted Frank Leslie's quote from McClymer (p. 195). Nathaniel Parker Willis's quote is a combination of two quotes taken from Braude (p. 94) and McClymer (p. 196), and the final one about "sacred emotion" is from Barrett (pp. 182–183).

The accounts of B. F.'s treatment of Cora are taken from "Supreme Court City & County of New York, Cora L. V. Hatch agst Benjamin F. Hatch" and several news articles. Highlights of the articles include "Separation of Cora L. V. Hatch and Husband," published in the September 14, 1858, edition of New York's *Evening Post*, which includes the quote about her getting "pale as death." The article "The Hatch Divorce Case. Mrs. Hatch, the Medium's, Complaint Against her Husband," published in the January 5, 1859, edition of New York's *Evening Post*, describes a "female of abandoned character" whom Hatch was intimate with and with whom he forced Cora to socialize.

Information about the "penny" press comes from "American Newspapers, 1800–1860, City Newspapers," published in the University of Illinois's History, Philosophy, and Newspaper Library and accessed here: https://www.library.illinois.edu/hpnl/tutorials/antebellum-newspapers-city/, and from William A. Dill's *Growth of Newspapers in the United States*, 1928, accessed here: https://kuscholarworks.ku.edu/bitstream/handle/1808/21361/dill_1928_3425151.pdf?sequence=1&isAllowed=y.

"Toward freer thought" is from Cox (p. 3).

"In 1856, it seems more likely . . ." is from John Weiss, ed., *Life and Correspondence of Theodore Parker* (London: Longmans, Green, and Co., 1863), vol. 1. I excerpted from McGarry (p. 3).

Emma Hardinge Britten's descriptions of Cora come from her book *Modern American Spiritualism: A Twenty Years' Record of the Communion Between Earth and the World of Spirits* (New York: New York Printing Company, 1869), 170, 264.

Issues with Cora's lungs are attributed to her "delicate constitution" in Barrett (p. 270).

The story of the doctor intervening on Cora's behalf can be found in the 1991 introduction to Barrett. It is one of the only references to B. F. Hatch in the biography. I find it interesting the main mention of B. F. is the moment Cora got free of him.

"Radical and essential . . ." is from "Is There Such a Thing as Sex?," published in *The Nation*, February 4, 1869. I excerpted it from McClymer (p. 209).

Discussion of some of Cora's attributes as "masculine," as well as her run-in with Walt Whitman, are from McGarry.

"A curse and a disgrace . . ." is from Barrett (p. 132). "Reconstructed health . . ." is from Britten. I excerpted it from McGarry (p. 50.)

"The terrorizing and ultimate deprivation . . ." is from Barrett (p. 221).

The account of the McKinley scandal is taken from multiple news stories. The details of the young man jumping up to accuse his father come primarily from "Particulars of the Last Cora Hatch Scene," published in the *San Francisco Bulletin*, February 19, 1864. The account of the trial is taken from "The Cora L. V. Hatch-McKinley Scandal Case," published in the *New York Herald* on January 28, 1864. The reference to her return to the podium one week after the original incident is from "The Cora Hatch Sensation," published in the *New York Herald*, February 1, 1864. The quote that Cora visited "a house of assignation" is from Hatch's divorce filing against Cora and is cited in McClymer.

"The experiment of masculine rule . . ." is from "The Three Great Problems of the Nineteenth Century," published in the *Banner of Light*, July 4, 1868. I excerpted it from McGarry (p. 51).

Chapter 6: The Fall

The reference to the articles mocking Mary Todd Lincoln and the description of the Red Room séance is from Horowitz (pp. 58–59).

The details of Cora's life in DC and New Orleans are from John B. Buescher's *Across the Dead Line: Lincoln and the Spirits during the War and Reconstruction Era Washington*, which I accessed here: http://iapsop.com/spirithistory/jb_buescher_across_the_dead_line.pdf. The Quartermaster General's quote is also excerpted from this book (p. 36), as is the information about Cora channeling Lincoln's "horse" laugh during meeting with President Johnson (p. 71).

Dr. Frederic Marvin's quote is from his *The Philosophy of Spiritualism and the Pathology and Treatment of Mediomania: Two Lectures Read before the New York Liberal Club* (New York: Asa K. Butts & Co., Publishers, 1874). I excerpted it from McGarry (p. 125).

"One common brotherhood . . ." is from Britten. I excerpted it from Cox (p. 8).

"Through archways of perfect light" is from Barrett (p. 752).

Cora's quote naming the New Age is from an 1897 public address. I excerpted it from Buescher's *The Other Side of Salvation* (p. 218).

PART III: Madame Blavatsky, Cofounder of the Theosophical Society

The details of Madame Blavatsky's life and the Theosophical philosophy and society are, by and large, taken from four books:

Lachman, Gary. *Madame Blavatsky: The Mother of Modern Spirituality*. New York: Penguin Group, 2012.

Meade, Marion. *Madame Blavatsky: The Woman behind the Myth*. New York: Open Road Media, 2014. First published 1980.

Personal Memoirs of H. P. Blavatsky, compiled by Mary K. Neff. London: Rider & Co., 1937.

Washington, Peter. *Madame Blavatsky's Baboon: A History of the Mystics, Mediums, and Misfits Who Brought Spiritualism to America*. New York: Schocken Books, 1995.

I relied most on Lachman's account. The story I call the "alternate theory" of HPB comes primarily from Meade's account of Blavatsky's life. Neff's book is a compilation of various letters, writings, and publications from HPB and the main players in her life, with commentary from Neff.

Additional sources and specific citations are listed chapter by chapter below.

Chapter 7: Once Upon a Time, When East Met West

"Ragged street boys" is from Sylvia Cranston's *HPB: The Extraordinary Life and Influence of Helena Blavatsky* (New York: Tarcher/Putnam, 1993). I excerpted it from Lachman (p. 8).

"At least I shall be spared . . ." is from Neff (p. 17).

The quoted Kris Kristofferson song is "The Pilgrim, Chapter 33," released by Monument Records in 1971.

"Mischievous, combative . . ." is from Neff (p. 26).

"Whole linen . . ." is from Jean Overton Fuller's *Blavatsky and Her Teachers* (London/The Hague: East, West Publications, 1988). I excerpted it from Lachman (p. 17).

"When I was young . . ." (p. 32), "I had engaged myself . . ." (p. 33), "Surely, I shall not," (p. 35), and "a liberal outlay of rubles" (p. 38) are all from Neff.

"Gentleman student" is from Lachman (p. 34).

HPB's account of first seeing Master M in person has taken various forms over the years. Sometimes she said she saw him on the bridge at this critical moment, others that she just saw him walking down a street in London. The account on the bridge is taken from a letter HPB wrote in 1882, published in *H. P. B. Speaks, Volume 2* (London: Theosophical Publishing House, 1951). I excerpted it from Meade (p. 117).

"Slip of the foot . . ." is from Lama Anagarika Govinda's *The Way of the White Clouds* (London: Rider, 1984). I excerpted it from Lachman (pp. 63–64).

"I hereby certify that . . ." (p. 187) and "venomous mad-dogs . . ." (p. 175) are from Neff.

Chapter 8: The Famous Heathen of Eighth Avenue

"Feelings not unlike those of a Mohammedan . . ." is taken from "Madame Blavatsky: Her Experience—Her Opinion of American Spiritualism and American Society," published in the *Spiritual Scientist* I, no. 3, December 1874. I excerpted it from Horowitz (p. 53).

I found information on the conditions of Lower East Side tenements during the late nineteenth century from Jacob Riis's *How the Other Half Lives* (New York: Dover Publications, 1971 [first published 1890]). Other accounts of New York at the time come from various online sources and the documentary *New York: A Documentary Film*, directed by Ric Burns.

"I have been to Tibet" is taken from Neff (p. 189). The description of HPB during the interview is based on Lachman's account (p. 89). It was documented that HPB frequently lounged in her tenement common room chain-smoking, as described, and Lachman supposes she likely did so during this interview, as the reporter, Anna Ballard, states she called upon HPB. However, it is not certain.

The insults to Spiritualism come from various sources. "Weak, sick minds" (p. 156) is from Lachman; "filthy weeds" (p. 249) and "necromancy" (p. 256) from Neff; and "crude" from Robert Ellwood and Catherine Wessinger's "The Feminism of 'Universal Brotherhood': Women in the Theosophical Movement," in *Women's Leadership in Marginal Religions* (p. 69).

"It is not I who talk and write . . ." is from Neff (p. 244).

"I had a volcano" is from a letter HPB wrote to her friend Prince Alexander Dondukov-Korsakov, published in Blavatsky, 1951. I excerpted it from Lachman (p. 30).

The quotes from the varied reviews HPB received for *Isis Unveiled* are from Meade (p. 325).

"Flapdoodle" is known to have been one of HPB's favorite sayings. "Tame subservience . . ." is from Olcott's inaugural address to the Theosophical Society in 1875. I excerpted it from Ellwood and Wessinger (p. 70). "A stepping-stone for ambition" is from HPB's *Studies in Occultism: The Esoteric Character of the Gospels* (Boston: New England Theosophical Corporation, 1895), 337.

The quote about "the mother, the wife, and the daughter" is from HPB's *The Secret Doctrine: The Synthesis of Science, Religion, and Philosophy* (London: Theosophical Publishing Company, 2010), 131. First published 1888.

"The liberation of the mind . . ." is from *The Key to Theosophy* (Wheaton, IL: Theosophical Publishing House, 1972), 6. First published 1889.

In addition to discussing the intersection of queer culture in Spiritualism, McGarry also discusses it in the context of Theosophy and HPB.

Susan Sontag's *Notes on "Camp"* was first published in *Partisan Review* in fall 1964.

The *New York Sun* called HPB "the famous heathen of Eighth Avenue" in "Silence in the Lamasery," published December 19, 1878. I excerpted it from Horowitz (p. 47).

I found backing for Theosophy's international membership crisis here: http://www.theosophy.world/project/mainstreaming-theosophy-0.

"Only land of true freedom in the world" is from Neff (p. 284).

Chapter 9: Prophet or Fraud or Both

"I am repeatedly reminded . . ." is from Neff (p. 175).

"Crumbling away like an old sea biscuit" is taken from Washington (p. 86).

I saw the cover of the *Theosophist* here: https://www.theosophy.world/resource/publications/theosophist.

I excerpted Gandhi's quotes about Theosophy from Horowitz (pp. 190–191).

"Foolish is the gardener . . ." is from HPB's *The Key to Theosophy* (1972 ed., 136).

"Oh my dear Mrs. Besant . . ." is from *Annie Besant: An Autobiography* (London: T. Fisher Unwin, 1893). I excerpted it from Lachman (p. 258).

Much of the information on Besant and Tingley comes from Ellwood and Wessinger.

HPB's final words are from an article in *The Path*, July 1894, volume IX. I excerpted it from Lachman (p. 269).

"All the top congressmen . . ." is from Louis Fischer's *The Life of Mahatma Gandhi* (New York: HarperCollins, 1997). I excerpted it from Lachman (p. 292).

The Matilda Joslyn Gage quote is from her *Women, Church, and State* (Amherst, NY: Humanity Books, 2002), 235–236. First published 1893.

PART IV: Zsuzsanna Budapest, Author, Activist, Lesbian Witch, and Feminist Goddess Worshipper

My primary sources for the story of Z's life are writings and recordings by Zsuzsanna Budapest, as well as an interview I conducted over the phone with her on November 2, 2018. Z's *My Dark Sordid Past as a Heterosexual: First Destiny* (California: Women's Spirituality Forum, 2014) tells the story of her life, from childhood to her arrival in California. For information on her later life, I relied on anecdotes in two books she wrote, *The Holy Book of Women's Mysteries* (San Francisco, CA: Weiser Books, 2003 [first published 1980]) and *The Grandmother of Time: A Women's Book of Celebrations, Spells, and Sacred Objects for Every Month of the Year* (San Francisco: HarperSanFrancisco, 1989). I also used autobiographical accounts found in blog form here, ZBudapest.com/autobiography, and in recorded form in *Bring It On!: Tales from the Revolution* (iM Zsuzsanna E. Budapest: 2017).

The text that played the most integral role in my explanations of both feminist Goddess worship and witchcraft is Starhawk's *The*

Spiral Dance: A Rebirth of the Ancient Religion of the Great Goddess: Twentieth Anniversary Edition (New York: HarperCollins, 1999).

Other main sources with information about Z, Dianic Wiccan, and witchcraft that I used include:

Adler, Margot. *Drawing Down the Moon: Witches, Druids, Goddess-Worshippers, and Other Pagans in America*. New York: Penguin Group, 2006. First published 1979.

Coleman, Kristy. *Re-riting Women: Dianic Wicca and the Feminine Divine*. Lanham, MD: AltaMira Press, 2009.

Eller, Cynthia. *Living in the Lap of the Goddess: The Feminist Spirituality Movement in America*. Boston: Beacon Press, 1995. First published 1993.

Salomonsen, Jone. *Enchanted Feminism: Ritual, Gender and Divinity among the Reclaiming Witches of San Francisco*. London: Routledge, 2002.

Additional sources and specific citations are listed chapter by chapter below.

Chapter 10: Welcome to the Machine

My account of the decline of the Goddess is based on Starhawk's *The Spiral Dance*; Mary Daly's *Gyn/Ecology: The Metaethics of Radical Feminism* (Boston: Beacon Press, 1990 [first published 1978]); Silvia Federici's *Caliban and the Witch* (Brooklyn: Autonomedia, 2004); Eller's *Living in the Lap of the Goddess*; and Gloria Steinem's

Revolution from Within: A Book of Self-Esteem (Boston: Little, Brown and Company, 1993).

The "chalice" and "blade" metaphor is taken from Riane Eisler's *The Chalice and the Blade: Our History, Our Future* (San Francisco: HarperSanFrancisco, 1988).

"Alienated women from our bodies . . ." is from Adrienne Rich's *Of Women Born: Motherhood as Experience and Institution* (New York: W. W. Norton, 1976), 13.

"The Gods love the brethren . . ." and "that youth is necessary . . ." is from Doreen Valiente's *The Rebirth of Witchcraft* (London: Robert Hale, 1989). I excerpted it from Salomonsen (p. 92).

The observations about white flight and TVs as the new pulpit are mine. The rest are from Z's *Dark Sordid Past*, which also includes the details of the TV shows she watched. In addition, the comments about "walls closing in" and "shutting out the past" are mine, not Z's, as are the comments about New York City's rubble being similar to the Budapest of her youth. My source for how the city looked during this era is Burns's *New York: A Documentary Film*.

"Fuckable broad" is from Budapest, 2014 (p. 179).

"Cunt juice" is from Budapest, 2014 (p. 180).

Z does not talk of this suicide attempt in any of her texts. She did tell Adler about it, who then wrote about it. "I regained my true perspective of a Witch . . ." is from Adler (p. 77).

I found reference to Timothy Leary and Allen Ginsberg enjoying sensory deprivation tanks in Ahmed Kabil's "Meet the Psychedelics-Obsessed Scientist Who Wanted to Learn Dolphins' Language," published on Timeline.com, November 29, 2016.

"Runaway housewife" is from Budapest, 2014 (p. 190).

Chapter 11: The Cocoon

"Casualties of the gender war" is from Budapest's "More Life at the Women's Center" episode on *Bring It On!*

"If God is male, then male is God" is from Mary Daly's *Beyond God the Father* (Boston: Beacon Press, 1973), 19.

"Religion is the soil of culture" is from Starhawk's *Dreaming the Dark: Magic, Sex, and Politics* (Boston: Beacon Press, 1982). I excerpted it from Salomonsen (p. 82). "Evoking power-from-within" and "liberation psychology" are from Starhawk's *Truth or Dare: Encounters with Power, Authority, and Mystery* (San Francisco: HarperSanFrancisco, 1987), 6.

"I didn't have my twenties as a girl . . ." is from Budapest's online autobiography, "Chapter 3: 1974."

"Folk Art, search those archives . . ." (p. xii) and the Susan B. Anthony Manifesto (pp. 1–2) are from Budapest, 2003.

In *Grandmother of Time,* Z states that "The Goddess is alive! Magic is afoot" is her favorite chant (p. 246).

Chapter 12: The Witch Trials

"I thought my new-found integrity . . ." is from "The Tarot Trial" episode on *Bring It On!* "Hands off wimmin's religion" was the official slogan Z gave the trial and is referenced as such in Adler (p. 187).

The main source I used for the fracturing of the Women's Liberation movement in the midseventies is Alice Echols's *Daring to Be Bad: Radical Feminism in America 1967–1975* (Minneapolis: University of Minnesota Press), 1989.

The statistic that the ranks of female lawyers doubled comes from the United States Census Bureau, https://www.census.gov/library/stories/2018/05/women-lawyers.html.

I read several online accounts of the 2011 PantheaCon incident, but the main sources were Roz Kaveney's "Why Won't Pagans Accept Trans Women," published on TheGuardian.com, March 8, 2011, and Christine Hoff Kraemer's *Conference Report: PantheaCon 2011*, accessed here: https://www.academia.edu/1117503/PantheaCon_2011_Report.

The positions of Z and the Dianic brass come from Patti Wigington's *Origins of Dianic Wicca*, https://www.learnreligions.com/what-is-dianic-wicca-2562908, and *Gender and Transgender in Modern Paganism*, edited by Sarah Thompson, Gina Pond, Philip Tanner, Calyxa Omphalos, and Jacobo Polanshek (Cupertino, CA: Circle of Cerridwen Press, 2012).

"How is a binary transsexual man . . ." (p. 41), "Unlike most Budapestian Dianics . . ." (p. 88), and "Take all the religious freedom you need" (p. 115) are all from *Gender and Transgender in Modern Paganism*.

The information about the murder of trans women in 2017 and 2018 is taken from "Killings of Transgender People in the US Saw Another High Year," published on CNN.com, January 17, 2019.

The statistic that thirty-five is the average life expectancy for trans women comes from the 2015 report *Violence against LGBTI Persons in the Americas*, by the Inter-American Commission on Human Rights (IACHR).

"Sexual reproduction is an elegant method . . ." is from Starhawk, *The Spiral Dance* (p. 20).

I excerpted "The original witch was undoubtedly black . . ." from Eller (p. 73).

The information about Sarah Good and her daughters is from Gordon Harris's "Four-Year-Old Dorothy Good Is Jailed for Witchcraft, March 24, 1692," on HistoricIpswich.org.

The quotes and information about Salem were initially taken from interviews and tours undertaken during a trip to the township in October 2018. The tour I most recommend is No Wage Travel's WITCHES: 1692–NOW (https://hauswitchstore.com/shop/weekly-tour-witches-1692-now/). The information was confirmed via various online sources.

PART V: Marianne Williamson, New Age Sage and Presidential Candidate

For details on Marianne's life from childhood through the early nineties, I relied primarily on Elena Oumano's *Marianne Williamson: Her Life, Her Messages, Her Miracles* (New York: St. Martin's

Press, 1992) and anecdotes found in three of Marianne's books: *A Return to Love: Reflections on the Principles of "A Course in Miracles"* (New York: HarperCollins, 1992); *A Woman's Worth* (New York: Ballantine Books, 1993); and *Healing the Soul of America: Twentieth Anniversary Edition* (New York: Simon & Schuster, 2018). In addition, I took information from several articles, including Terry Pristin's "The Power, the Glory, the Glitz," published in the *Los Angeles Times* on February 16, 1992, and Monica Corcoran Harel's "The New Age of Marianne Williamson," published on LAMag. com on May 27, 2014. Some details also came from Marianne's live lectures I attended between July 2018 and January 2019.

Additional sources and specific citations are listed chapter by chapter below.

Chapter 13: A New Age of What Exactly?

"Talking to God" is from Oumano (p. 32).

"The problem that has no name" is from Betty Friedan's *The Feminine Mystique* (New York: W. W. Norton, 1997), 57. First published 1963.

My main sources for the sections about Helen Schucman and the *Course* are Ann Taves's *Revelatory Events: Three Case Studies of the Emergence of New Spiritual Paths* (Princeton, NJ: Princeton University Press, 2016), *A Course in Miracles* (Mill Valley, CA: Foundation for Inner Peace, 1976), and Marianne's lectures and writing.

"A better way" is excerpted from Taves (p. 162).

"If I were you, I'd take notes" is from a lecture Marianne gave on January 15, 2019, at New York City's Marble Collegiate Church. It is a variation on what Helen wrote in her *Autobiography* (California: Foundation for Inner Peace) accessible here: https://acim.org/acim/acim-scribing/helen-cohn-schucman-ph-d-autobiography/.

"By my midtwenties I was a total mess" is from Williamson, *Return to Love* (p. xv).

I excerpted "if you bring forth what is within you" from Steinem, *Revolution from Within* (p. 153).

"A single heartbeat" is from Williamson, *A Woman's Worth* (p. 126).

New York City crime statistics are from New York Crime Rates 1960–2016, accessed here: http://www.disastercenter.com/crime/nycrime.htm.

"Who cried all the time . . ." was said by writer Albert Goldman and is from Oumano (pp. 65–66).

"The rich boys get their money back . . ." is from OK Go's song "Louisiana Land," released by Capitol Records in 2010.

"A nervous breakdown is a highly underrated vehicle . . ." is from Oumano (p. 74). "Until this happens . . ." is from Williamson, *Return to Love* (p. 12).

The theory of the origin of the term *faggot* is taken from Steinem, *Revolution from Within* (p. 184). It is unproven.

The described church on Franklin Avenue is Hollywood United Methodist Church. The description is taken from my own visit there in 2018, not from Marianne's own experience in the early 1980s.

"This woman who look[ed] like one of [them] . . ." was said by Howard Rosenman and is excerpted from Oumano (p. 132).

"Go meditate. Charles Manson ate apples . . ." is from James Servin's "Prophet of Love Has the Timing of a Comedian," *New York Times*, February 19, 1992. "The only trouble was . . ." is from Pristin, "The Power."

The dialogue between Marianne and her mother is from her lecture on January 15, 2019.

Chapter 14: The Bitch for God

"That kind of spiritual transformation . . ." is from *The Oprah Winfrey Show*, February 4, 1992. I accessed it here: https://www.youtube.com/watch?v=vSO9veY96Ts.

"Hollywood's ticket to God" is from Oumano (p. 13).

"Scorned woman" and "militant attitude" are from Grace Segers's "Here Are Some of the Questions Anita Hill Answered in 1991," published on CBSNews.com on September 19, 2018. They are excerpts from questions Senator Howell Heflin (R-AL) asked her.

"A little bit nutty . . ." is from an article conservative commentator David Brock wrote in the *American Spectator* in 1992. It is widely cited.

"Our deepest fear . . ." is from Williamson, *Return to Love* (p. 190).

The statistic that 75 percent of the New Age market is women is from Karlyn Crowley's *Feminism's New Age: Gender, Appropriation, and the Afterlife of Essentialism* (Albany: State University of New York Press, 2011).

"Something out of Ibsen" and "like watching a 3-year-old . . ." is from Susan Schindehette's "The Divine Miss W," *People*, March 9, 1992. The reference to run-on sentences is found in Lynda Gorov's "Faith: Marianne Williamson Is Full of It," *Mother Jones*, November/December 1997.

"Egomaniac" is from Harel, "The New Age." "Tyrannical" is from Tim Appelo and Frank Spotnitz's "Marianne Williamson Has Almost Everything," *Entertainment Weekly*, March 6, 1992. "The epitome of a Southern snake oil salesman" and "platitudes gleaned" are from Pristin, "The Power."

"America's latest Mary Magdalene" is from Simon Sebag Montefiore's "Marianne Williamson: Who Is She & Why Do We Need Her Now?," *Psychology Today*, July 1, 1992.

The account of the fundraiser, including "bark" and "hiss," is primarily taken from Schindehette, "The Divine Miss W."

"I'd do it again . . ." is from Appelo and Spotnitz, "Marianne Williamson."

During the May 1992 presidential campaign, Dan Quayle publicly criticized the TV character Murphy Brown for her own unabashed single motherhood, calling her "a character who supposedly epitomizes today's intelligent, highly paid professional woman, mocking the importance of fathers by bearing a child alone and calling it another lifestyle choice."

"Jewish unwed mother" and a "bitch for God" are from Pristin, "The Power."

"Slowly but surely, generation after generation" is from Williamson, *A Woman's Worth* (p. 16).

"Hear what they want to hear . . ." is from *Publishers Weekly*, accessed here: https://www.publishersweekly.com/978-0-679-42218-1. "A return to gibberish" is from Steve Salerno's *Sham: How the Self-Help Movement Made America Helpless* (New York: Three Rivers Press, 2005), 54.

"Women are at the forefront of the spiritual . . ." is from Williamson, *A Woman's Worth* (p. 86).

The information about Hillary and Camp David is from Jessa Crispin's "The False Promise of the 'Yoga Voter,'" published on NewRepublic. com on April 25, 2019.

"Dirt under her fingernails again" and "if [she] saw one more beautiful" are from Harel, "The New Age."

Chapter 15: Healer-in-Chief

"A light unto the world" (p. xvii), "that there can be a land . . ." (p. 246), "making things better . . ." (p. 127), and "a storm ahead" (p. 194) are from Williamson, *Healing the Soul of America*.

"It was a commercial failure . . ." is from Marianne's talk in the LA Marriott in August 2018.

"How about me?" is from Harel, "The New Age."

"Our political salvation . . ." (p. 20) and "yet where does one start" (p. 2) are from Williamson, *Healing the Soul of America.*

"This woman has a direct line to God!" and the account of Steven Tyler are from Hawke Fracassa's "Marianne Williamson, Spiritual Director of Warren's Renaissance Unity, Will Move On," *Detroit News*, September 3, 2002.

The details of her time at Renaissance Unity are from "Radical Spirit," *Detroit Metro Times*, May 9, 2001, Fracassa and Harel.

"An egomaniac control freak" is from Harel, "The New Age."

The list of influential baby boomers is from "The Baby Boomer Hall of Fame," *Newsweek*, December 17, 2006.

"I got caught in the same unfortunate . . ." and "such a powerful force of darkness" are from Harel, "The New Age."

"When I first started talking . . ." is from a lecture Marianne gave in October 2018 at New York City's Rubin Museum of Art.

Marianne Williamson made the call for a "moral and spiritual awakening" in America repeatedly throughout her presidential campaign.

"Martin Luther King said it was . . ." is from Richard Leiby's "Marianne Williamson, Hollywood Self-Help Guru, Wants to Heal Washington," published on WashingtonPost.com, March 11, 2014.

The statistic that the average New York City rent had spiked 75 percent since the turn of the millennium is from Corinne Lestch's "NYC Affordable Housing Is Vanishing as Rents Skyrocket, Incomes Decline: Report," published on NYDailyNews.com, April 23, 2014.

The description of Marianne's apartment is from Marianne's Instagram and Laura Pullman's "Oprah's Guru, Marianne Williamson, Gears Up to Defeat Donald Trump with Love," *Sunday Times*, February 10, 2019.

"Today, we have a culture of death . . ." and "All manner of goodness, truth . . ." is from Williamson's October 2018 lecture, though she said variations of these quotes during the January 15 lecture, and throughout her presidential campaign. "It stunts the collective psyche . . ." is from Williamson, 2018 (p. 80). All the other quotes in this section are from the January 15 lecture. "Mighty companions are gathering all over this country . . ." is also from that lecture.

"I am not anti-vaxx . . ." is from Marianne's official Twitter account, July 17, 2019.

"People are so invested in creating this false narrative . . ." is from "Marianne Williamson: I Am Not a 'Wacky New-Age Nutcase,'" published on TheHill.com, July 30, 2019.

ABOUT THE AUTHOR

Photo © 2019 Laurel Golio

L ucile Scott is a Brooklyn-based writer and editor. She has reported on national and international health and human rights issues for over a decade. Most recently, she has worked at the United Nations and amfAR, the Foundation for AIDS Research, and has contributed to such publications as *VICE* and *POZ* magazines. In addition, she has written and/or directed plays that have been featured in New York City, Edinburgh, and Los Angeles. In 2016 she hit the rails as part of Amtrak's writers' residency program. *An American Covenant* is her first book. She hails from Kentucky and moved to New York after graduating from Northwestern University.